THE TRIALS OF EVIDENCE-BASED EDUCATION

The Trials of Evidence-based Education explores the promise, limitations and achievements of evidence-based policy and practice, as the attention of funders moves from a sole focus on attainment outcomes to political concern about character-building and wider educational impacts.

Providing a detailed look at the pros, cons and areas for improvement in evidence-based policy and practice, this book includes consideration of the following:

- what is involved in a robust evaluation for education
- the issues in conducting trials and how to assess the trustworthiness of research findings
- new methods for the design, conduct, analysis and use of evidence from trials and examining their implications
- what policy-makers, head teachers and practitioners can learn from the evidence to inform practice.

In this well-structured and thoughtful text, the results and implications of over 20 studies conducted by the authors are combined with a much larger number of studies from their systematic reviews, and the implications are spelled out for the research community, policy-makers, schools wanting to run their own evaluations, and for practitioners using evidence.

Stephen Gorard is Professor of Education and Public Policy at Durham University, UK, and a Fellow of the Academy of Social Sciences.

Beng Huat See is Senior Research Fellow in Education at Durham University, UK, and a Fellow of the Royal Society of Arts.

Nadia Siddiqui is Research Fellow in Education and Sociology at Durham University, UK, and a Fellow of the Royal Society of Arts.

THE TRIALS OF EVIDENCE-BASED EDUCATION

The Promises, Opportunities and Problems of Trials in Education

Stephen Gorard,
Beng Huat See and
Nadia Siddiqui

Routledge
Taylor & Francis Group

LONDON AND NEW YORK

First published 2017
by Routledge
2 Park Square, Milton Park, Abingdon, Oxon OX14 4RN

and by Routledge
711 Third Avenue, New York, NY 10017

Routledge is an imprint of the Taylor & Francis Group, an informa business

British Library Cataloguing in Publication Data
A catalogue record for this book is available from the British Library

Library of Congress Cataloging in Publication Data
A catalog record for this book has been requested

ISBN: 978-1-138-20965-7 (hbk)
ISBN: 978-1-138-20966-4 (pbk)
ISBN: 978-1-315-45689-8 (ebk)

Typeset in Bembo
by diacriTech, Chennai

Printed and bound by CPI Group (UK) Ltd, Croydon, CR0 4YY

CONTENTS

TABLES

ABBREVIATIONS

3ie	The International Initiative for Impact Evaluation
AFA3As	Achievement for All 3As
AfL	Assessment for learning (formative feedback)
APA	American Psychological Association
AR	Accelerated Reader (an intervention)
ASA	American Statistical Association
BTEC	Business and Technology Council (UK vocational qualification)
CAT	Cognitive Abilities Test
CCF	Combined Cadet Force
CI	Confidence interval (a confusing measure of uncertainty)
CKLA	Core Knowledge Language Arts
CU	Children's University (an intervention)
DfE	Department for Education (England, UK), formerly also DfEE and DfES
EBE	Evidence-based education
EEF	Educational Endowment Foundation (UK)
ES	Effect size (measure of impact)
ESRC	Economic and Social Research Council (UK)
FS	Fresh Start (an intervention)
FSM	Free school meals (measure of poverty)
HEFCE	Higher Education Funding Council England
IES	US Institute of Education Sciences
KS2	Key Stage 2 (phase of schooling leading to end of primary school in England)
KS4	Key Stage 4 (phase of schooling leading to 16+ examinations in England)
M|D|	Mean absolute deviation (measure of dispersion)
MDES	Minimal detectable effect size

NCRM	National Centre for Research Methods (UK ESRC-funded centre)
NFER	National Foundation for Educational Research
NGRT	New Group Reading Test
NNTD	The number of counterfactual findings needed to disturb a research finding
NPD	National Pupil Database (England)
P4C	Philosophy for Children (an intervention)
PALS	Peer-Assisted Learning Strategies
PiE	Progress in English (a standard outcome measure)
PiM	Progress in maths (a standard outcome measure)
QM	Quantitative Methods (a UK research initiative)
RCT	Randomised control trial (a powerful design for causal studies)
RDD	Regression discontinuity design (as powerful in design as an RCT)
RTI	Response to Intervention (an intervention)
SD	Standard deviation (measure of dispersion)
SEN	Special educational need
SENCO	Special educational needs co-ordinator
SES	Socio-economic status
SJA	St John Ambulance
STAR	Standardised Assessment of Reading (see AR)
TA	Teaching assistant
TLRP	Teaching and Learning Research Programme (UK)
WWR	World and Word Reading (an intervention)
YSA	Youth social action
YUF	Youth United Foundation (an intervention)
ZPD	Zone of proximal development (see AR)

PREFACE

There has been a recent worldwide move towards demanding evidence-based policy and practice in education, with policy-makers and practitioners wanting more practical and coherent answers from research. Funding schemes such as the International Initiative for Impact Evaluation, the US Institute of Education Sciences, and the Educational Endowment Foundation in England have been set up to provide the kind of robust practical evaluation research that more traditional funders – such as the research councils and charities in the UK – have tended to ignore. There are even new funding streams (such as the pupil premium for schools in England) allowing schools and others to take advantage of the new evidence generated by implementing evidence-based reforms.

The authors of this new book have been involved with all of these initiatives from the outset as researchers and advisers, and on funding and commissioning panels – and in previous incarnations such as the UK ESRC Teaching and Learning Research Programme. The moves towards evidence-based education (EBE) are welcome and well intended, and many improvements have been made as a result. However, progress has been sketchy for a number of reasons, including continued resistance from university academics, which means that the funding is disproportionately going to bespoke companies and organisations with an unhealthy reliance on repeat 'business'. There have also been important methodological wrong turns. In trying to make this new approach to evidence more widely accessible and politically acceptable the funders have picked up too many of the bad aspects of the kind of research they were intended to replace.

This book presents innovative methods for the design, conduct, analysis and use of evidence from robust evaluations like educational trials. The book describes the promise, the problems and the new opportunities as the attention of funders moves from only being interested in attainment outcomes to political concern about character-building and wider educational impacts. The latter is novel and also too frequently misunderstood, as explained in the latter part of the book. The results and implications of around 20 studies conducted by the authors are combined with a much larger number of studies from our systematic reviews, and their implications are spelled out for the research community, policy-makers, schools wanting to run their own evaluations, practitioners using evidence, and the wider public (who pay for research and who are the participants in education).

The book should appeal to those interested in the substantive areas of educational promise covered in the book, or needing to understand the advantages and limitations of evidence-based policy-making and practice, with reference to education. This will include those reading and wanting to critique the research evidence of others, and those thinking about conducting robust evaluations for themselves. It will be a key text for any school wanting to undertake their own evaluations, or for their research leads trying to pick their way through evidence for use in practice. Some of the design and method proposals in this book, such as the quality sieve and the simple sensitivity analyses, are innovative and have never before been presented together as a solution to the kinds of problems encountered in trials.

As described in the book, there are problems with the way evaluations are often envisaged by others, and then commissioned, conducted, reported and synthesised – these are the 'trials' of evidence-based education. Opportunities for real advancements in education research have been missed so many times due to reluctance by some to change, and pressure from influential quarters to retain the *status quo*. Really only the funders of research have the power to change this. We hope that this book will help them to decide to act before more money is wasted and more opportunities are missed.

The authors are grateful to the Educational Endowment Foundation, the Nuffield Foundation, and the Economic and Social Research Council who funded a lot of this work, and to everyone who participated in the research described in this book, including the developers but especially the staff and pupils of the hundreds of schools taking part in the trials.

PART I

Introduction

1

INTRODUCTION

The state of evidence in education

What kind of evidence is this book about?

This is a book about the use of evidence to improve education for its participants, including improvement sought via changes in education policy and the development of more effective educational practices. Education is a lifelong process, affecting all of us in various ways, and education is clearly not primarily about the evidence for its improvement, efficacy or equity. There is much more to education than that, and there is also a great deal of other evidence used in the practice of education – sources in history, research reports in science, texts in first language instruction and so on. But, in addition, practitioners and policy-makers routinely use, or ought to use, evidence of many kinds to help decide on or to justify actions taken to improve the conduct of education.

Evidence on education is, and presumably always has been, used in this way with the best of intentions. And relevant evidence abounds. A politician could be influenced by what they thought voters wanted to happen in education, or by what a section of the media reported that voters wanted to happen in education. Their decisions and policy declarations might be affected by apparently successful policies used in other countries or contexts, and by summaries of evidence presented by advisers and think tanks. The behaviour of teachers and managers in education could be swayed by brochures with evidence of effectiveness from commercial publishers, picked up from stands at educational conferences, or by a new text, new theories, or ideas proselytised by their peers. Practitioners may feel that they have to do what they are told by someone senior who was influenced by any of the above kinds of evidence, or they may simply reflect on how something appeared to work previously when they tried it out in the classroom.

These anecdotal, third hand, observational, and commercially or politically motivated kinds of evidence may appear useful, and could be occasionally effective.

They are more often confused, poorly understood, distorted, unbalanced and unwarranted. Perhaps most importantly, these kinds of evidence are at least as likely to cause harm as they are to do any good, and mostly they will just waste effort, time and money that could have been used to make the lives of each cohort of participants in education better. This sounds and indeed is unethical.

Much of the published research on education is of such poor quality that it might do more harm than good overall (Gorard 2002). Policy-makers, government, funding bodies, schools and parents make decisions informed by such research. If the research findings are doubtful and the evidence is weak, then people are making decisions based on a false promise. If an intervention or a programme of activity does not work, but still claims to be effective, then this becomes an ethical issue. It constitutes a waste of time and effort for everyone involved. It is also a waste of taxpayers' money. And, in the worst-case scenario, it may be harmful to the participants. In education research these participants are very often schoolchildren. But because in education research, children do not die from these harmful programmes and the adverse effects are not immediately apparent, people do not seem to pay much attention to it. Such bad practice continues to be perpetuated and harm is being done while we wait to do something about the problem of poor evidence. The situation is worsened by the fact that serious syntheses of evidence that do exist and are more deserving of attention can have limited impact on policy and practice compared to exciting new initiatives (Green et al. 2016). Therefore, any book on research ethics should have a chapter or more on the importance of the quality of research. Publishers, journal editors and peer reviewers should now make it their policy to demand the highest quality of research. By this, we mean making sure that the claims made are supported by the data presented and that appropriate methods of data collection and analyses are used. A major problem with research quality lies in its unwarranted conclusions (Gorard et al. 2007).

There are a number of reasons why the confused forms of evidence listed here are used so widely. Probably the simplest explanation is that there is too often little alternative. We cannot expect all politicians, advisers, school leaders or nursery teachers, for example, to generate safe evidence on the effectiveness of their actions in education for themselves. They will contribute to it, feature in it, and use such evidence where it is available, but it is not their main job to produce it. Secondly, much of what is produced by professional researchers, both academics and those employed by research organisations, is very weak research and very poorly reported. In some respects, ignoring such research is the most rational and safest thing for potential research users to do. This is especially so because it is hard for users to decide what research to trust. However, there *is* good and useful research of all kinds hidden among the forest of wasted opportunities. It is hoped that this book will help all research readers to be able to decide which research results and conclusions can be trusted, which cannot, and when it is that we genuinely do not know the answer to a research-relevant question in education.

Surely academic/professional research just needs to be used more?

We have conducted many large-scale critical reviews of evidence, including on the impact of pupil attitudes, aspiration and behaviour on attainment (Gorard et al. 2011), literacy interventions during transfer to secondary school (See and Gorard 2014), parental engagement in their child's education (Gorard and See 2013), and primary school pedagogy (Gorard et al. 2016a).

Conducting any such review, it soon becomes clear that a majority of published and unpublished 'research' is of no consequence or use for any real-life purpose. It can be safely ignored and should not influence the findings of an empirical review. It may, of course, have other uses but its prevalence and predominance in the field of education suggests that a considerable sum of public and charitable funding is being spent for no gain. Biased reporting is common. Studies frequently make bold claims about 'impact' despite having biased or very small samples, no counterfactuals and large amounts of data missing, and without establishing any form of baseline equivalence. These issues are discussed in Chapter 4.

Even worse, so much in education that could be evaluated robustly has not been, or has been and continues to be used in practice despite testing negative. Much policy and practice today seems to be less evidence-based or evidence-informed as evidence-resistant – content to rely on asking those with a vested interest whether they think a policy or practice is effective. The latter is a very poor kind of evidence – as illustrated in examples throughout this book.

For example, Aim Higher and other forms of widening participation to higher education in the UK are routinely assessed in terms of whether participants in widening participation activities enjoyed them, or reported being more likely to apply to a university than they were before (Gorard et al. 2007). What is needed instead is a simple comparison between the participants and an equivalent group of young people to see how many more of the participants actually do apply to university later. But the poor existing approach satisfies uncritical research users and generates easy funding for research organisations, so it prevails. In an 'evaluation' of the work of STEMNET (to attract more young people into studying science and maths), Straw and Macleod (2015) used a pupil, teacher and ambassador survey plus case studies to assess 'impact' but had no measure of how effective the schemes were in actually attracting more STEM students.

The field of educational 'effectiveness' rarely if ever includes a study in which students are randomly assigned to classes, schools or teachers (Paufler and Amrein-Beardsley 2014). In fact, such so-called effectiveness studies seldom use any form of active allocation of students. Where such studies have been attempted the random allocation of students has been subverted by teachers or school leaders, and the teacher and student dropout from the study has been so high as to make the results meaningless (Raudenbush 2015). Where they have been more successful, robust studies can produce results at variance with the majority of school effectiveness and school improvement models (Clark et al. 2015).

Instead, most school effectiveness studies try to assess differential effectiveness from existing data in naturally occurring groups. But this approach has serious limitations, and the supposed educational 'effects' could easily be artefacts (Marks 2015a, 2015b). The models usually take no account of measurement error, which can produce spurious 'effects' (Televantou et al. 2015), and these unacknowledged errors can propagate dangerously, producing completely meaningless results (Gorard 2010a). Further evidence of the spurious nature of these kinds of results comes their volatility (Johnson et al. 2014, Darling-Hammond 2015). Despite these limitations, value-added school effectiveness models are still being used to hold schools and teachers accountable, for example.

There must be a better way to evaluate educational interventions, purported improvements, programmes and policies.

Outline of the rest of this book

With these few illustrations (from so many ranging from learning styles to multiple intelligences), we have summarised why we need more robust evaluations in education research. People already use evidence from commercial producers, anecdotes, their own observation of classes, and so on. They just tend to use it unsystematically, uncritically and therefore badly. The move towards evidence-based education (EBE) is not towards evidence as such, because evidence of a kind is already widely used. It is towards the better and more discriminating use of existing evidence, and the generation of better evidence in the future. However, the kind of work described in this book forms only one part of the work of education research.

Chapter 2 in this book shows how robust evaluations of the kind now being sought by some governments and practitioner bodies fit into a larger cycle of research. Chapter 3 discusses some of the main problems in current EBE work, and Chapters 4 and 5 look at some of the solutions to these problems. Chapters 6 to 9 use the suggested approaches to describe new evidence from our own evaluations in three different areas – bespoke interventions for low attainers, whole school approaches to improvement, and the wider outcomes of schooling such as character formation. We describe 12 robust evaluations in detail. Chapter 10 summarises what has been learnt from these, specifically in terms of recommendations for the wider public, practitioners, policy-makers, and researchers themselves.

2

THE CHANGING INCENTIVES AND INFRASTRUCTURE FOR ROBUST EVALUATIONS

This chapter looks briefly at the state of education research in developed countries like the UK, and at some recent improvements in the funding and commissioning of evidence-based education work.

In the UK, there is a long-standing concern about the quality and utility of social science research (Platt 2012). The same kind of concern appears in many other countries. In education research, for example, US journal editors and others have long reported that very few published papers were really worthy of acceptance. Wandt et al. (1965) deemed most published studies to be trivial or invalid, and often both. The key issues were lack of appropriate study design, incorrect methods of analysis, and lack of reporting assumptions or limitations. Forty years later, Ioannidis (2005, p. 1) reported concerns that most current published research findings in medicine, science and social science are simply false. 'For many current scientific fields, claimed research findings may often be simply accurate measures of the prevailing bias'.

For several decades (Hillage et al. 1998, Tooley with Darby 1998), and probably much longer (Gorard 2004a), UK education research has been criticised for not providing the kind of evidence base necessary to improve education especially by raising attainment for disadvantaged pupils. More recently, such concerns have been allied also to a claimed lack of 'quantitative' (i.e. working with numbers) skill in UK social science and beyond (Adeney and Carey 2011). Despite high profile resistance by apparently threatened education researchers, in fact these concerns were and are shared by a wide range of stakeholders including policy-makers, funders and some senior academics (McIntyre and McIntyre 2000, Taylor 2002). Despite the level of taxpayer and charitable funding, education research has been described as failing to deliver answers to even some of the most basic questions of interest to policy-makers and practitioners. Similar concerns about the lack of usable research evidence have emerged in the US (NRC 1999, NERPP 2000), and elsewhere.

A new era for evidence-based education?

In response to these problems and claims, a number of research capacity-building initiatives have been attempted. In the UK, one of the first major responses was the then huge ESRC-funded Teaching and Learning Research Programme (TLRP), set up to permit applicants to have their projects funded at a level that the generation of safe evidence on improving learning was deemed to require. The Chair of the Programme was a trials advocate with experience in health sciences, and the Steering Committee included experts in field trials, experimental psychology and psychometrics.

There have been several other promising starts previously (including the brief National Educational Research Forum). The Evidence for Policy and Practice Information and Co-ordinating Centre (EPPI) was set up in the UK to lead and support systematic reviews, and to work on how to make evidence more usable. Now, the Department for Education (DfE) is citing Goldacre (a medic and journalist) in setting up a list of research priorities and requesting evidence of the same form that McIntyre and McIntyre (2000) and so many others described as missing 25 or more years ago (Wrigley 1976, Broadfoot 1985, National Science Foundation 2002, Goldacre 2013).

In 2010, the UK government set up the quasi-independent Educational Endowment Foundation (EEF), funded by a combination of DfE research money, charitable contributions and co-operation with other funders. The EEF is intended to meet the long-term demand for robust evidence on school improvement. Linked to this is the EEF Teaching and Learning Toolkit, providing a dynamic portrayal of the weight, cost and effect of summaries of evidence for a wide range of school-based interventions. The Toolkit was developed to help schools and teachers make informed decisions on which programmes to adopt. The emphasis is on low achievers, and the most disadvantaged 20% of the school population. The funding to permit schools to use the most effective interventions comes from a parallel policy – the Pupil Premium – where schools in England receive further funding for every disadvantaged pupil in their intake.

In addition, a number of key funders of social science in the UK have set up a National Quantitative Methods (QM) Initiative, intended to boost knowledge and research using numeric evidence including big datasets, and large-scale evaluations. It is funded by the ESRC, the Nuffield Foundation, HEFCE, and the British Academy, and adds to a number of related capacity-building initiatives such as the ESRC Researcher Development Initiative, and the ESRC National Centre for Research Methods (NCRM).

Many other countries have similar reforms and initiatives such as the Norwegian Knowledge Centre, Danish Clearinghouse for Educational Research, Australian Teaching and Learning Toolkit, and New Zealand Best Evidence Synthesis. However, perhaps the biggest moves have been in the US, with the Institute of Education Sciences (IES) described as the statistics and evaluation arm of the US Department of Education, which leads the What Works Clearinghouse for education (a role now undertaken in the UK by EEF). The IES also funds randomised trials, with some success (Spybrook et al. 2016).

The Campbell Collaboration was founded in the US to review, synthesise and advise about evidence in public policy areas like education (and so is similar to but much larger than EPPI). It is now international in nature. The International Initiative for Impact Evaluation (3ie) is funded by a mixture of US charity and UK aid, and has a deliberate focus on robust policy and practice evidence in developing countries.

How has it worked out?

One of the main problems with all of these initiatives lies in finding the capacity among traditional researchers in university departments of education to conduct and even appreciate such work. The lack of ability among traditional education researchers to conduct such work, and their apparent unwillingness to learn or adapt, means that such departments have more often been sites of resistance to the newer ideas and approaches. In the US, this has meant that in practice many education departments stopped applying for the federal funding that demanded evidence-based approaches. Instead, the funds have been taken up by the grow-ing sector of not-for-profit organisations. This damages the integrity of university departments. And, unfortunately, it can lead to dangerous interdependence. IES (and EEF in the UK) need the capacity that these organisations offer in order to conduct evaluations, and the organisations need the external funding maintained in order to pay the salary of the staff employed to do the evaluations. This might make the organisations more likely to provide what they feel the funder wants (for exam-ple, all EEF press releases so far at time of writing have emphasised positive results), and for the funder to condone that docility, so inhibiting the innovation and dis-sension that blue-chip funding for universities permits and can even encourage.

In the UK, as in the US, the capacity to conduct the kind of work needed did not exist in most schools of education. Unlike the US, the schools of education in the UK effectively took over the TLRP instead. Within a few years all of the key players had left the programme. They were replaced by a historian as Chair and theorists and 'qualitative' researchers on the Committee, and the second Director was another 'qualitative' researcher. No one in charge of TLRP had ever run a randomised control trial or used an alternatively rigorous evaluation design such as regression discontinuity. None had even done a systematic review of evidence. In that, they represented the majority of UK education research, and hence the very gap in skills that the programme was intended to address (Walford 2002, Schuller 2007). Not surprisingly, the TLRP failed to have the kind of impact that Sir Iain Chalmers and others had wanted.

Despite these many well-intentioned innovations internationally, large-scale reviews of international evidence suggest that, so far, little has changed in 15 years or more (Gorard et al. 2016a). Putting aside the majority of work of no conse-quence, and the remaining majority of work of a descriptive or explanatory nature, there is much less work that even tries to test out an intervention or approach. Of this minority of evaluation work, most is still next to useless due to threats to design, minimal scale, or high attrition. In addition, there is the problem of which trials are funded and conducted (as discussed in Chapter 3).

Most actual trials that have been conducted seem to emerge from the ground upwards – such as testing the product of a company, or the idea of an academic. We know more about some relatively small and sometimes even trivial issues, and much less about some of the key issues emerging from strong descriptive work. There is also the widespread problem that trials from the ground up can be conflicted, either because a company wants their product to be successful or an individual does not want their idea to be shown not to work for prestige reasons. This lies behind the use of outcome tests produced by the intervention developers themselves, and may motivate the partial reporting encountered in any review of studies. In the reported outcomes of studies that are unable to test a causal model by design, it is notable that the vast majority of poor studies nevertheless report an 'impact', and that most of these report positive impacts. Many studies have tried to find some positive results on some sub-scales or sub-tests, or by using a more complex analytical approach than necessary. Evaluations tend to be better when the researchers have nothing to gain or lose from whatever the result is, but gain or lose from whether the result is trustworthy or not.

Biased reporting is frequent – even to the extent that the success claimed in the abstract and conclusion of a report do not match the findings actually reported. Positive results are often highlighted in the abstracts or pulled out for more extensive discussion in the conclusion. For example, the paper may be an evaluation of literacy, testing different components sometimes using different tests for different outcomes. Almost invariably bigger or positive effects are found for outcomes measured using researcher or developer-constructed assessments. It is often the case that when standardised tests are used such positive effects disappear. The issue of different results depending on the independence of the test is widespread and noted in most reviews (e.g. Li and Ma 2010).

Another general finding is how small much of the work is (even in the category of appropriately designed evaluation work, which is among the best to be found). What is clear is that there is overall sufficient funding for large studies but that it is being frittered away on many small ones. This is why initiatives such as the IES in US and the EEF in England should be important – and indeed their studies are often among the best to be found. But these still suffer from the lack of strategic vision that the studies prompted from ground upwards display. As with the former ESRC TLRP, they seem to fund disproportionately those individuals and companies who want evidence that their own idea or product works, to the detriment of funding the big unresolved issues for improving learning.

What new kind of work is needed?

Overall then, the general standard of education research is poor, with too much funding frittered away on very small studies that would never be able to answer important research questions, but which seldom chart innovative new routes, ideas or approaches either. What is needed is better work across the board. However, there are more specific needs than that.

Research in any field or programme can be envisaged as a cycle of different phases – from synthesising what we already know about a topic, through developing a new theory and testing an intervention or educational artefact, to monitoring how well a new approach works in practice (Gorard 2013a). The cycle is more properly a spiral which has no clear beginning or end, in which phases overlap, can take place simultaneously, and could iterate almost endlessly. Within this cycle, different types of research have different purposes, and different research designs will be particularly suitable for these different types of research.

The cycle might start with an evidence synthesis, which should use existing datasets and previously published literature in an unbiased way to produce a summary of what is already known in relation to the research question(s). Once the existing evidence synthesis is complete, it should be clear what remains unanswered in the area of interest, and this can lead to a definition of the problem to be solved, the research purpose, and new research questions. The cycle might also end there, if existing evidence answers the question satisfactorily. Currently, while it remains true that most researchers do not bother with this phase, and a few seem stuck only in this phase, there is some good work being done with secondary datasets and in systematic reviews.

Prototyping and trialling of any new idea is vital, if resources are not to be wasted on a large-scale definitive study that has no chance of success. Trying ideas out in a development stage will tend to be done via smaller-scale work, to minimise the risk and cost in case the idea does not work. With minimal risk and cost, several alternative ideas can be tried out in parallel. Feasibility studies can be as cheap as thought experiments or as simple as case studies, or they can be complex designs for multi-method data collection. Their purpose in the cycle is to assess the likelihood of success of the idea, and so to assist with the decision whether to proceed further in the cycle, or not. Unfortunately, a high proportion of existing education research seems to be in this phase of the cycle. Very little of this work currently starts with a serious attempt at research synthesis, offering instead only partial literature reviews and confusing 'conceptual frameworks'. Even less of it moves on from this development work towards the preparation of a definitive large-scale study, or to creating something clearly useful from the knowledge gained.

The biggest gap in the kinds of work being conducted is still in the robust evaluation of artefacts from previous phases. Each prior phase might lead to a realisation that little more can be learnt and that the study is over, or that the programme needs radical revision and iteration to an earlier phase, or progression to a subsequent phase. However, the overall cycle can be envisaged as tending towards an artefact or 'product' of some kind. This product might be a theory (if the desired outcome is simply knowledge), a proposed improvement for public policy, or a tool/resource for a practitioner. In order for any of these outcomes to be promoted and disseminated in an ethical manner they must have been tested properly. A theory, by definition, will generate testable propositions. A proposed public policy intervention can be tested realistically and then monitored for the predicted benefits, and for any unwanted and undesirable side effects. However, only a tiny minority of education research is of this kind, and as we show in later chapters, much of the work of this kind that does exist is of poor quality.

The need for randomised control trials within the cycle

Logically, legally and philosophically, a causal model can be envisaged as being formed by evidence of an association (where two things X and Y are clearly related), an appropriate sequence of events (X occurs before or at the same time as Y), an explanatory model (how might X cause Y), and then evidence that altering or introducing the purported cause changes the purported effect (deliberately varying X produces otherwise unexplained variations in Y). There is quite a lot of education research describing the first three components of a causal model in most fields. For example, descriptive work may have suggested that a successful teacher tends to use a certain approach. The key question for policy or practice is whether other teachers can be encouraged to use that approach as well, and if so whether the results improve for their students.

We cannot fairly propose or test a causal model via case study designs (Gorard 2013a). Such passive observational approaches belong at a very early phase of the research cycle or in conjunction with other more powerful designs. Similarly, a correlation is not sufficient to identify causation, and so a study with a correlational design cannot be used. For example, children from families with several cars or a tennis court in their back garden may well do better in maths at school than their peers, but this does not mean that buying more cars or building more courts will improve national maths results. Yet this is the inadequate and misleading approach used in so much educational effectiveness research (see Chapter 1). We cannot test causation with only a longitudinal (before and after) design. For example, Bennett (2015) looked at the 'impact' of Singapore Maths Mastery with 40 third-grade students in the US. The group were taught maths using this approach and in later years were found to know more maths than at the start. The author confuses the reader with complex statistical approaches like ANOVA that have no place with these non-randomised cases (as discussed in Chapter 3). But this does not disguise the fact that they made causal claims about the effect of Maths Mastery without any idea of what would have happened in the absence of the new type of maths. In fact, the intervention could have reduced the amount by which children improved over time compared to normal teaching.

The approach used by Bennett is distressingly common, even in the minority of education research work supposedly trying to assess whether something works. Yet it should be obvious that some form of counterfactual is needed. The counterfactual cannot be a naturally occurring group, else we end up with a mere correlation. Instead we need at least two large groups of cases which are comparable at the outset and only one of which receives the intervention. It is possible to try and match cases to create comparable groups, but this involves considerable practical difficulties, and of course can only succeed in matching cases in terms of things that are known about (in order to be matched on). It is far better either to randomly allocate cases to treatment or comparison groups (for a randomised control trial), or to use a measure that creates a threshold to define the two groups (a regression discontinuity design). These are not gold standards or anything like that because the design needed in any study depends upon the research question(s). But they are the best available for addressing causal questions, and they are currently in short supply. The rest of this book looks at how such causal studies are conducted and what we can learn from them. First, we consider some of the things that are already going wrong with attempts to enhance the evidence base for education in this way.

PART II

Issues in conducting trials

3

PROBLEMS, ABUSES AND LIMITATIONS IN THE CONDUCT OF TRIALS

As suggested in the previous chapters, there are major problems with the conduct of education research worldwide, and with the trustworthiness of the evidence that such research generates. Therefore, moves towards the generation and use of safer evidence on educational effectiveness are welcome and overdue. However, they also reveal problems of their own. Ill-founded objections to safer evidence continue, and at some level probably pervade the majority of professional education research. The evidence-based movement is far from dominant, as some have suggested. But some of the criticism of the EBE movement is well founded, and partly due to the clear weaknesses of the ways in which it has been operationalised and reported. These weaknesses range from the kind of evidence being evaluated, practical problems in conducting trials, how the results are being analysed, and how they are being aggregated and used. This chapter is devoted to a discussion of some of the main weaknesses.

What do we need evidence on?

In theory, it is possible to evaluate any policy or practice intervention no matter how trivial or implausible it is. But, in reality, we need more clarity about which things to test and which things to ignore. The IES in the US (as described in Chapter 2) has a series of phases for their grant funding. Applicants can apply for relatively small amounts of funding for developing an idea and testing its feasibility. If results look promising they can apply for a larger amount to test the efficacy of the intervention developed from their idea, and if that looks promising they can apply for an even larger amount to test its effectiveness at large scale. While not ideal, this scheme does prevent public money being wasted on ideas that have no real chance of success, and forces those who wish to pursue their early ideas to develop their intervention and demonstrate its promise. However, there is little strategic direction. Priority funding is not routinely offered for the most important or the most urgent areas of investigation. The system depends largely on evaluating the merit of the projects that individuals and groups happen to apply for.

In England (UK), the EEF is more problematic. It does not have such a strictly phased scheme as the IES, and although it funds pilot, efficacy and effectiveness trials, the amount of funding does not vary in such a clearly phased way. About as much can be spent on an idea that quickly proves to have no merit, as on a large trial of an already very promising and fully developed intervention. There is also almost no encouragement or funding for replication studies of the kind promoted by 3ie, for example. The EEF depends mostly on individuals or groups applying for funding to have their ideas tested, with little or no strategic direction. And most of the rest of their evaluations are co-funded by organisations, policy departments and pressure groups who want their own pet concerns to take centre stage whether or not these are the most important current issues in education. IES and EEF both focus on formal education, and on school-age students, leaving the actual learning happening to most individuals in society, whether informally or as adults, not funded at all well.

This scattergun approach to evaluations ignores any hierarchy of needs – that could start with so many 'bread and butter' issues even in formal schooling that we do not know about. We need to use robust evaluations of academic selection at a young age (as in the grammar school system in the UK) to decide whether there is any merit in it. A linked series of studies could address the value and pitfalls of setting and streaming by ability within schools. We need to know whether whole class or small group teaching or some combination is best at each age – and how best to use homework, if at all. Are different kinds of schools – mixed or single-sex, all-age, 11–16 or 11–18, faith-based, specialist, independent and so on – actually any more or less effective with equivalent pupils? There are a large number of serious issues that have not been properly evaluated by randomised control trials or similar. Instead, we have a plethora of very small trials about some rather trivial issues, while the big issues continue to be debated fruitlessly over decades because they are not being properly tested. The bigger issues continue to be assessed using passive non-experimental designs, such as in the educational 'effectiveness' movement, that generate passion and publications but little real progress.

What can go wrong with trials that have been commissioned?

Even where trials have been conducted – and the work of IES, EEF, 3ie and others has led to considerable progress – they can be problematic. They often do not address key issues, and are frequently so small or have so many treatment groups that they have no practical value (see Chapter 4). They may test complex or vaguely defined approaches so that even when a trial shows that an approach is successful it is unclear what that means. They are often poorly reported, missing key information such as the amount of missing data or even the basic results such as the outcome scores for each group. They too often use outcome measures created by the researcher or intervention developer, which are well known to produce more favourable results than standardised tests and official qualifications.

The What Works Clearing House (see Chapter 2) routinely collects and identifies studies meeting a minimal threshold of quality on key topics – to summarise the current state of evidence on the effectiveness of a specified educational intervention. This makes it a useful one-stop shop for any topics covered. However, there are concerns that there may be serious estimation bias in such studies because of the complex real-world nature of educational interventions. For example, Ginsburg and Smith (2016) looked at 27 RCTs of mathematics interventions that met WWC minimum standards, and reported that 26 of them face important threats to their trustworthiness and usefulness. They propose that evaluations and outcome measures must be independent of the intervention developer, and that the outcome measures must not intrinsically favour one group or the other. These are the kinds of standards that IES and EEF adhere to. In addition, Ginsburg and Smith (2016) propose that the intervention and comparator groups must have equivalent resources and curriculum or teaching time, that curriculum changes are introduced for a whole school year (for example) before being evaluated, and that the evaluation only goes ahead if the in-depth evidence suggests that prior implementation of the intervention has been high quality. All three of these suggestions are clearly sensible, yet are not currently standard practice for evaluations run by any funder.

Perhaps the most prevalent problem for all evaluations concerns missing data. A situation where cases are selected for a random sample (or are randomly allocated to groups for an experiment), but some do not actually participate or do not provide responses for a key variable, leads to the sample being non-random in nature. There may be non-response, refusal to take part, untraceable cases, errors in the sampling frame, and unreadable or undecipherable data. In our own trials (such as those in Chapters 7 to 9) we have encountered cases missing either pre- or post-test data, or contextual data such as eligibility for free school meals. We had erroneous data such as an incorrect version of the pupil's name or year. We had two or more pupils with the same 'unique' identifier and the same pupil with more than one identifier. We had tests given to the wrong pupils, scripts sent to the wrong address, and on one occasion a school inadvertently shredded the completed test forms. Sometimes pupils were absent, and schools would not follow them up, or they had moved abroad. Sometimes a pupil was permanently excluded during the trial, or moved under a protection scheme so that their destination was secret. We even had schools closed during a trial, with the children scattered between other schools in the area. These, and many more examples, are all possible in any school-based trial. No large field trial can avoid all of them.

If cases from a random sample drop out or do not provide responses for a key variable after a study has started, the resulting sample is necessarily non-random by definition. In general, the larger the study, the more data it collects and the longer it lasts, the more likely it is to have substantial missing data. Many commentators suggest that 100% participation, of the kind required by statistical sampling theory, is unheard of in practice (Cuddeback et al. 2004). For example, Lindner et al. (2001)

examined all of the articles published in the *Journal of Agricultural Education* 1990–1999. All empirical reports had issues of non-response even though most made no mention of the threat that this caused to the validity of their findings. Most, if not all, evaluations have missing data. In our many and varied systematic reviews *all* studies we encountered had issues of missing data (e.g. Gorard et al. 2016a). Some studies do not report how much data is missing in a clear manner. Many of the rest do not report how the missing data was handled. And most of the remainder do not appear to have handled it well (Powney et al. 2014).

This is partly because of poor advice. For example, the EEF (2014) quality guidelines state in relation to attrition that 'For cluster randomised trials, the number of clusters that dropped out will determine the threshold, not the individual pupils'. This means that a school-level RCT with no school dropout would be reported as having no attrition even if 80% of the pupils in the treatment group did not provide final scores. This is clearly absurd. The EEF has been misguided in their treatment of attrition, once citing the WWC as claiming that up to 30% missing data was 'low' attrition as long as the number of cases missing was about the same between groups. But if the 29% highest attaining pupils dropped out of one group and the 29% lowest attaining from the other, this would seriously threaten the security of any trial findings. It would be nothing like 'low' attrition. In reality, we would not know which cases were missing, but there is no reason to assume balance any more than imbalance in terms of the types of cases missing. For example, there can be post-allocation demoralisation in any trial. In a study of an intervention to improve the literacy of low-attaining students, the higher attaining students allocated to the intervention may drop out because they feel patronised, while the lower attaining students allocated to the control may drop out because they are disappointed not to receive the help. Dong and Lipsey (2011) agree with us – bias is linked to *any* level of attrition and not just to differential attrition between the groups.

Researchers need to be more explicit about missing data in their studies, and more aware of the bias that this can cause (Dumville et al. 2006). All non-response creates a potential for bias in the results from the remaining cases (Peress 2010). It is most unlikely that the cases dropping out from a random sample are randomly distributed, and that is part of the reason why the residue is no longer a 'random' sample (Hansen and Hurwitz 1946, Sheikh and Mattingly 1981). Therefore, data based only on the achieved respondents in any study is almost certainly biased to some extent, and non-response can have a 'dramatic impact' on the data (Behaghel et al. 2009, p. 1, Dolton et al. 2000, Gorard 2015a).

Bias in the substantive results caused by missing data generally cannot be corrected by technical means (Cuddeback et al. 2004). Missing data cannot be accurately replaced by using the evidence that has been collected. In fact, attempts at such replacement often make the bias worse. Weights can only be used *post hoc* to correct for variables for which all true population values are known anyway, making weighting for these pointless, while weighting a sample in this way clearly cannot correct the values of other variables for which the true population value is not known (Peress 2010). Multiple imputation often makes little substantive difference to the results of a study anyway (Pampaka et al. 2016). It should therefore be avoided as complex, harder to explain and justify, and potentially misleading. Because there is no secure way to 'replace' missing data, preventing it and working harder for 100% completion are key elements of good quality research (Dziura et al. 2013). We explain in Chapter 4 how missing data can be accounted for and handled in analyses.

How are evaluation results mistreated?

Significance testing with missing and inappropriate data

The use of significance tests is a widespread misuse of statistics in the analysis of trials. Statistical significance testing – such as the use of t-tests, ANOVA, chi-squared and similar – is a commonly used, taught and published procedure when researchers are analysing numeric data. It is routinely used to assess the importance of a difference between groups, or a correlation between measures, or some other kind of pattern or trend in the data. Traditionally it operates by assuming that there is no difference, correlation or other pattern in the real world (the population), and that any apparent pattern in the achieved data must be solely the result of the vagaries of randomly selecting or allocating cases from that population. This crucial prior assumption is known as the nil-null hypothesis, and it clearly entails another, which is that the cases involved in the research must have been selected or allocated fully at random. There must be no bias in the study design, and no measurement error, non-response or sample dropout. It is on these bases that the steps (or the algorithm in any software) to compute a significance test result are defined. 'This is not a matter of debate or opinion; it is a matter of mathematical necessity' (Berk and Freedman 2001, p.2).

Some commentators attempt to defend the use of significance testing (see below) with incomplete samples by drawing a purported distinction between data missing randomly (an unlikely scenario), which they term missing completely at random, and data missing at random, which they claim is data whose 'missingness' does not depend upon its value (Brunton-Smith et al. 2014). This then 'permits' them to use their favoured statistical approaches with over 60% of the relevant data missing (for example, see Pampaka et al. 2016). The distinction is a false one. Randomness is a very simple concept, meaning that events happen by chance. Since we are sure from empirical studies (see above) that missing data does not occur by chance, it cannot and must not be assumed to be random in nature.

A random sample with missing data is no longer a random sample, and so cannot form the basis for significance tests. Nor should significance tests be used with population data, convenience samples or any other non-random cases such as snowball samples. Gibbs et al. (2015) show that the misleading and invalid practice of using inferential statistics with population data is widespread in top education journals (part of the reason for the perpetuation of this ridiculous practice is the demand by some journals and reviewers for significance tests regardless of context).

It should be easy to see that using inferential statistics with either population or incomplete data is wrong. There can be no standard error under these circumstances. Complete randomisation of the cases under consideration is an absolutely necessary pre-condition (Camilli 1996, Freedman 2004, Glass 2014). Therefore, estimating the p-value for any kind of non-random sample is pointless (Filho et al. 2013). The answer does not and cannot mean anything.

It follows that, in practice, significance tests should never be used. But their abuse is widespread. We have collectively conducted a large number of systematic reviews on a wide range of topics, involving perhaps 50,000 individual studies, and have never come across a piece of research in which significance testing was conducted and reported correctly. But this is not just a problem in general research. It is actually worse in EBE work, and worst of all in work funded and used by the very organisations described in Chapter 2 as having been set up to improve the quality of evaluations.

For example, the Director of the ESRC-funded NCRM (Chapter 2) conducted an analysis of a survey with 40% of the cases missing because they used 'data from the April 2007 to March 2010 rounds of the survey, with a total achieved sample of 57,345 and an average response rate over the three years of 60%' (Sturgis et al. 2014, p. 1291). However, they then carry on to conduct significance tests for what is clearly not a random sample, and take no further account of the missing data itself. Yet the NCRM was set up to improve the quality of research.

Chamberlain et al. (2015) were funded by the ESRC to help improve the use and quality of quantitative methods in the UK as part of the QM Initiative, and yet they made an elementary error in evaluating their success by computing p-values for incomplete census data. For example they say:

> At Loughborough University, first-year students must complete a 12-week introductory quantitative method statistics course as part of their BSc (Hons) Sociology or BSc (Hons) Criminology and Social Policy degree studies . . . Students completing the module were asked to complete a project questionnaire at the beginning of the module (Week 1) and the end of the module (Week 11) . . . Data collected were on the Likert-type scale of ranked ordinal level of measurement, so a paired sample t-test can be used to measure the difference (if any) in respondents' mean responses at the beginning and end of the introductory statistics module . . . A total of 66 first-year undergraduate students completed the introductory statistics module. Of these, 55 completed the initial questionnaire (83%) and 44 (67%) fully participated by completing a questionnaire at the beginning of the module and at the end . . . Respondents agreeing that they were anxious decreased from 55% to 43%, while, reciprocally, those disagreeing increased from 21% to 35%, a statistically significant if small change (T-test result: $T(43) = -1.730$, $p = 0.05$). (Chamberlain et al. 2015, pp.5–6)

This is nonsense – there is no sample and no randomisation and therefore there cannot be any probabilistic uncertainty to assess via a t-test or anything else.

In a report for an evaluation funded, and peer-reviewed, by the EEF, Sibieta (2016, p. 3 and throughout) describes the evaluation as a randomised control trial. But on page 14 they say:

> Random assignment will, on average, lead to small and statistically insignificant differences between each group in terms of gender, age and SWRT score. However, in any particular random draw it is possible that larger, significant differences can arise purely by chance . . . The randomisation process was repeated 1,000 times, resulting in 1,000 different allocations. To identify the optimal randomisation, we first restricted our attention to the random assignments that led to zero significant differences between groups in terms of age, gender and SWRT score. Among this set of assignments, we then selected the one that yielded the smallest value of the total differences in average characteristics.

The purpose of randomising cases to groups for a trial – in a true randomised control trial – is so that the characteristics of the cases in each group are not biased (via volunteering, selection or subversion). A researcher could try to match the two groups without randomisation, by considering all of the variables known about all cases, and this is effectively what happened in this EEF trial rather than randomisation. But this is inferior to fair randomisation for a number of reasons, and should anyway not be described as the same as a randomised control trial. Playing a random game 1,000 times and then picking one outcome does not lead to a random outcome even though that outcome was generated randomly itself. The eventual outcome was matched and selected, not random. And this kind of matching can only be done using variables that are known about for all cases. It is not clear that it can help to create unbiased distributions of the infinite number of other variables not known about. In fact, it may make the balance of those variables worse. Anyway, a strong constraint when matching is that it can really only be done with a few variables, and so makes little difference in practice. If matching is attempted with many variables it is easy to find cases or groups that have nearest equivalents whose nearest equivalents in turn are not those same cases or groups, which creates a major practical problem (Gorard 2013a).

The issue here appears to be that the EEF evaluator (and the EEF methods advisers and reviewers) does not know what fair randomisation is. They could have done what they did, and described it as something else, like randomised matching, and argued that this was superior. But then they should not have even attempted to use significance tests, which they did. When they say that after a sample is drawn randomly (one iteration) 'it is possible that larger, significant differences can arise purely by chance' this is clearly nonsense. If the cases are truly randomised then any differences must have occurred by chance and so no differences can be what they term 'significant'. If the cases have not been randomised the evaluators cannot even begin to justify using a significance test. The evaluation reports 30% attrition from the pupil sample, and then blithely goes on to run post-intervention significance tests, even though the achieved allocation was not random to start with (above), and even if it had been it is now only 70% intact and would no longer be random. There are serious flaws in this analysis at almost every step and yet it is defended by EEF, which is meant to be an organisation funded to improve the quality of education evaluations.

In another example, Williams et al. (2016) were funded by the ESRC to overcome the 'quantitative deficit'. Like Sibieta they checked their baseline scores in a small evaluation using p-values. If they had randomised their cases to treatments, then a significance test would not be needed because the only differences between treatment groups *must* be due to the randomisation (as above). As they did not randomise in fact, they should not be using significance tests at all. What they say is:

> In social experiments, particularly those in education, randomisation is also difficult to achieve . . . The research described here was conducted across one academic year (2012/13) in two universities . . . In both universities the second level research methods module constituted the control group and was compulsory for all students. The 'experimental' modules were also in Year Two . . . Students taking the experimental modules opted to do so voluntarily . . . To check for selection effects we tested for significant differences in attainment, experiences and attitudes between the control and experimental groups. There were no significant differences . . . confirming that there were no academic or pre-university selection effects. However, there was a difference in attitudes that may have been influenced during the first year of university and the experimental group were significantly more confident in using numbers in everyday life than the control group ($t = 1.97$, 190 d.f., $p = 0.05$). The experimental group were also significantly more inclined to see their main degree subject as closer to science/maths than the control group ($t = 1.94$, 191 d.f., $p = 0.05$).

The paper is awash with significance tests for these naturally occurring (not randomised) groups with high attrition. How will research improve if even those employed to improve it do not understand how to do it?

Misunderstanding the logic of significance tests

However, such abuse is not even the worst problem. In significance tests, the p-value is the probability of finding a difference as large or a pattern as strong as that shown in the given sample, assuming that the pattern is just a fluke introduced by the randomisation of cases from the population to the sample. This is based on a prior assumption that the sample is completely random (which is highly unlikely) and other assumptions about the distribution of the values in the dataset and the nature of the measurements involved. Not only are these assumptions underlying the calculation of the p-value very unlikely to be true in any real piece of research, it is not at all clear what use this peculiar probability is to analysts. It is clearly *not* the probability of the null hypothesis being true. Why do so many researchers continue to calculate and cite it?

They continue to use and cite it because they misportray what the p-value is. They imagine that it is the probability of the nil-null hypothesis being true given the data observed in one sample. They, therefore, feel able to use it to decide whether to accept or reject the nil-null hypothesis. But these two conditional probabilities are very different. A significance test computes the probability of the data observed in one sample given that the nil-null hypothesis (H_0) is true. What analysts want is the probability of the nil-null hypothesis being true given the data observed. No one wants to know the probabilistic answer the tests actually provide, and the test cannot provide the answer analysts really want (Falk and Greenbaum 1995). But researchers so much want the second that they allow themselves to pretend it is the same as or closely related to the first. This is clearly false − $p(A \mid B)$ is not the same as or even closely related to $p(B \mid A)$. Cohen (1994, p. 998) illustrates the absurdity of ignoring these facts when interpreting NHSTs and p-values. The logic underlying the false but still widespread interpretation of a 'significant' result is as follows:

- If H_0 is true, then the data obtained would probably not occur.
- But this result has occurred.
- Therefore, H_0 is probably not true.

The problem with this line of reasoning is that it is formally identical to:

- If a person is an American, then he is probably not a member of Congress.
- But this person is a member of Congress.
- Therefore, he is probably not an American!

Written like that it is clear that the two probabilities in each version are different. The 'inverse probability error' is an obvious logical fallacy. Pretending these two things are the same or even closely related in scale, as so many analysts do, would lead to serious errors in practice. The desire to include some quantitative measure of credibility has prompted this illegitimate use of statistical significance as an inadequate and misleading surrogate for such a measure (Matthews 2001).

Significance tests are therefore widely misinterpreted by researchers, students and their teachers, as well as by professional statisticians (Watts 1991, Murtonen and Lehtinen 2003). These mistakes are not isolated errors but a normal part of statistical discourse (Oakes 1986). Again 'experts' appear not to get this, and again the problem is prevalent even (or perhaps especially) among those funded by government and charities to improve the use of evaluations and their analysis.

At a conference designed by EEF to give expert advice to their panel of evaluators, one of the experts, who was also a REF panel member for education on the basis of statistical expertise, showed that they believed a significance test portrayed the likelihood of the nil-null hypothesis being wrong. See, for example, the fourth slide in Connolly (2013) which states that the 'Significance of b_4 indicates whether there is evidence of an interaction effect (i.e. in this case that the intervention has differential effects for boys and girls)'. Members of the audience, including the lead evaluator from NFER, agreed, and when the inverse probability error was pointed out, stated that it made no difference.

The same error is routinely made in interpreting confidence intervals (discussed in Chapter 4). An example appears in resources produced by WISERD (2013) who had been funded by the ESRC National Quantitative Methods Initiative to improve the use and understanding of statistics. For example, in explaining what a confidence interval (CI) is, Slide 5 says that 'We can use these properties of the sampling distribution of sample means to determine what interval the population mean probably falls in, based on the sample mean and sample standard deviation'. Slide 6 says that 'For example, we can determine the interval in which we can be 95% confident that the population mean falls. We call such an interval the "95% confidence interval"'. This explanation is completely wrong, and again is based on the inverse probability error.

This last example leads to consideration of what follows from abandoning the use of significance tests – as we must. We must then also abandon the multiple testing done almost invisibly as part of more complex analyses such as regression (relying instead only on effect sizes to retain or exclude explanatory variables). We must abandon the current notion of statistical power and minimal detectable effect sizes (MDES), as described on Chapter 4, both of which rely on conducting significance tests. And we must abandon confidence intervals that are so like significance tests and share the same reverse logic, but are even harder to understand. 'There are no interpretations of these concepts that are at once simple, intuitive, correct, and foolproof', especially the confidence interval (Greenland et al. 2016).

There are many other problems with significance tests, covered in the references given here and thousands of others. The problems include data fiddling, publication bias, false positives, misuse of power analyses to deny non-significant results, post hoc dredging, and the multiple use of tests designed for one-off use. The use of significance tests also tends to reduce the value of small studies, favouring one large 'significant' study over a large number of less than significant smaller ones.

The ethics of the situation

None of this is new. The fact that significance tests and similar related approaches do not work as intended (or as used) has been clear for more than 90 years in the social sciences and beyond (Boring 1919, Jeffreys 1937, Berkson 1938, Rozeboom 1960, Bakan 1966, Meehl 1967, Morrison and Henkel 1969, Carver 1978, Berger and Sellke 1987, Loftus 1991, Daniel 1998, Tryon 1998, Nickerson 2000, Gorard 2003a, Hubbard and Meyer 2013).

Thousands of pieces have been written since the adoption of significance tests, warning against their use both because they do not work as used to test a nil-null hypothesis, and because they should not be used with non-random cases even if they did work. Methods experts in medicine, psychology, sociology and education, including the APA, ASA and other bodies, advise against their use (Walster and Cleary 1970, Nix and Barnette 1998, Fidler et al. 2004). *The American Journal of Public Health, Epidemiology, Basic and Applied Psychology*, and numerous medical and ecological journals, have banned their publication, as have most US medical journals (Starbuck 2016). Hunter (1997, p. 3) called for a ban in Psychological Science, stating simply that 'The significance test as currently used is a disaster'. Guttman (1985, p.4) argued 'that it be abandoned by *all* substantive science'. Nester (1996, p. 407) said that 't-tests, analyses of variance . . . linear contrasts and multiple comparisons, and tests of significance for correlation and regression coefficients should be avoided by statisticians and discarded from the scientific literature'. The volatile results produced by such testing are so prevalent in epidemiology that Le Fanu (1999) suggested that all departments of epidemiology be closed down as a service to medicine. For the IES, Lipsey et al. (2012) stated that significance testing and p-values give misleading results about the substantive nature of results, and are 'best avoided'. Even Field (author of a popular statistics book for undergraduates in psychology that used to promote testing) now agrees that null hypothesis significance testing 'is flawed because the significance of the test tells us nothing about the null hypothesis' (Field 2013, p. 76). These results are more often wrong than right.

Yet the misuse of significance testing, and all that follows from it, continues to cause widespread damage, denying improvement, wasting research time and funding, and creating unimaginable opportunity costs. Advances are stalled and scientific discoveries threatened by the 'ubiquitous misuse and tyranny' of the p-value (Stang et al. 2010, p. 1). It prevents the public as students or patients from obtaining the most appropriate treatment, and therefore harms many of them either by omission or commission at some stage in their lives.

In addition, the misuse of significance testing is corrupting to researchers themselves. We all learn that significance tests are based on conducting one test, pre-specified, with completely randomised cases (Schmidt and Hunter 1997, Starbuck 2016). But usage is clearly different to that even for purported experts (as above). Many researchers report pretending that the key assumptions do not matter as a kind of ritual in order to get published and further their careers. Students and new researchers are usually more confused at the end of a course on statistics, which makes them use significance tests wrongly, and ignores more logical and simpler approaches (Chatfield 1991). In order to pass such a course, students must accept something which does not make sense, and the most talented may find it the hardest to cope with for that reason (Deming 1975). The use of significance testing encourages game-playing and even a lack of integrity (Simmons et al. 2011), where researchers are less likely to publish insignificant results, and journals are less likely to accept them – leading to the file-drawer problem (Rosenthal 1979, Pigott et al. 2013, Kuhberger et al. 2014). And they seem to be used *instead* of crucial considerations of sample quality, design bias, measurement quality and so on

(Gorard 2015a) in the mistaken belief that statistics can solve the problems of poor research and weak designs.

Significance tests just do not work – even when used as their advocates intended, with fully randomised cases. They cannot be used to decide whether a finding is worthy of further investigation or whether it should be acted on in practice. They are providing vast numbers of false results, leading to vanishing breakthroughs in all of the fields in which they are used. Where their research has no real-life implications, those researchers relying on significance tests are simply wasting the time of those who read the work, and the money of those who fund them. These are serious opportunity costs, because the time and money could otherwise have been spent on something that was valid and perhaps even useful. But where the research matters, as it should, the damage caused by using significance tests is even worse. The use of significance tests means that progress is being hindered, and real lives are being damaged, in areas from law and epidemiology to education and social justice.

This is now a serious ethical issue (Gorard 2016). It is not due to ignorance of the problems. Nor is it a mathematical or logical debate, because that has been over for a long time (Thompson 2004). Significance testing appears to derive from a psychological flaw among its advocates and defenders. Schmidt (1996) considered it an addiction to false belief.

> It does not tell us what we want to know, and we so much want to know what we want to know that, out of desperation, we nevertheless believe that it does! (Cohen 1994)

We now need research funders, taxpayers and charity givers to demand change, and that researchers no longer use the money given to their studies to stifle progress and harm the lives of those intended to benefit from research.

What difference do evaluations make?

For a number of good and not very good reasons, robust evidence from attempts to evaluate improvements in education does not usually have the impact that it should. This issue is considered in more detail in Chapter 10. Perhaps the main reason for this is that potential users are confused by the amount of evidence of different kinds and quality, and are not able to make appropriately critical discriminating choices between the robust evidence and the rest. This is not in their preparation or even their role as users of evidence, after all. However, academics seem to have no appropriate mechanism to make these decisions either. The peer-review system cannot work while the majority of work remains so poor, because the academics producing such work then form the majority of peers judging the quality of each other's work. Some may not be competent, some will practice clique or competitor peer review, and some will have conflicts of interest.

We need an appropriate conduit between front-line research and the users of research evidence that can convert the evidence into more usable forms while focussing on the best and safest work and largely ignoring the remaining majority that could mislead badly. Some commentators believe that systematic reviews and meta-analyses of studies in particular fields are the way forward, but these do not eliminate most of the problems (Egger et al. 1998, Glass 2016). Most such syntheses of evidence are insufficiently careful about the quality of each study, and try to collapse evidence on studies that are too dissimilar to each other. Examples appear in Chapters 6 to 9.

Worse than all of this, much of the weaker work *does* have impact even though it should not. Partly this is due to low standards being set. For example, in the UK academics are required to demonstrate impact from their research in order to obtain competitive national funding via the Research Excellence Framework (REF), and yet the research basis for the impact is permitted to be as much as two categories of quality below the best work available (a low 2* as opposed to the best 4* grade). Demanding that academics demonstrate impact may therefore worsen things (Moss 2013). We need to ensure that the interventions actually used in policy and practice are the most useful and the least harmful available. We should demand 4* work for our policy-makers and practitioners to act on.

Some of the solutions to the various problems for EBE are presented in Chapter 4.

4

ASSESSING THE TRUSTWORTHINESS OF A RESEARCH FINDING

This chapter concerns what are sometimes called 'impact' evaluations (as opposed to the 'process' evaluations discussed in the next chapter). It looks at how the impact of a controlled intervention is estimated, and then how to judge the security of that estimate of impact. It looks at 'effect' sizes as a way of estimating impact, and their limitations, as well as sensitivity analyses especially for handling any missing data or measurement error. It then describes a general procedure for assessing and comparing the trustworthiness of research findings. These approaches are used in the remaining and substantive chapters of the book to judge the quality of research. However, the first section on the importance of clear presentation and several other key points throughout are relevant to all forms of research, not just intervention studies.

Clear presentation of research findings

To be able to judge the quality of any piece of research its report has to be presented clearly. A major purpose of reporting research is to enable the widest possible relevant readership to understand what has been done and found out in the research being described. Therefore, the keys to any presentation of results are its simplicity of expression and its clarity as a narrative or argument. Presentation matters, because it is impossible for a research reader or user to assess how trustworthy a piece of research is unless it can be understood fully. If crucial information is omitted from a report or presented in such a way that it may as well have been omitted, then the research that it describes must be assumed to be untrustworthy.

This may sound harsh, but it is necessary in the context of evidence-based education. For example, as is shown throughout the book, missing cases or missing data from any study can have a huge influence on the apparent results. If a study reports (and reports clearly) the level of missing data then this can be taken into account when judging the results. If a study does not state (clearly) how much data is missing then it is impossible to judge how trustworthy the results are. This is similar to not having a report, or indeed not doing the research in the first place.

Of course, the research reporting also needs to be truthful. If the research is fabricated, distorted or exaggerated, for example, then none of the other things matter. The focus of ethics committees ought to be much more on keeping research honest than it currently is.

As well as being truthful and containing all relevant information, research reports should be expressed and presented as simply as possible. This allows the widest readership, and makes it more likely that any errors or leaps in logic are exposed. The explanation provided by researchers for any findings should always be the simplest one that requires no further assumptions. An easy way to consider whether any conclusion is 'warranted' is to consider how the evidence for it could be explained if the conclusion were not actually true (Gorard 2013a). This process is both creative and logical.

While they may sound obvious, all of these principles need to be kept in mind constantly when considering more technical issues, such as which 'effect' size to use.

Presenting results as 'effect' sizes

Moving away from the flawed approach of significance testing should encourage researchers to consider and report a much wider range of issues – such as the possible importance and methodological soundness of their findings (Greenwald 1975, Kline 2004). What is needed is some idea of the scale of any difference or pattern or trend (Yates 1964, Lecoutre and Poitevineau 2011), the methodological limitations underlying it, and a judgement about its substantive importance (and perhaps also the cost-effectiveness of accepting the finding's implications or not).

When looking at impact evaluations, a common method of presenting the results is to use 'effect' sizes (Lipsey et al. 2012). 'Effect' is written in inverted commas like this because an effect size is really just a standardised difference between groups. It could portray how much better the exam results are for a group of girls compared to a group of boys, for example. But this would not suggest that the difference was necessarily the effect of being a girl or a boy. It would perhaps be better to use a different name in this book, but the term effect size (ES) is already in widespread use and so the confusion from changing it might be even greater. An 'effect' size does not imply a causal relationship. Nor does it provide a test of anything. It is simply a way of presenting results, in the same way as drawing a graph. Effect sizes can give a good idea of the standardised size of any difference, pattern, trend or correlation. They do not rely on the same unlikely assumptions as significance tests – so that they can be used legitimately with non-random cases, where substantial data is missing, and so on. They emphasise the scale of the finding (pattern, trend or difference) rather than the scale of the study (as significance tests and confidence intervals do).

Effect sizes *are* open to publication bias and abuse, just as significance tests and confidence intervals are. For example, effect sizes are theoretically independent of sample sizes. Yet in a study of 1,000 articles, a correlation of −0.45 was found between the sample size and reported effect size (Kuhberger et al. 2014). Perhaps this is because small samples are more likely to produce aberrant or extreme 'effect' sizes which, like significant results, are then more likely to be published (Slavin and Smith 2009). 'Effect' sizes also tend to be larger when the outcome measurement is not an independent and otherwise standard measurement (Cheung and Slavin 2015). In themselves, ES offer no direct assessment of a finding arising by chance and give no indication of the quality of the study that led to the finding.

Some commentators, in scrapping significance tests, have suggested using confidence intervals (CIs) with effect sizes, on the basis that CIs offer at least a likelihood estimate (Cumming 2014). But, as suggested in Chapter 3, the problems with CIs are largely the same as for significance tests. CIs are, in fact, disguised significance tests. CIs also say nothing about the quality of the study, cannot account for missing data, apply only to complete random samples and, like p-values, are the reverse of what most commentators want and believe them to be. They are mainly the size of the sample converted into a less comprehensible format.

All of these issues can be avoided (see below) by having well-designed evaluations with large numbers of cases (N) in each cell for any comparison and with minimal attrition. In this context, ES and N are sufficient.

There are 'effect' sizes for correlations and regression models (such as R^2), and for categorical frequency data (such as odds ratios). But the most common type used in impact evaluations is 'effect' sizes expressing a difference between the scores of two or more groups. There are a number of variations on this kind of ES, but all have as their numerator the difference between the means of the two groups of cases being compared (such as the mean post-test score for the treatment and control groups in an experiment). This difference between means is then divided by a measure of the variability of the scores that make up the mean scores. Probably the simplest estimate of such variation is the mean absolute deviation (M|D|). This is calculated by working out how far each data point is from the overall mean of all data points, adding the results together but ignoring whether the results are positive or negative, and then dividing the total by the number of data points.

Gorard (2005a) showed that an error had been made nearly 100 years ago in using the standard deviation as the basic summary of variation for a distribution rather than the M|D| favoured by Eddington. The idea of such a robust and simple approach to measuring variation dates back to at least 1757 but was perhaps not really practical then due to lack of computing power (Li and Arce 2004). The mean absolute deviation is now growing in use and areas of applicability – including astronomy, biology, engineering, dentistry, IT, physics, imaging, geography and environmental science (e.g. Anand and Narasimha 2013, Hao et al. 2012, Hižak J. and Logožar R. 2011, Sari et al. 2012, Ashith and Acharya 2014). In fact, a whole alternative statistics is growing up around this simple and intuitive indicator of variation, including methods for correlations, covariance and regression techniques

(Falie and David 2010, Gorard 2015b, Elamir 2015). The M|D| is less sensitive to distortion from extreme scores in the data than the more usual standard deviation, and it does not rely on the assumptions made in least squares modelling such as that the model has normally distributed errors. It involves fewer computations, meaning less chance of propagating errors in the measurements involved.

Gorard (2015c) proposed an effect size based on M|D|, which was simply the difference between means divided by their overall M|D|, and which has all of the advantages listed above. This effect size (A) is now being used in practice in a variety of fields of science and engineering (although interestingly very little in education and social science research). However, ES 'wars' have long been fought over exactly what the denominator for an effect size should be. More common forms of ES include Cohen's d with the pooled standard deviation of both comparator groups as the denominator. Glass' delta uses only the standard deviation of the control group, on the basis that these cases are unaffected by the treatment in an experiment and so represent the more usual pattern of variation. Hedges' g is a variation of Cohen's d but with the pooled standard deviation purportedly adjusted for sampling variation (which is of no relevance for population data and non-random or incomplete random samples). These varieties sound and indeed are very similar. With a good study and a large number of cases in each group the substantive findings from using Gorard's A, Cohen's d, Glass' delta, Hedges' g or any other sensible variation will always be the same. Put another way, the direction of any difference between the two groups is determined by the numerator which is common to all ES listed here. Therefore, the results cannot change sign depending upon the precise ES used. The exact decimal places in the ES can then change depending upon which measure of variation is used as the denominator – but not by much in practice.

For example, Xiao et al. (2016) conducted a re-analysis of 22 findings from 17 randomised control trials. Where they used the same outcome variables in each calculation, the results for each trial were the same whether the Hedges, Glass or Cohen version of the effect size was used. They did not compare results with the mean absolute deviation ES (but see Gorard 2015c for such comparisons). This suggests that it really does not matter which ES is used in practice. Gorard's A involves the fewest assumptions, has the simplest algebra for explanation (largely because there is no squaring and then square-rooting involved), and is more intuitive for practitioners.

Xiao et al. (2016) went further and compared the 22 results based on a simple effect size with those based on linear regression, multi-level modelling, and Bayesian approaches including Bayesian multi-level modelling. Again, for these well-structured randomised controlled trials (RCTs) with relatively large N, and using the same outcome variables in each calculation, these different approaches made no difference to the substantive result. Put another way, any result that varied substantially depending upon exactly which of these plausible approaches was used would not be a safe result (presumably it would stem from a small cell size creating volatility). Although neither of these comparisons had their true implications highlighted by the authors of the paper, these are useful illustrations. It seems that a simple effect size gives the same results in a well-designed large study as any of the more complex methods of presenting an analysis. For that reason, effect sizes should always be used, based on the simplest ES suitable for the data involved, while more complex analyses are not needed for the results of randomised control trials.

In RCTs the design does the heavy lifting and entails a simple comparative analysis (Gorard 2013a), with no need for the more complex forms of analysis designed for use with less secure datasets. In fact, these more complex analyses are more dangerous and could be misleading. This is partly due to the increased propagation of errors, and partly because the link between an outcome and a pre-test variable can be reversed when controlling for a third variable, as happens in multivariate analyses – leading to Simpson's Paradox, Lord's Paradox, or suppression effects (Tu et al. 2008). Therefore, a simple difference in outcomes ES is preferred when presenting the results in the substantive chapters of this book.

Some commentators and methods resources appear overly concerned with the impact of 'clustering' when analysing the results of a trial. They claim that the standard error of the outcomes scores will be misleadingly small when the scores are collected from cases nested within units or areas that have themselves been randomly allocated to treatment groups (Gorard 2009). This is rarely if ever an issue in robust evaluations for a number of reasons. Most real-life samples have no standard error (Chapter 3). The standard error only matters when conducting significance tests or similar, and these techniques should not be used anyway, so there is no problem. If cases have been randomised at cluster (e.g. school) level, then the clusters are the cases, and can be analysed as such. Again, there is no problem. As Xiao et al. (2016) show, the intra-cluster correlation that supposedly causes the reduced standard error is anyway often zero for a decent multi-site trial. In practice, the substantive results from using multi-level modelling and simpler approaches are the same anyway. The mean score for all pupils in one group in a trial must be equal to the weighted mean for all schools, based on the mean score for all pupils in that group in each school. The two results will obviously be exactly the same, unless for some spurious reason the size of each school is ignored. In summary, simple random allocation of cases is to be preferred where possible. Where it is not possible, any possible difference in the findings caused by using a complex analytical technique will not compensate for the lack of readability in the results.

A further issue concerns which version of the outcome variables should be used to create an effect size. This, of course, depends chiefly upon the outcomes and the design pre-specified for each trial. Suitable designs include 'post-test only', in which the outcome measure is the variable pre-selected to be assessed for both groups after the treatment group has received the intervention. If the trial is large, the two groups will tend to be reasonably balanced in terms of the outcome variable before the trial, and so using only a post-test and assuming initial balance between groups is simpler. It is also somewhat safer than a pre- and post-test analysis, since it involves fewer subtractions of similar sized values, and so reduces the chances of the propagation of any initial errors in measuring the outcome variable (Gorard 2013b).

However, on occasion, the two (or more) groups in a trial will be large but still unbalanced at the outset. This is an inevitable consequence of random allocation to groups; indeed it is an important part of what 'random' means. Therefore, it cannot be prevented by constraining the randomisation (because that would merely produce non-random allocation). It is not possible to halt the trial at this stage, partly because that would be a waste of the resources used so far, but mainly again because it would destroy the randomisation of trials over the long-term. For the same reason, the trial cannot be continued with a new randomisation, repeated until there is initial balance. Neither of these two decisions would be fair. It would be like playing a dice game with someone who was permitted to re-roll any die whose result they did not like. Under the circumstances of initial imbalance the most suitable practical approach is to look at the improvement or change scores for each group in the trial, by comparing the pre-test and post-test scores for each group.

The simplest way of doing this is to compute the gain score for each case, which is their score on the post-test minus their score on the pre-test. The mean of these gain scores for each group then provides an appropriate outcome variable. Since it is important to pre-specify the analysis, and because there is no way of knowing beforehand whether the groups will be balanced at the outset, it is better in many ways to pre-specify a gain score analysis as a default. If the groups are unbalanced this will be fairer, and if the groups turn out to have been balanced then using gain scores instead of post-test only will obviously make no substantive difference. Always using gain scores as the default also means that the results of different trials can be more easily compared.

Some commentators are concerned that using gain scores (or similar) entails a danger that any substantive finding could be due to 'regression to the mean'. They seem to ignore the fact that the same thing can happen even if there is no pre-intervention score and so gain scores are not used – it will simply be unobserved. When a set of scores has an extreme mean value (perhaps near a threshold like 0 or 100%) there is a genuine danger that taking a new set of scores from the same cases will yield a mean further away from that extreme even if the variation is somewhat meaningless (Gorard 2013a). As an analogy, a sprinter who breaks a world record is unlikely to match or improve that time on their next sprint. While this phenomenon is a genuine consideration in evaluations, it is very unlikely to happen in a randomised control trial. With large N, initial balance is likely, initial imbalance does happen, but extreme scores for only one group of the kind needed for regression to the mean are implausible unless something went very wrong with the initial random allocation of cases to treatment groups.

Some researchers use, and some commentators and 'authorities' call for, significance tests with pre-test data to help determine if there is serious imbalance. Using this approach is clear evidence that such 'experts' can have no idea what a significance test is or does. Having randomly allocated the cases to the treatment and control groups they then want to run a significance test to estimate the likelihood that any imbalance between the groups is due solely to chance. This is absurd. They know exactly what this likelihood is. It is 100%, because the cases were randomly allocated. If the cases have been randomly allocated and the significance test does not give a p-value of 100% this is a further indication of the failure of p-values, not that the cases are not random. If the cases were not randomly allocated then the assumption for using a significance test has not been met anyway. If non-response or dropout means that there is a danger of bias then a significance test could not assess this, even if it worked as intended. This use of significance testing at pre-test is therefore further evidence of the blind, mechanical approach to EBE noted in Chapter 3 that endangers the very thing it hopes to achieve.

A much easier way of dealing with *post hoc* realisation of initial imbalance is to consider the direction of change and, if necessary, run a simple before and after comparison. So, if there is little or no initial imbalance then there is no problem (the most likely situation). If there is imbalance but the lower-scoring group at the outset makes the lowest gain, then this cannot be regression to the mean by definition, and the use of gain scores is perfectly safe. If there is gross imbalance and the lower-scoring group at the outset makes the highest gain (a tiny minority of trials), then the cases can be divided into the top and bottom half in terms of their pre-test scores irrespective of treatment group. If the higher attainers at the start make the greater gains (or there is no difference) then there is again no problem. There is only a danger of regression to the mean, if the lowest scoring half makes the highest gain (and by an important amount). This can then be reported with the findings, and used to add some caution to the substantive conclusions. It is, however, good practice to report both post-test and gain score outcomes, as appear in this book, where the relevant figures are available.

Judging the trustworthiness of findings

An effect size from a trial provides an indication of what difference the intervention would make compared to the control group in a future implementation, or if it were rolled out more widely. The financial cost of the intervention also needs to be considered alongside the estimated ES, and brief cost analyses appear in the next section of this book. Interventions can also have unintended consequences and side effects, and these have to be a factor in any real-life decision as to whether the intervention is feasible and useful. Evidence of these unintended consequences is one of the things addressed by process evaluations of the kind described in Chapter 5.

However, one of the most difficult but important things to decide upon for each evaluation result is how trustworthy or secure the findings are. 'Trustworthiness' here is something like how convincing the finding is, or even how much one would be prepared to bet on it being true or replicable. How can researchers portray the trustworthiness of their results, or judge those of others?

We present here a process of judging the quality or trustworthiness of evidence. This is summarised in Table 4.1, which is derived from Gorard (2014, 2015d). The table has five main columns representing the kinds of issues that might usefully be taken into account when judging how secure the findings of any piece of research are. Using the descriptors in each column it is possible to decide on a

TABLE 4.1 A 'sieve' to assist in the estimation of trustworthiness of descriptive work

Design	Scale	Dropout	Data quality	Other threats	Rating
Strong design for research question (RQ)	Large number of cases (per comparison group)	Minimal attrition, no evidence of impact on findings	Standardised, pre-specified, independent	No evidence of diffusion, demand or other threat	4★
Good design for RQ	Medium number of cases (per comparison group)	Some attrition (or initial imbalance)	Pre-specified, not standardised or not independent	Little evidence of diffusion, demand or other threat	3★
Weak design for RQ	Small number of cases (per comparison group)	Moderate attrition (or initial imbalance)	Not pre-specified but valid in context	Evidence of diffusion, demand or other threat	2★
Very weak design for RQ	Very small number of cases (per comparison group)	High attrition (or initial imbalance)	Issues of validity or appropri-ateness	Strong indication of diffusion, demand or other threat	1★
No consideration of design	A trivial scale of study, or N unclear	Attrition huge or not reported	Poor reliability, too many outcomes, weak measures	No consideration of threats to validity	0

broad classification for each study, ranging from 0 (not research or equivalent to not having done the research) to 4★ (the most trustworthy a piece of research can be in real life on this scale). The issues included are study design, scale of the study, bias through loss of data, the quality of data obtained for the study, and other threats such as conflicts of interest. Judgement of these issues assumes that the study has been reported fully, clearly and without bias. If the study has not been reported properly, so that a fair judgement could not be made on these factors, it would automatically rate as 0.

The procedure starts with the first column, reading down the design descriptions in Table 4.1 until the study is at least as good as the descriptor in that row. For a causal question, an RCT or Regression Discontinuity Design (RDD), for example, might lead to the first row. A propensity score matched design might lead to the second row. If the design is not reported or there is no comparator this would lead immediately to the final row. Staying in the row achieved for the design, attention moves to the next column and down the scale descriptions until the study is at least as good as the descriptor in that row. An RCT with only 12 cases in each group would end up in row 5 at this stage. This process is repeated for each column, moving down (never up) the rows until the study is at least as good as the descriptor in that row. The final column in the table gives the estimated star rating for that study.

This means that an evaluation will be judged to be as good as the lowest classi-fication it has achieved for each of the five categories. For any column, if it is not possible to discern the quality of the study from the available report(s) then the rating must be placed in a low category. In using this aid, the emphasis throughout is intended to be on judgement. The ratings represent how much one might be prepared to stake on an intervention working or not, based on a single evaluation, in the same context or setting again (or for descriptive work how 'accurate' the results are).

The cell descriptions are therefore deliberately non-specific (but discussed in more detail in the remainder of this chapter). This is not lack of care, but passing of control to the user. For example, the phrase 'a large number of cases' might be interpreted rather differently, depending upon the precise context, question or payoff. There is also an interaction between the simple number of cases, their com-pleteness, representativeness of a wider set of cases, and the integrity of the way they have been allocated to groups. 'A large number of cases' would certainly be in the hundreds, but there is no precise figure such as 400 that can be set, other than as a rough guide. An excellent study might have one case below whatever threshold is suggested (399) and a weak one might have one more (401). Similarly, a true RCT might be considered a 'fair design for comparison' but there will be other designs of equal ability to discriminate between effect and noise. Some may not even have been thought of yet. There is no limit to the ingenuity of research design. An attrition rate of 2% might be crucial if the missing cases all had extreme scores in the same direction, whereas 10% might still yield reasonably secure results if there was an obvious reason for the dropout that was unbiased across groups and types of cases. There is no clear threshold between 'minimal' attrition and worse that can be defended. But there is a clear difference between trivial attrition and non-trivial attrition. Where precisely that difference lies is a matter of judgement, based on what is known about the context and the nature of the missing cases and where they appeared in the research process. The following suggests how the table columns might be interpreted.

Column 1 – Design

Issues of design, and the fit between the research question and the design (White 2009), were introduced in Chapter 2. What this table makes clear again is that no one design is ideal. A descriptive study might properly use a comparative design, and so on. But this book is primarily about robust evaluations to address causal questions, and these are assumed from hereon.

Although a valid causal model may start with a correlation, and may include an explanatory model and a proposed sequence of events, it is fundamentally based on a comparison between two or more groups of cases (Gorard 2013a). One (or more groups) is exposed to one level of the purported cause, and another is exposed to a clearly different level of the cause. All other things being equal, a difference in the relevant outcomes between the two groups can be interpreted as evidence of cause and effect. One key element of such an interpretation is that the comparison between groups is a fair one. This fairness can be achieved in a number of ways. One is to randomly allocate all participating cases to the initial groups, in an RCT. Another is to allocate cases to groups in terms of a threshold or cut-off point, in a regression discontinuity design (RDD; for explanation see Gorard 2013a). Alternatively, the technique of matching cases between the two groups, in terms of their known characteristics, can achieve superficial balance but is demonstrably more likely to lead to bias or substantive imbalance than either RCT or RDD. Not matching cases and simply having two (or more) naturally occurring groups is clearly even weaker. And weaker still is to have one group and to compare only the before and after data. Case studies and research with no apparent study design at all would be completely inappropriate.

There is therefore a hierarchy of designs for causal questions. No researcher can be blamed for not using a stronger design if it is genuinely not possible, and research does not become useless simply because it uses an inferior design. But an inferior design must then limit the kinds of claims made by the researcher, and the trust-worthiness of the findings as viewed by others. The crucial thing for column one is whether the study design matches the nature of the research question.

Column 2 – Scale

Perhaps the next single most important factor in judging the quality of a research study, all other things being equal, is its scale. A claim is commonly made that in some ways research in the social sciences is harder than in natural science because the cases are more variable and less inherently predictable (Nash 2004). This may be so, but it is seldom pursued to its logical conclusion. In order to make believable claims, social science research would therefore need a larger number of cases than used in other areas of investigation (perhaps where clones or identical particles are possible).

The scale of any study is not judged in terms of total N, but in terms of the number of cases in each analytical group (such as treatment and control in a trial). It depends on the smallest cell size used in any comparison or contrast. A large study reduces the volatility of small numbers, and so provides a better estimate of what is being measured or observed, and its true variability (Gorard 2003b). Both figures are needed to compute the estimated ES. The advantage of larger scale is subject to a law of diminishing returns. A study with 505 cases per group is better than a study with only 500 cases per group, but not by much – at least not as much as the difference between a study with 5 cases per cell and another with 10 cases.

Table 4.1 is deliberately vague about how large is enough for a study, since the purpose of the table is to allow the reader to judge. But everyone knows that a trial with only 10 cases per group is trivial, while a trial with 500+ cases per group is not. If the groups are unbalanced in size then it is the size of the smallest group that should drive the judgement about study scale.

There is a widespread practice of calculating 'power' to assess how large a sample needs to be for a secure research result. As with most aspects of trials, this step tends to be used unthinkingly and mechanically. 'Statistical power is the probability that if the population ES [effect size] is equal to delta, a target we specify, our planned experiment will achieve statistical significance at a stated value of alpha' (Cummings 2013, p. 17). There are two complementary ways of using this idea of power. The first is to estimate the ES being sought (perhaps based on prior studies), and then compute a number of cases needed to be able to detect such an effect size, at a chosen level of statistical significance (such as 5%) with a chosen level of likelihood (such as 80%). The second is to compute, for a given number of cases, with chosen levels of significance and likelihood, the smallest ES that might be found – the minimum detectable effect size or MDES. As well as being very sensitive to slight changes in any of the parameters, such power calculations clearly suffer from three major defects.

The first and most obvious problem is that the logic of power calculations is internally contradictory. As the definition above shows, a power calculation starts by envisaging a non-zero effect size (the estimated effect of the treatment in an RCT). The researcher assumes this non-zero effect size as the bedrock for the calculations that follow. The calculations themselves are also predicated on a significance test, which was shown in Chapter 3 to assume as the basis for its own calculation that there is no effect size (the nil-null hypothesis). Put another way, the p-values generated by significance tests assume an ES of precisely zero. Both of these initial assumptions cannot be true in the same calculation, by definition. Therefore, 'power' does not make sense.

The second fundamental objection is that power calculations should not be used because they rely on significance tests. Significance tests do not work, and therefore power is also an illusion. Power calculations would only make any sense if an analyst were planning to conduct a significance test. Since such tests do not work, it follows that power calculations do not work.

Cox (1958) defined a statistician as 'one who will not accept that Columbus discovered America because he said he was looking for India in the trial plan. Columbus made an error in his power calculation—he relied on an estimate of the size of the Earth that was too small, but he made one none the less, and it turned out to have very fruitful consequences'.

The key variation in a well-conducted trial is that of the condition the treatment is intended to influence, not the variation in the treatment itself (Senn 2002).

Thirdly, as with significance tests, because many researchers do not seem to have thought much about the logic of power calculations, the process is widely abused. Hoenig and Heisey (2001) describe a plethora of articles and 'experts' suggesting that power calculations should be conducted whenever a test of significance yields a non-significant result. The idea seems to be that such an inconvenient 'negative' finding can be dismissed on the grounds that its power was too low (Smith and Bates 1992). Hoenig and Heisey (2001) show that this approach is fundamentally flawed – it is tantamount to cheating – but as widespread as the other abuses of significance tests such as p-hacking. We really are better off without significance tests in all of their disguised forms including power calculations.

The EEF (2014) have developed (with acknowledgement) our ideas on the trustworthiness of research as expressed in Table 4.1, but they have taken it in a direction warned against by the original authors at the outset. They do not like the element of judgement necessary in each cell, have removed the column on data quality for some reason (it is hard to imagine that they do not think this is important), and replaced some factors to make the table much more mechanical. Part of what they did was to corrupt the idea of a research scale suitable to the research question into a minimum detectable effect size (MDES), clearly based on the notion of significance testing, which they had originally eschewed. In this respect, they are making negative progress for EBE from their fine ambitions at inception. Unfortunately for those wanting simple rules to conduct research, there is no calculation to perform to decide in advance if the number of cases is sufficient. The sample should always be the largest possible given other constraints. But this is only one factor. A high quality medium-size sample could well be better than a low quality larger one.

When considering scale, the cases are the units that would be randomised or otherwise allocated to the two (or more) groups but not necessarily the units from which data is collected. For example, if 60 hospitals were randomly allocated to two groups, and then data was collected from all patients, the cases would be the hospitals not the patients. The important 'N' would be 60. A research report needs to clarify the N for each and every analysis, since N is rarely a constant in practice, largely due to missing data for different variables.

Column 3 – Missing data

As important as scale is the completeness of the cases involved in the study. If the design has worked thus far, the research has two sizeable and very similar groups of cases ready for a comparison to take place after only one group has received the 'treatment' level of the purported cause. Any dropout from the study is serious after the cases have been allocated to comparison groups, because there is no reason to believe that the dropout will be either random or balanced (see Chapters 2 and 3). In social science, it can often be the knowledge of which group a case has been allocated to that creates the imbalance. For example, if the cases are people, knowing that being in the treatment group involves some effort might make less motivated cases in that group more likely to drop out. Or, if being in the treatment group is seen as exciting or beneficial there may be more attrition of disillusioned cases from the other group. Either way, those dropping out may be busier, more mobile, more likely to be homeless, less motivated, less literate, less concerned and so on.

Therefore, despite the lax WWC (What Works Clearinghouse) guidance to the contrary (https://ies.ed.gov/ncee/wwc/Docs/referenceresources/wwc_procedures _v3_0_standards_handbook.pdf), bias can easily arise even if the amount of drop-out is equal in number between the groups. Imagine a study looking at a remedial reading intervention for primary school children. The higher attaining children allocated to the treatment group might find the intervention programme patron-ising and unnecessary, making them more likely to drop out. The lower attaining children in the other group may be demoralised at not getting the extra help given to their peers in the treatment group. They may be less likely to continue to co-operate with the study. Even if the numbers dropping out are small and identical between the groups, the fact that the kinds of children dropping out in each group tend to differ will then create considerable bias for the results. It can create an apparent post-test difference between the groups even if the treatment has no impact.

An RCT with 100 randomly-allocated participants receiving the interven-tion and a further 100 randomly-allocated participants not receiving it, and 100% completion rate has N=200. An RCT with 200 randomly-allocated participants receiving the intervention and a further 200 randomly-allocated participants not receiving it, but only a 75% completion rate has N=300. In any synthesis of evi-dence, the first study must be treated as far more trustworthy than the second despite the reported N being smaller. The missing 100 cases in the second study could completely transform the findings if their data were available. Yet this crucial difference would be largely ignored in traditional approaches to analysis and con-ducting so-called reviews of evidence.

In fact this leads to a sensible approach to considering the possible impact of attrition – how different would the data from the missing cases have to be to negate the apparent finding from the cases that *are* available? One way of assessing this is to estimate the number of counterfactual cases that would be needed to disturb the finding (NNTD). This approach is described later in the chapter.

Column 4 – Data quality

The data used to represent the trial outcome needs to be reliable in the true senses of being repeatable/replicable and of being judged to be the same by different observers (rather than merely internally consistent). In this respect, real-life mea-sures such as length tend to be better than counts such as how many cases had a certain clear characteristic (Gorard 2010b). Worse in turn are standardised tests of attainment which tend to be somewhat better than questionnaires used to estimate latent concepts such as motivation. Weakest of all will be impression data (although as with all forms of data collection this may have other advantages, but just not for the trustworthiness of the study).

It is important that the outcome(s) of interest is specified and made clear before the study is conducted, if at all possible. This is to prevent researchers or users subsequently dredging a larger number of variables for those that show 'success' or 'failure'. The outcome also needs to be independent of the intervention itself. A key threat, especially when the outcome measure is tied in any way to the intervention, is that the treatment group might practice the post-test or a close proxy for it, in a way that the control group does not.

In social science it is best to assume that all measurements are inexact. For any dataset there will be errors in the measurements. It is important to consider how large these errors might be, whether they are biased, and whether they could affect the results in a similar way to missing data. For example, if two sets of measurements were only 90% accurate and the difference between them only 5% then it is obvious that this difference could easily be the result of error.

The next step is to consider the propagation of any errors when conducting the computation part of the analysis (whether caused by inaccuracy in measurement or recording, or by missing cases or data). Where data contains errors, any calculations conducted with the data will also be conducted with the error components. Subtraction (or adding negative values) is a particular threat to the validity of findings, because it tends to create numbers that have an increased error component. We do not usually know whether our measurements are in error by being too large or too small. Therefore the error in any measurement is initially treated as being positive or negative. If e_x is the error in measuring the positive number x, then the measurement in our research is actually $x \pm e_x$. If we add this to a positive measurement y with error e_y, the maximum error in the result of x+y is $e_x + e_y$. The maximum error has risen in line with the answer. But if y is subtracted from x, the maximum error is still $e_x + e_y$, but now it is the error in a smaller number (x−y). The error component has grown as a proportion of the answer, on the basis of one subtraction. Consider the complex computations that some researchers use in their reports. It is quite easy to end up with findings in which the error component completely outweighs the substantive findings – examples appear in school effectiveness studies (Gorard 2010a), and in more complex experimental designs (Gorard 2013b). Such error propagation needs to be monitored and considered when explaining the results.

Further threats to safe findings

There are a large number of further issues that could enhance or reduce the trustworthiness of research results (Shadish et al. 2002). In practice the overall level of research quality is already set by this point, as the various elements of quality are related in practice to some extent. For example, it is unlikely that a design based on a very weak comparison group would bother with whether the participants were 'blind' as to which group they were in when the outcome data was collected. Perhaps the single greatest threat to any study is a conflict of interest (CoI) for anyone involved. Traditionally this has been interpreted as concern where stakeholders stand to gain financially from the results of the study.

Just as one would be sceptical of research on the dangers of tobacco sponsored by tobacco companies, we, as consumers of research, should also be aware of research on innovations conducted by people who have a vested interest in that innovation. One example is recent research on the use of interactive whiteboards in classrooms by an institute funded by a developer of the interactive whiteboard. The latter would have been more acceptable if researchers declared the CoI so that readers were aware of it. Such practices are quite common. Some researchers have sold their intellectual property rights to commercial companies, but retain a financial interest in the success of the product.

However, CoIs are wider than this. Researchers can have prestige or prior claims wrapped up in a study intended to test their own, perhaps well-known, theory. This might make them reluctant to face a robust and independent test of their claims. Oddly, practitioners can become unreasonably enthusiastic about an intervention even though ostensibly they have nothing to gain from an untrustworthy finding. The solution is, of course, that evaluators must be unconcerned about the nature of the results other than their quality, and that all interested parties should be 'blinded' as far as is feasible.

Other threats to validity include having so many possible outcomes that some must be positive, the unintentional experimenter effect, accidental diffusion of the treatment between allocated groups, and post-allocation demoralisation (Shadish et al. 2002).

Generalisation

Having settled the security of any finding, it may be interesting to consider to what extent the finding could also be true for any other set of cases – such as those in different times, places or institutions, or with different characteristics. Traditional inferential statistical techniques require assumptions that are rarely met with social science or indeed any real-life data, and the techniques do not provide an answer to these questions of generalisation anyway (Kern et al. 2016). Rather, whether findings generalise must be a judgement (Gorard 2006a). We do not know what the findings would have been for the wider cases we are considering (else we would not be seeking to generalise). We can only imagine what they are.

This judgement may be aided by considering how similar or different the other cases are to those in the actual study – in terms of the values and variables that we *do* know about. For example, if the research findings are based on a mixture of individuals with characteristics also found elsewhere then it is plausible to imagine that cases elsewhere will also be similar in terms of the substantive findings. The closer the match, the less variable the findings actually are between cases, and the more relevant the matching variables appear to be, the more likely the findings are to generalise.

Of course, if the findings of any study do not seem to generalise, or a judgement is not possible, this does not mean that the findings of the research are not valid, or useful and interesting in their own right. Whether this is so would be a separate judgement. The generalisability of findings comes a clear second to internal validity – if the results are not trustworthy then it does not matter, or usually even make sense to ask, whether they would also apply to some other setting.

Sensitivity analysis

One way of aiding a judgement encompassing many of the factors above is to consider how different the data obtained would have to have been in order for the finding of interest to disappear. If little would have to change then the finding is clearly not a strong one, unless the finding is that there is no difference (pattern or trend). There are a number of ways of implementing this approach. The method proposed here is simple, standardised, and takes into account in one summary figure the sample size, the magnitude of the finding and the level of missing data. It involves calculating the number of counterfactual cases needed to disturb the finding.

Imagine a piece of research comparing the mean scores of two groups. Perhaps these are the outcome scores in a simple trial comparing an intervention and a control group. Assuming that the study design was good, the measurements secure, and that there are no obvious threats to validity, then the difference between the means yields an estimate of the impact of the intervention given to one group but not the other (the effect size).

In general, how much attention is paid to the difference between means in situations like this should depend on the number of cases in the smallest group, the size of the difference in the outcomes between groups, and the level of missing data. Large studies with little missing data are preferable to small studies or studies with high rates of attrition. For an effect to be meaningful the difference between the means must be considered substantial, and robust in the face of missing data, chance and design issues such as bias. The number of counterfactual cases needed to disturb the finding (NNTD) allows all of these factors to be encompassed in one summary figure.

This can be achieved in a number of ways. One way would be to create a counterfactual score such as the mean score for the largest group plus or minus the overall standard deviation for both groups. The SD would be added if the mean of the smaller group (in scale) were smaller than the mean of the larger group, and subtracted if the mean of the smaller group was the largest. The ensuing counterfactual score can then be repeatedly added to the smaller group of cases until the ES disappears (as it must eventually). The number of these imaginary counterfactual scores needed to make the ES disappear is the measure of sensitivity. A simpler way that does not require direct access to the datasets (only the means and standard deviations) would be to set NNTD as the absolute value of the 'effect' size multiplied by the number of cases in the smaller group in the comparison. The two approaches anyway tend towards exactly the same answer when N is large. The number needed to disturb is the number of counterfactual cases needed to change the effect. Therefore, the bigger NNTD is the more stable is the finding because it would mean that it takes many more counterfactual (or missing cases) to completely reverse the effect.

NNTD provides a clear and useful interpretation of an effect size. An effect size represents the proportion of cases in the smaller group that need to be made more counterfactual (or that need to be added as counterfactual cases) before the 'effect' disappears. Multiplying the effect size by the smaller N yields a single statistic that incorporates the absolute size of the difference, the variability in measurements, and the scale. The number needed to disturb (NNTD), however computed, is expressed as a number of cases. Therefore, it can be compared directly with the number of cases missing key data, or missing entirely through dropout or non-response. The initial result from the steps above should be therefore reduced by the number of cases missing data. The final result would then take attrition into account as well, on the assumption that any missing data will tend to be counterfactual. This assumption is a somewhat pessimistic one, but it does mean that any finding that still looks robust after this process deserves to be taken very seriously. It means that the 'effect', difference or trend cannot have been caused simply by missing data, even in the unlikely scenario that *all* of the missing data had been counterfactual.

The calculation of NNTD can be extended to almost any analytical situation where there is a concern to assess the robustness of a difference, trend or other pattern in the data. As already shown, the process does not depend on equal sized groups. Nor does the data have to represent that from a random sample, or mimic a specific distribution (such as the normal curve). It can be used where there are more than two groups to compare, simply by pairwise consideration. It can even be used in modelling of the kind based on correlation/regression by asking how much the data would have to have differed to disturb a coefficient, or eliminate an increase in R linked to the inclusion or exclusion of a specific variable. The process can also be used to estimate the sample size needed in order to detect a pre-specified 'effect' size with a pre-specified NNTD. And it can be used as a basis for meta-analysis of several results – using the ES, N of the smallest cell, and number of missing cases.

It is reasonably simple to apply NNTD to data based on frequencies, since frequencies are real numbers in the same way as measurements are. In analytical terms the difference, between a comparison of groups of measurements classified in terms of which group they are in (as above) and a comparison of groups of frequencies classified in terms of which group they are in, is often over-emphasised (Gorard 2010b). One way to approximate the NNTD as outlined above, but for frequencies, would be to add new counterfactual cases to the smallest group. However, it would probably make more sense to use the difference between the observed and expected values in each cell, as is traditional, and which can be computed using the marginal totals. Either way, the NNTD can then be compared directly to levels of non-response and missing data, also expressed as a number of cases.

This section has introduced the computation of a 'number of counterfactual cases needed to disturb the finding' to help assess the robustness of a pattern, trend or difference in numeric data. The idea of the number of counterfactual cases needed to disturb the safety of an empirical finding is a simple one. It is presented here as a superior alternative to the failed approach of significance testing and confidence intervals, and to the limitations of using 'effect' sizes alone. Unlike the permutation test it is not predicated on complete random sampling. In fact, creating NNTD requires no particular underlying assumptions, creates no threshold of acceptance/rejection, is comparable between studies of different sizes using different outcome measures, and uniquely it takes into account in one figure the sample size, magnitude of the finding and the level of missing data. It can be used with any form of numeric data, and any number of groups or classifications. It is easy to understand, and simple to compute. The heuristic approach allows a minimum value to be estimated even when there is no access to the actual data (such as when conducting a review or meta-analysis). Regardless of how the details are worked out, the principle of NNTD has a lot to recommend it (Gorard and Gorard 2016).

Summary: aids to judging trustworthiness

The issue of trustworthiness arises when researchers are considering each other's work as well as assessing their own. A synthesis of existing evidence must take more than the author's conclusions or the reported findings (such as an effect size) into account, otherwise weak evidence will be bundled along with strong evidence, leading to invalid and possibly dangerously misleading conclusions. 'Strong' and 'weak' here refer not to size of the difference, pattern or trend uncovered but to how convincing the evidence for it is. Meta-analyses and systematic and narrative reviews of existing evidence are invalid when each study is merely given equal weight. But they are also invalid where only some studies are included while others are rejected as not reaching some threshold of trustworthiness.

Both reasons for needing an assessment of research trustworthiness currently face similar problems. Policy-makers, practitioners, advisers, think tanks and other research users generally do not understand enough about the reported research base in their area to make the kinds of judgement necessary. And the main reason for this is that researchers do not present their findings and the evidence for them in a form that others can readily understand. Researchers do the same to each other, presenting results with undigested output from statistical software, long paragraphs and sentences, and needless verbiage and neologisms (Gorard 2013a). Partly because of this some researchers may think that they are providing a comprehensible estimate of trustworthiness when they are not.

The ratings should take no account of whether the intervention itself was deemed successful. That is part of the impact assessment. Nor should they take into account the practicalities, or otherwise, of the intervention. That is part of the cost: benefit analysis. A low rating should not be interpreted as necessarily the 'fault' of the researcher – who will often be faced with practical, resource and ethical constraints. The researcher can however be deemed at fault in three common ways:

- If the rating is low because the reporting of research is poor or incomplete, or cannot be understood by the audience for which it is intended

- If there is clearly a better, simpler or more powerful approach the researcher could have used with the same resources
- If the researcher tries to make claims or draw conclusions unwarranted by their study

There is no technical or push-button solution that will decide whether to include a study in a synthesis of evidence or not, or how much weight to give it if it is included. Either decision is necessarily a judgement (Gorard 2006a). This judgement should be justified and made clear to others so that they can decide if they agree, or where exactly it is that they disagree. It is perhaps here that the 'sieve' in Table 4.1 might be most useful. Unfortunately there is also a danger that it becomes a complex or extensive technical checklist (https://v1.educationendowmentfoundation .org.uk/uploads/pdf/Classifying_the_security_of_EEF_findings_FINAL.pdf). This is not the intention and not how it will be best used.

Part of what is achieved by the procedures described here is a way of retaining more evidence in an evidence synthesis while being careful and scrupulous about the quality of evidence. Ten studies of reasonable quality each involving 10 cases must be at least as important as one reasonable quality study of 100 cases. Yet many traditional approaches to evidence synthesis would reject each of the ten smaller studies on account of scale (examples from https://eppi.ioe.ac.uk/cms/). Similar rejections often occur because of deficiencies of design or even because of the nature of data collection or analysis. These same syntheses may, rather strangely perhaps, also make great play about including all studies, even those that are not published, because of the bias caused by the file-drawer problem (Torgerson 2003). All readably reported studies should be considered in a synthesis, published or unpublished and despite deficiencies of scale and quality. All studies can help the aggregation towards the best possible bet on whether a finding is true or whether an approach works or not. At the same time, however, a synthesis cannot be a simple vote count. The quality of each study needs to be taken into account explicitly, as well as it 'effect' size and costs. It is such judgements of quality that the NNTD plus sieve procedure is intended to assist with.

5

IN-DEPTH EVIDENCE AND PROCESS EVALUATIONS

For any research design, but perhaps especially for a trial, it is important to collect more than the presumed outcome data (Gorard with Taylor 2004), such as that discussed in Chapter 4. In-depth and contextual data can help explain why an intervention does or does not work, how to improve it, or which sub-groups of learners it is most appropriate for. In fact, one could argue that the in-depth data, helping to create the explanatory causal mechanism (Chapter 2), is an essential part of any secure causal model (Pearl 2014).

Chapters 3 and 4 were primarily about impact evaluations but, as the following chapters show, it is usual to combine these with parallel process evaluations, gathering different kinds of data to address different questions. An impact evaluation might address a question like 'Does this intervention work as intended?' or 'How much better does the treatment group do as a result of the intervention?'. Process evaluations address questions like:

- How well is the intervention implemented in the treatment group?
- How good are the training and resources for the intervention?
- Are there any barriers to implementation?
- Was the intervention subverted in any way?
- Were there any unintended consequences?
- Did the participants appreciate the intervention?
  - And did this appreciation vary between different groups of students?
- What happened to the control group during the period of the intervention?
- Is there any evidence of diffusion such that the treatment became more widely used (outside the treatment group)?

These are very different questions to those about impact, and it is quite clear from all prior studies that the kinds of data collected by a process evaluation cannot be used to assess impact any more than the scores for impact can be used to assess barriers to implementation and so on. Each part of the dataset in a trial has its own function(s).

What are the different forms of 'evidence' in evidence-based education?

In Chapters 7 to 9 we present the findings of a large number of attempted robust evaluations in education. Each one involved a process evaluation, and in each study these were very similar. The remainder of this chapter describes in general terms what we did in all such studies. Specific details of the methods and a summary of the results of each process evaluation appear in Chapters 7 to 9.

For each trial, we looked at prior evidence relevant to the intervention, and at how the topic had previously been investigated. Before the trial, we generally gathered the age, sex, free school meal eligibility, special needs, first language and ethnic origin of all pupils involved (as these measures would appear on the pupil-level annual schools census in England).

Our process evaluations were generally light-touch and conducted in co-operation with the developers of each intervention. Schools agreed to be part of the evaluation when agreeing to be part of the intervention. We consulted with the programme organiser in each case, and were happy to accept from them literature and documents relating to the intervention, curriculum or activities, and the results of any information-gathering they have conducted or have access to via the schools (such as pupil attendance records at intervention events).

A substantial part of the evaluation fieldwork was to assess how closely schools adhered to the intended intervention, and what the short term or intermediate impacts were (such as changes in classroom interaction). In several trials, the developers also monitored the interventions in schools to ensure that delivery adhered to the protocol, and they provided regular feedback reports about the quality and the level of implementation in the schools. Each school was then given a score by the developer, based on the frequency of intervention lessons, and observed adherence to the protocols.

Our primary fieldwork on site included observations of training, implementation, classroom lessons and testing, plus semi-structured interviews with developers, teachers, school leads, pupils, and as far as possible parents, and *ad hoc* focus groups with pupils. The latter were loosely structured to get a sense of pupils' perceptions of the programme and to allow respondents to talk about what they thought was important, and not be constrained by a more structured interview protocol. Resources and protocol tools used in the programme were also collected. Most of the fieldwork took place in intervention schools, because its purposes included:

- Checking that those randomised to treatment received the treatment as intended and for the required number of sessions in order for intervention effects to be realised.
- Providing intermediate indicators to enable us to explain why the intervention had the effect that it did

- Identifying the features of successful implementation, as well as highlighting potential barriers
- Identifying potential issues which could be addressed for any future scaling up

We also needed evidence on control schools and the nature of standard activity there. Usually, we would visit 10% to 20% of all schools in a trial to ensure variety, and of these we would visit around half twice per year in order to assess changes and progress over time. We have however read many trial reports by others that have conducted purported process evaluations only via documents, surveys or telephone interviews and even statistically. We fail to see how this is possible. It is only via observations that we can see problems that people fail to report, and can also see and take away materials.

For these reasons the observations and focus group interviews were intentionally kept minimally structured so that we were not constrained by only pre-set questions that could bias our observations. We wanted to let the interviewees focus on things that mattered to them – not only things we thought were important. The interviews and field notes were part transcribed and shared between the evaluation team. The process evaluation data was collated and analysed by evaluators initially blind to the trial outcomes and independent of the impact evaluation. But the findings of the process evaluation were later used to help explain the impact outcomes, and any barriers to implementation.

If the programme was found to have positive effects, using all of this data we could then understand more about the mechanism behind it. On the other hand, if the evaluation found no effects, the process evaluation could help to identify potential limitations. For example, children may not progress as expected either because the programme was intrinsically ineffective, or because the teachers were not implementing it in the way they should. It could also be that the amount of time devoted to the programme was not long enough for effects (if any) to be manifested. Or it could be that the measures used for assessing impact were not appropriate – for example, the tests are not related to the skills trained.

PART III

What do trials show?

6

A SHORT SHARP SHOCK? THE TRANSITION TO SECONDARY SCHOOL

The remainder of this book concerns substantive work of the kind discussed in general so far, and forming the basis for evidence-based education. This chapter is about the prior evidence base for catch-up projects. Catch-up projects are educational interventions intended for pupils struggling to reach what are officially deemed the age-appropriate levels in reading (and maths). They are important because struggling pupils entering secondary school are more likely to remain behind, or fall further behind, their classmates, which can also lead to other issues such as disruptive classroom behaviour (Gorard et al. 2011).

In the UK, and elsewhere, there is concern that too many young people are moving into secondary education without the basic skills necessary to make progress with the wider secondary school curriculum. Most importantly, too many are considered not to have achieved the expected threshold level of literacy. Around 25 per cent of primary school pupils in England do not achieve the expected level 4 at Key Stage 2 (KS2) in English, and many mainstream primary schools do not achieve the minimal expected level in terms of pupils reaching level 4 (Department for Education 2013). Of course, these expectations may have been set too high (or too low) but this is still evidence of a potential problem for secondary schools and their lowest attaining pupils.

Such children are not likely to catch up and will continue to fall further behind their peers (Sainsbury et al. 1998, Galton et al. 1999). Pupils struggling to achieve their 'expected' reading level at primary school would generally find it difficult to access the full secondary curriculum, since literacy is such a fundamental gateway for further study (Good et al. 1998). Pupils who read well in early stages of their education are more successful in later years compared to those who fall behind (Hirsch 2007). This differential reading ability is a key determinant of patterns of subsequent learning (Wolf and Katzir-Cohn 2001, Pikulski and Chard 2005). Poor reading ability can have harmful psychological, social and economic consequences, with implications far beyond those directly associated with education (Adams and Bruck 1993). Societal demands for reading ability are increasing in the information age (Cunningham et al. 2004), and a minimal level of literacy is an entitlement for all.

Improving children's reading ability is therefore necessary. This chapter provides a brief critical overview of the evidence base on what can be done to improve literacy for pupils at transfer to secondary schools, before focussing on six promising or widespread interventions. We begin with a summary of recent and relevant policy in the UK, and then present existing evidence for a range of catch-up interventions aimed at raising literacy at the transition phase. This evidence is based largely on two systematic reviews we have conducted (see Gorard 2014, Gorard et al. 2016a).

Policy and context

Children and young people with low levels of basic skills are disproportionately, although far from exclusively, from disadvantaged family backgrounds – such as those living below the official poverty line. The Department for Education (DfE) and others have implemented a range of policies to try and reach national targets for reading at KS2, including the National Literacy Strategy, and giving extra funding to schools since 2010 in proportion to their level of disadvantaged (mostly free-school meal eligible) pupils. This 'pupil premium' money must be used to help raise the attainment of disadvantaged pupils who are more likely to be struggling than their more advantaged peers. This might involve hiring extra teaching assistants, or purchasing resources or interventions to support children at risk of not reaching an appropriate level of literacy. Such interventions and approaches need to be both effective and practical in the sense of being able to be integrated within the wider school timetable and curriculum.

In 2012 the government in England made an extra £10 million available to the Educational Endowment Foundation (EEF) via the Department for Education, for a grants round dedicated to literacy catch-up projects for children at the primary-secondary transition. It was intended to benefit pupil premium children who enter secondary school with below Level 4 in literacy (Gov.UK 2012). Schools and other educational organisations were encouraged to develop programmes that could support disadvantaged pupils to 'catch up' with their peers and societal expectations. Four of the interventions discussed in Chapter 7 were part of this.

How effective are 'catch-up' interventions?

What does the existing evidence say about how effective catch-up interventions are? A lot of the existing and even widely used approaches to improving literacy (and numeracy) for children aged 9 to 12 either have no good evidence that they are effective, or have evidence that they are ineffective. The various approaches found in our reviews of evidence (and not covered in later sections) are reasonably well balanced in terms of reported effectiveness (Table 6.1). Interestingly, however, a clear majority of the studies that claimed to be effective are of poor quality.

Table 6.2 summarises those studies noted in Table 6.1 that are of medium or high quality. These are aimed at improving literacy at the transition phase. The quality assessment (last column) is based on the sieve discussed in Chapter 4 (see Table 4.1). The studies in bold are the higher quality studies (rated 3* and above). The same style of summary tables is used throughout the book. No one approach or intervention emerges here as having evidence of effectiveness with repeated evaluation. Some of the larger studies show quite convincingly that approaches like READ180, for example, do not work.

TABLE 6.1 Quality and impact summary: improving literacy

	Effective	Ineffective/unknown
Higher quality 3* or better	1	2
Medium quality 2*	2	3
Lower quality 1*	24	7

TABLE 6.2 Quality and impact detail: improving literacy

Reference	Intervention	Smallest cell	Attrition	ES	NNTD-attrition	Quality
Horsfall and Santa 1994	Project CRISS	111 pupils	20%	+	0	2*
James-Burdumy et al. 2009	Project CRISS	1,155 pupils	Unknown	0	0	2*
Puma et al. 2007	Writing Wings	1,500 pupils	Unknown	0	0	2*
White et al. 2005	**READ180**	**617 pupils**	**Unknown**	**0**	**0**	**3***
Kim et al. 2010	READ180	132 pupils	Unknown	+	Unknown	2*
Sprague et al. 2010	**READ180 (Grade 6 to 10)**	**2,775 pupils**	**Large**	**0**	**0**	**3***
Cantrell et al. 2010	Learning Strategies Curriculum	431 pupils	24%	0.22	0	2*
Coe et al. 2011	**6+1 Trait Writing**	**1,931**	**Unknown**	**0.13**	**Unknown**	**3***

Project CRISS (Creating Independence through Student-owned Strategies) is a programme where teachers model learning strategies for students to help develop independent learning. The strategies used by teachers include monitoring learning, and building on prior knowledge with new information. This programme has been the subject of extensive research, but only two studies out of 31 met WWC minimal evidence standards (WWC 2010). Horsfall and Santa (1994) reported a positive effect on comprehension for students in grades 4 and 6, but only using a teacher-developed 'free recall' comprehension test. James-Burdumy et al. (2009) found no benefit from Project CRISS on a standardised norm-referenced diagnostic test (GRADE), or on the science or social studies reading comprehension assessments. Overall, there is no good evidence of beneficial impact from Project CRISS.

Writing Wings, a structured writing programme, was evaluated using 3,000 students in the third, fourth and fifth grades in 39 schools across the US (Puma et al. 2007). No positive effect was found on the writing ability of disadvantaged students. *The Rainbow Repeated Reading* programme was also found to have no added effect on reading skills (Wheldall 2000). This was an add-on to an existing programme, MULTILIT (Making Up for Lost Time in Literacy). The programme emphasised repeated reading of short sections of texts, which were graded, to increase accuracy and fluency. Another bespoke programme involving instruction on the learning environment used videotaped lessons showed that although the intervention encouraged students to use reading comprehension strategies, it did not improve comprehension skills (De Corte et al. 2001).

READ180 is a small group reading programme designed for both primary and secondary students not achieving the expected level of proficiency. The programme involves a combination of tracking students' progress via the computer, reading practice using a computer program, reading of storybooks and direct instruction on reading, writing and vocabulary in two 90-minute sessions. It has been evaluated in 111 studies listed by What Works Clearinghouse (WWC) (2009). Many of these did not meet WWC standards for evidence, and those that did were not able to provide clear evidence of impact.

A small number of studies portrayed positive effects, but the evidence is not always clear due to compromises made in the research. For example, Interactive Inc. (2002) reported mixed results, but a re-analysis by WWC found no clear differences. In a trial involving 16 US schools, READ180 was offered to 617 grade 4 to 8 students who were not achieving the expected grade level in literacy (White et al. 2005). Results on standardised English Language Arts and Reading tests showed that the treatment group made greater progress in reading compared to an unmatched comparator group of 4,619 students from the same schools. However, the average effect across the three grades was not large enough to be considered important.

Another evaluation of READ180 involving 384 grade 6 to 8 students from one middle school found no intervention effect in the first year, although greater gains were reported for the intervention group compared to the control group in the second and third years (Woods 2007). A smaller study by Caggiano (2007) involving 120 grade 6 to 8 (age 11–14) students found no clear differences between groups in all three grades on standardised tests in reading. One study conducted by Scholastic Research (2008), the same organisation who created and marketed the intervention, reported clearly different results in general literacy for 285 students in grades 6, 7 and 9 after one year of READ180, compared to 285 matched students. All were considered to be struggling readers, and a majority had English as a second language. The outcome measure was the gain score in the English Language Arts subtest of the California Standards Test.

Two fairly large studies using standardised assessments found no positive effects of READ180 on students' literacy. For example, Kim et al. (2010) involved 264 grade 4 to 6 students identified as struggling readers and found no effects on all outcome measures, including reading fluency, reading comprehension and vocabulary, using norm-referenced and standardised tests. In the most extensive evaluation of the READ180 programme covering five sites in different states of the US (Sprague et al. 2010), no differences were found in all the sites apart from one, which had a very high dropout rate of 55%. This finding is important as it is one of the largest studies of READ180 involving 5,551 students randomly assigned to either READ180, Extreme Reading (alternative reading programme) or 'business as usual' where they received regular instruction. The outcome measures in all sites were the standardised, state-level assessments.

The overall evidence for READ180 is therefore not promising. It is shown to work chiefly with assessments designed by the developers but not on standardised assessments. It did not work in the few randomised control trials, or for those students most at risk.

Learning Strategies Curriculum (LSC) is a supplementary reading intervention to improve reading comprehension for sixth to ninth graders (age 11 to 15) where students receive 50–60 minutes of LSC per day for the entire school year. Cantrell et al. (2010) evaluated this intervention for 862 students in 12 middle and 11 high schools. The intervention was found to be effective in improving reading comprehension for sixth graders (effect size of 0.22), but not for ninth graders on both outcome measures. It has to be noted that there was a relatively high attrition rate of 24%.

6+1 Trait Writing is a supplemental writing programme that complements the schools' existing writing curricula. Coe et al. (2011) examined the impact of this programme with 4,461 (2,230 intervention students and 1,931 control) students in 74 US schools. The results showed that experimental students increased their writing scores in a year, by a small overall effect size (0.12 to 0.14). Only three of the six outcome measures were reported as improved.

In summary, very few interventions for literacy catch-up have been rigorously evaluated at scale and 'survived' in terms of providing evidence of benefit. Many have only been evaluated once.

The remainder of this chapter describes the existing evidence on six of the more promising, or at least popular, catch-up interventions that we have evaluated using a robust design of the kind described in Chapter 2. The results of our evaluations are described fully in Chapter 7. All involve attempts to improve reading and sometimes numeracy for year 6 and 7 pupils over a very short period of time, but they represent a considerable variety of approaches.

The prior evidence on Switch-on Reading

The first approach is Switch-on Reading, which is reportedly derived from a long-standing intervention called Reading Recovery (RR). RR is an intensive one-to-one intervention for the lowest performing 20% of first graders, and has been widely used in the US, Australia, New Zealand and the UK (Kelly et al. 2008). The What Works Clearinghouse (2013) found only four out of 78 evaluations of RR that met minimal evidence standards, and even these RCTs were rather small in scale (Table 6.3). They involved 168, 91, 79 and 74 students respectively (Baenen et al. 1997, Pinnell et al. 1988, 1994, Schwartz 2005). One other study (64 students) met WWC criteria with reservations because it was not a randomised control trial (Iverson and Tunmer 1993). Of these five studies, four reported positive effects for RR on first-grade general reading achievement, using the Observation Survey subtests for Dictation and Writing Vocabulary. Baenen et al. (1997) did not find positive effects using grade retention as an outcome measure. In addition, Tanner et al. (2011) compared 57 RR schools with 54 other schools, and reported that pupils at the RR schools had performed better. However, the schools were not randomised to treatment and baseline equivalence was not established.

Subsequently, May et al. (2013) reported an effect size of +0.68 for RR with 866 randomly assigned low achieving first graders, based on measurements using the Iowa Tests of Basic Skills. May et al. (2015) looked at one-to-one RR and found an effect size of +0.47. Holliman and Hurry (2013) looked at the impact of Reading Recovery on 73 Year 1 children in England who had received RR three years earlier and 48 pupils who had been in RR schools but had not received the intervention. This was a longitudinal study to assess the impact on literacy progress and subsequent prevalence of SEN in Year 4. The findings showed that RR children were more likely to be on track for Level 4 at the end of KS2 and less likely to have been diagnosed with SEN. Effect sizes of 0.53 were reported for reading and 0.43 for writing. Attrition was 17%.

Overall, there is only weak evidence that such an intensive one-to-one approach is effective (Table 6.4).

TABLE 6.3 Quality and impact summary: studies of Reading Recovery/Switch-On

	Effective	*Ineffective/unknown*
Higher quality 3* or better	0	0
Medium quality 2*	1	0
Minimal quality 1*	4	1

TABLE 6.4 Quality and impact detail: studies of Reading Recovery/Switch-on Reading

Reference	Intervention	Smallest cell	Attrition	ES	NNTD-attrition	Quality
May et al. 2013	**Reading Recovery**	433	17%	0.68	220	3*

Switch-on Reading is reported by its developers as a modified version of RR but is shorter in duration than the traditional Reading Recovery. Unlike RR there has been less research on Switch-on Reading itself. One previous study (Coles 2012) with Key Stage 2 primary age children reported an effect of +0.8 on reading. In this study 100 pupils were randomised to treatment or control, but 8 were unaccounted for (7 from the control).

It was this suggestion of success that led to EEF funding to replicate the intervention with fresh secondary school pupils and at a considerably larger scale. This was a rapid efficacy trial to test the impact of Switch-on with the developer from Nottinghamshire LA leading the training and overseeing the delivery of the intervention, and the authors as an independent evaluation team. The new evaluation is over twice the scale of anything done previously, it looks only at the reading element of Switch-on, and for the first time it is tried with pupils just arriving in secondary school (i.e. it is used as a transitional literacy catch-up scheme). As with the five following interventions, the precise intervention, methods and results of this new evaluation appear in Chapter 7.

The prior evidence on Accelerated Reader

Accelerated Reader (AR) is a widely used web-based intervention produced by the Renaissance Learning Company, which monitors and manages pupils' reading practices and encourages them in independent reading. It is a computerised reading programme which includes elements of explicit and systematic teaching and differentiated instruction (all believed to be effective instructional practices) to address phonemic awareness (PA), phonics, fluency, vocabulary, and reading comprehension, in addition to writing and spelling. AR incorporates a number of strategies thought to be best practice – direct instruction, and understanding by design which is teaching and testing for understanding (a form of feedback from pupils to teachers). In the UK, over 2,000 schools are using AR on a regular basis (Topping 2014). However, it is not clear that the implementation of AR at such a large scale can be justified solely on the basis of the pre-existing evidence of effectiveness.

Our review suggests that there is little convincing evidence that Accelerated Reader is effective in raising the academic outcomes of primary school children (Table 6.5). Even where there is evidence that AR as a package worked, it is not possible to identify which aspect of the programme is the driver because AR is a multi-component intervention including explicit and systematic teaching, use of technology and differentiated instruction and self-regulated reading. So it is not clear which of these components are the key ingredients, or is it a combination of all of them.

TABLE 6.5 Quality and impact summary: studies of Accelerated Reader

	Effective	Ineffective
Higher quality 3* or better	1	0
Medium quality 2*	0	0
Lower quality 1*	12	6

TABLE 6.6 Quality and impact detail: Accelerated Reader

Reference	Intervention	Smallest cell	Attrition	ES	NNTD-attrition	Quality
Ross et al. 2004	AR	286	Not known	0.25	–	3*

In addition to simple snapshot surveys suggesting that AR participants read more than other pupils (Clark 2013), there have been several weak evaluations reporting success for AR (such as with no comparator group, Johnson and Howard 2003). Scott (1999) involved only 28 pupils, had unbalanced groups at the outset, and the report is unclear how the cases were allocated to AR or not. There are also studies showing no effects or even a negative impact. Mathis (1996) compared the progress of 37 AR pupils over one year with the whole year cohort, using the Stanford Achievement Test. There was a large negative effect size for AR pupils on reading comprehension.

AR is one of 24 reading interventions listed by the What Works Clearinghouse (WWC) (IES 2008). According to the findings of their systematic review, AR has no visible effect on reading fluency, a mixed effect on comprehension and a possible positive effect on reading achievement (What Works Clearinghouse 2008). These results are based on only two studies that met WWC minimum standards (Bullock 2005, Shannon et al. 2010, 2014, 2015).

In the strongest study, 45 teachers (with 572 K-3 grade students, aged 11-14, in 11 schools) were randomised to teach using AR or another commercially available reading programme (Ross et al. 2004). The impact was estimated after one year. The authors reported what they termed a 'significant' impact on reading comprehension using the STAR reading test, but WWC recalculated and reported that they found it was not statistically significant, although the effect size was over 0.25. Similarly, there was no significant effect on general reading achievement based on the STAR Early Literacy test for each year group, but the overall effect size was over 0.25. The STAR tests are produced and marketed by Renaissance Learning as part of the AR programme itself (www.renlearn.co.uk/accelerated-reader/reports-and-data/). They should, therefore, not be regarded as independent assessments in any way (Krashen 2007). A second study involved only 32 grade 3 students attending one school in the Pacific Northwest (Bullock 2005). They were individually randomised to receive 90 minutes of AR reading or not per week for 10 weeks. At the end there was no difference in terms of oral reading fluency. As above, the author reports no 'significant' effect on reading comprehension using the STAR reading test, but the effect size is greater than 0.25.

Brooks (2007) conducted a meta-synthesis of UK studies involving reading interventions for pupils with reading difficulties. The synthesis for AR found 47 studies conducted mostly in the US, but only two were selected for inclusion (Vollands et al. 1996, 1999). According to the report, AR produced positive effects. However, the cell sizes in comparison were only 11 in one study and 12 in the other. This is too small to draw conclusions on the effectiveness of the intervention. It is not clear how the groups had been created, nor whether baseline equivalence was established between the treatment and control groups. And anyway in tests three months later, the control group had made more progress.

A more recent study was conducted with 108 primary age pupils from two schools in the US (Nichols 2013). Pupils were randomly allocated to AR in one (treatment) school, and to a literacy plan in the other (control) school. After one year, there was no difference (or rather a small negative effect of −0.02) between the two groups in terms of the Standards of Learning test. In contrast, an even more recent study in the US based on 19 teachers randomly allocated to AR or not (Shannon et al. 2015) reported a positive impact for the AR group. However, the groups were not balanced at the outset with the treatment group having markedly lower prior test scores. The outcome measure used in the study was again the STAR reading test, which is an integral part of the AR intervention itself – meaning that those in the treatment group had more practice at this kind of test.

There have been some larger studies, all with weaker designs and non-random allocation of cases (and that are incorrect in using 'significance' tests to determine differences between groups). For example, Paul et al. (1996) had a large sample of 6,000 schools in which 58 per cent were non-AR comparison schools in similar geographic locations. According to official records, the schools having access to AR had better pupil attendance records and reading performance scores compared to the schools not using AR. A similar study, based on schools that had already adopted AR or not was conducted by Peak and Dewalt (1994), who reported greater success for the AR group at both primary and secondary levels. Pavonetti et al. (2000) developed a test to measure the quantity of books read, called the Title Recognition Test (TRT). Pupils were asked to mark the book titles they had read and in order to check if they were guessing rather than giving true responses, some foils for book names were added in the list (25 titles were actual books and 16 were foils for book names). AR claims that pupils' quantity of book reading increases if they use AR in schools. This claim was assessed using a school-level matched comparison design, with 10 secondary schools. There was no increase in the quantity of reading for pupils using AR compared to those not using AR (reported mean difference was −.008) (see also Pavonetti et al. 2000). Goodman (1999) involved 282 pupils in one US secondary school with no comparator, and claimed a positive gain based on pre- and post-test only. Using a small sample, Facemire (2000) reported gains of five months for AR pupils compared to gains of only three months for comparison group on the STAR reading comprehension test. Given that the STAR comprehension test is part of the AR programme, the test is intervention specific, and may be practised more often by the intervention group, but not available to the comparison group.

Rudd and Wade (2006) used matched comparison schools, and found that the average gains in reading from using AR were lower than for the intervention schools, but this finding appears neither in their summary nor their conclusion. Instead, the authors reported that it needs 'to be emphasised that there were improvements in average standardised test scores in the treatment schools for mathematics (both secondary and primary) and in the primary schools for reading. These were not spectacular improvements, but they can be seen as an important step in the right direction' (p. 51). This is one of many examples of clearly biased reporting. The authors do not report attrition clearly either at school or pupil level, but it seems that the reading attainment results are based on only 11 schools of the 21 originally allocated.

Duke (2011) reported that AR pupils made significant progress in the Standardised Test of Assessment of Reading (STAR), but not in the Missouri Assessment Programme (MAP), the state standardised test. Participants were 99 children in the third and fourth grade taken from three districts. Pre-post comparisons were made, with no control group. So it is not possible to say if the children would have made similar gains if they had not had the intervention.

There is a considerable research base on AR, making it one of the most researched interventions in which reading is practised through online resources. Prior research has mainly been carried out in the context of US schools. Also, the quality of the evidence on the effectiveness of AR on attainment is mixed, with much of the research small, with high attrition, using AR-led measurements, or based on weak research designs. Much of it also shows no benefit from using AR anyway (Table 6.6). Given that the use of AR is widespread, there was therefore a role for a UK-based trial involving a larger sample, true random allocation where baseline equivalence between the two groups is established and using a test of attainment that is independent of the intervention. Such a trial has been conducted and is described in the next chapter.

The prior evidence on Fresh Start

How to teach reading has been hotly debated. Schools under pressure to show improvement in their literacy goals have various approaches available, but it is not always clear to them which approaches to teaching literacy will be the most effective, with national policies liable to change over time (House of Commons Education and Skills Committee 2005). From 1998, England had a National Literacy Strategy for primary schools, based at least partly on an 'analytic approach'. Children first learnt the alphabet, and words were then introduced to illustrate the sounds associated with each letter. Subsequently, children used the whole word as the context to work out the sound of each letter (Johnston and Watson 2004).

The Rose Report (2006), based on a large-scale review, suggested that there was no evidence that the analytic approach had been effective, and so proposed changes. This led to a greater use of phonics and teaching reading through phonics.

The evidence on generic phonics training is not entirely clear. It may be effective for some groups and for some measures (fluency, decoding and comprehension) but less effective for other measures, such as spelling. Most of the positive studies in two reviews also suggest that phonics training alone is not enough (Slavin et al. 2009, Slavin et al. 2011). Many programmes included other elements such as cooperative learning or phonological awareness as well. For English language learners, programmes involving phonetic small group or one-to-one tutoring have shown positive effects (Cheung and Slavin 2012).

Almost all of the studies uncovered in our review were of low quality in terms of research design, and as is usual with weak studies almost all of these reported positive effects (Table 6.7). Two 'experiments' seem have had a considerable influence on the move to phonics after the Rose Report. One involved 304 first-year primary school children, allocated to three groups to receive different literacy interventions (Johnston and Watson 2004). But the groups were not randomly allocated – indeed they were not even matched, and the most disadvantaged pupils received the synthetic phonics intervention (p. 12). This makes the finding less secure as the phonics group started from a lower base so more improvement was possible in a short time. The second experiment by the same authors allocated the groups via matching, but involved only 92 first-year pupils and these were divided into three groups – synthetic phonics, analytic phonics and analytic phonics with phonological awareness training. This is a small study with only about 30 pupils per group, and it was ended early for ethical reasons. Other commentators have suggested the implementation of the three conditions may have led to bias (Wyse and Goswami 2008).

A subsequent review of 20 RCTs on phonics interventions concluded that systematic phonics teaching (teaching letter and sound links in a clear sequence) was more effective than not using phonics or using phonics non-systematically (Torgerson et al. 2006). But importantly, it excluded the first Johnston and Watson 'experiment' (above) on the basis of their lack of a valid control (but included the second because the authors personally communicated that the cases had been randomised even though this contradicts what they said in the original paper). The overall effect size for systematic phonics compared to other approaches was estimated as +0.27, and the results largely confirmed a previous review by

TABLE 6.7 Quality and impact summary: studies of phonics

	Effective	*Ineffective/unknown*
Higher quality 3* or better	0	0
Medium quality 2*	1	1
Lower quality 1*	12	3

Ehri et al. (2001). The earlier review of effective reading programmes summarised the results of 68 experimental studies (22,000 children) for beginning readers. It identified the key features of successful programmes as those that included teacher development and cooperative learning where children work with other children on structured activities and where there was a strong focus on phonics and phonics awareness, although focus on phonics alone could not guarantee positive results. Effects were stronger for decoding (ES = +0.27) than for comprehension (ES = +0.2). Thirteen studies for kindergarten children all reported strong positive outcomes. However, a combination of relatively few trials, and poor evidence or poorly-reported methods in some existing trials, meant that the result cannot be seen as definitive.

Johnston et al. (2012) conducted two follow-up analyses using some of their cases from the assessment of the impact of synthetic phonics teaching in Scotland (see above) by comparing them with cases from England, unmatched on prior attainment. The cases being compared were therefore neither randomly selected nor randomly allocated so there can be no standard error by definition. Despite this, the authors analysed their results using techniques such as analysis of variance that are based on standard errors (and they similarly cited p-values erroneously in their 2004 study). This is a common mistake in the field.

Two generic meta-analyses of reading interventions for struggling readers, like the previous reviews described above, reported that phonics was a promising approach. Galuschka et al. (2014) found 22 randomised control trials of phonics interventions. McArthur et al. (2012) found 12 studies using a variety of evaluation designs. Their conclusion was that teaching phonics was more effective than other methods for reading accuracy, but not for spelling or reading fluency. See also, What Works Clearinghouse (2010).

More recently, two higher quality studies in England have come to opposing conclusions (Table 6.8). An evaluation of 'Rapid Phonics' – a popular synthetic phonics programme used as a catch-up literacy intervention for pupils moving to secondary school – found no benefit. In fact the pupils in the treatment group did worse than those in the control (King and Kasim 2015). However, 'Butterfly Phonics' was found to be effective for pupils who were not achieving expected reading levels in the transition stage from primary to secondary school (Merrell and Kasim 2015). The evidence is thus mixed. The generic phonics approach may be effective for some measures and in some contexts but not others.

TABLE 6.8 Quality and impact detail: studies of phonics

Reference	Intervention	Smallest cell	Attrition	ES	NNTD-attrition	Quality
King and Kasim 2015	Rapid Phonics	87 pupils	13%	−0.05	0	2*
Merrell and Kasim 2015	Butterfly Phonics	155 pupils	17%	0.43	40	2*

There have been several poorer quality studies on phonics training each introducing a different element, and most suggest some positive results. One was about additional phonics instruction in small groups on top of regular classroom instruction (Kerins et al. 2010), while another was about phonics instruction as a supplemental lesson on a one-to-one basis (Vadasy and Sanders 2011). Another was about integrating phonological awareness and phonics training into whole class mixed-ability classroom (Shapiro and Solity 2008). Kerins et al. reported mixed effects with effect sizes ranging from −0.74 and −0.38 to 0.69 and 1.00 for different measures. This study was rated low because it was small-scale (n = 23), based on one classroom teacher and her pupils plus an SEN teacher. This was also not a fair comparison as treatment children had additional instruction.

One relatively popular approach to phonics is Fresh Start (FS) produced by Read Write Inc. Fresh Start is a 'systematic synthetic approach' (sometimes known as rml2). In FS the individual letters are sounded out within words, and these sounds then blended to form the pronunciation of the word, so as to 'read' it. The 44 basic sounds, used as building blocks, are taught first rather than the letters. When writing, the combination of sounds is said aloud and then converted to letters and written on the page (Brooks 2003).

A study by Brooks et al. (2003) evaluating FS for use with low attaining pupils at Key Stage 3 (KS3) claimed success. But with only 30% of its initial 500 pupils retained, such claims cannot be taken seriously. One report of the FS programme adopted by all the secondary schools in one local authority, for pupils not meeting or not likely to meet expected levels of literacy, only evaluated the outcomes of pupils in one school using before and after results with no comparators (Lanes et al. 2005). Despite no proper evaluation the authors claimed that the approach was popular and considered effective by teaching staff. Oddly, a later summary of reading interventions for KS3 included these studies of FS, reporting effect sizes of +0.25 to +0.34 for reading comprehension (Brooks 2007). The study reported no benefit for spelling, perhaps precisely because of the phonic nature of FS. All of the samples were small, with one study having only 29 cases, and there was high dropout, with studies not clearly reporting comparator groups, the allocation of cases or whether the groups were equivalent at the outset.

Even more than phonics generally, the prior evidence related to FS is weak, again because studies have too often been small and non-randomised, with high dropout or poorly reported. Overall, therefore, the direct evidence for Fresh Start itself is limited but promising, and mostly from small-scale studies not randomising pupils to treatments. Given that it is widely used, a larger randomised control trial was appropriate. Such a trial has been conducted and is described in Chapter 7.

The prior evidence on our literacy software evaluation

We uncovered a very wide range of studies examining the effects of CAI (Computer Assisted Instruction) or IT on pupil achievement. Of these only two were of higher quality and both showed no benefit (Table 6.9). They are discussed in more detail below (Table 6.10).

TABLE 6.9 Quality and impact summary: studies of ICT/CAL

	Effective	Ineffective/unknown
Higher quality 3* or better	0	2
Medium quality 2*	0	3
Lower quality 1*	19	9

TABLE 6.10 Quality and impact detail: studies of ICT/CAL

Reference	Intervention	Smallest cell	Attrition	ES	NNTD-attrition	Quality
Bai et al. 2016	**Integrated CAL in English**	44 schools (2,000+ pupils)	6%	0	0	4*
Chambers et al. 2011	Tier 2 CAL in reading	274 pupils	Unknown	0 or worse	0	2*
Bebell and Pedulla 2015	iPad apps in literacy	8 classes, 130 pupils	0 (confused reporting)	Unknown	0	
Bakker et al. 2015	Computer games in maths	16 schools	47%	0.22 (but not ICT alone)	0	2*
Rosas et al. 2003	**Video games**	**169 pupils**	**Unknown**	0	0	3*

Many of the studies directly addressing the efficacy of ICT in literacy education have been descriptive in nature, relying on the impressions of participants. These studies often find an apparently positive impact on the acquisition of pupil literacy skills (Blok et al. 2002, Silverstein et al. 2000, Cox et al. 2003, Pittard et al. 2003, OFSTED 2004, Rose and Dalton 2002, Pelgrum 2001, Sivin-Kachala and Bialo 2000). But others have argued that the small sample sizes, the lack of comparators, indeed the lack of research design, and the passive retrospective nature of some of this work combine to offer a potentially misleading picture (Waxman et al. 2003).

In this light, it is interesting that experimental studies of the effectiveness of software packages in improving literacy skills tend to show rather different results. Rigorous intervention studies with suitable controls often find little or no positive impact from the use of technology-based instruction compared to standard or traditional practice. A number of studies and systematic reviews have found that software packages had no effect on reading achievement (Borman et al. 2009,

Rouse and Krueger 2004, Andrews et al. 2005, Torgerson and Zhu 2003, Angrist and Lavy 2002, Goolsbee and Guryan 2005, Dynarski et al. 2007, Lei and Zhao 2005).

Bai et al. (2016) used 6,304 fifth-grade pupils (age 10/11) from 127 primary schools in China to test the impact of computer-assisted learning complementing regular English lessons. The 40-minute sessions were conducted twice weekly, involving two pieces of software – animated reviews and game-based remedial exercises, and a collection of additional exercise questions. A lesson implementation protocol was developed to assist teachers to deliver the programme. 44 schools were randomised to receive either the CAL integrated into their lessons, or as a stand-alone intervention. 4,000 students in 83 schools forming the control did not receive any intervention and were blinded to the treatment condition of the other schools. Outcomes were measured using the standardised Endline English test. Attrition was just over 6% of cases, and there was baseline equivalence between the groups. The two CAL interventions provided no overall benefit compared to traditional teaching.

Bakker et al. (2015) looked at the impact of playing mathematics computer games on students' multiplicative reasoning ability as used in regular US second-grade and third-grade maths lessons. The intervention consisted of 4 game units, each lasting 10 weeks and in each unit 8 different mini-games were played. The mini games focussed on 'automatising multiplicative number facts and multiplicative operation skills (through practicing), and on developing insight in multiplicative number relations and properties of multiplicative operations (through exploration and experimentation)' (p. 59). The study recruited 66 schools but 19 dropped out at different stages. Schools were also excluded if classes in both grades did not complete more than half of the mini-games. Results are reported for 719 children from 35 schools, representing attrition of over 50%. Multiplicative reasoning ability was measured using the knowledge, skills and insight test. It seemed that mini-games played at home and debriefed at school had a positive effect in enhancing overall multiplicative reasoning compared to the control (ES = 0.22). However, it seems to be the school debriefing that works (if it does) and not the use of the technology itself. Use of the mini-games at home, school or both had no clear benefit.

Rosas et al. (2003) tested the effects of the use of video games in the classroom for maths and reading. Video games instruction was used daily for 20-40 minutes over 12 weeks alternating between maths and language content. Participants were 1,274 first- and second-grade children and 30 teachers and directors from six schools in Chile. Schools were paired by academic achievement, SES and level of vulnerability. Students were divided within schools to an internal experimental or internal control group matched by educational level. An external control group was made up of schools where the tool was not used, and with a similar education level as the experimental group. There were 758 experimental children from 19 classes, 347 internal control from 9 classes (teacher used regular instruction), and 169 external control from 4 schools. Attrition is not known. There was no clear difference between treatment and control children in maths, reading and spelling.

Chambers et al. (2011) evaluated the relative effects of computer-assisted tutoring in small groups (Team Alphie) and one-to-one tutoring provided to struggling readers in 33 high-poverty Success for All (SFA) schools. Team Alphie is a small group literacy intervention, providing daily 45-minute lessons in phonemic awareness, phonics, fluency, vocabulary, and comprehension, with the focus on decoding and fluency skills. In this year-long study, struggling readers in the Team Alphie schools were tutored in groups of 6. In the control schools, students were tutored using the standard one-to-one tutoring process used in SFA. Participants were the lowest 50% of first- and second-grade children. Students were replaced by the next lowest scorer if they left (and therefore attrition is not clearly reported). The CAL group had 372 pupils and the control 274. Pre-post data was only available for Letter Word Identification (Woodcock LWID), although the authors reported positive effects on all three reading measures (Letter Word Identification, Word Attack and Comprehension). They concluded that 'computer-assisted, small-group tutoring programme may be at least as effective as one-to-one tutoring and serve more struggling readers'. However, calculation of gain scores for our review shows that the CAL group actually performed worse.

The report by Bebell and Pedulla (2015) is an example of authors appearing to have a conflict of interest, or at least wanting the use of technology to be shown as successful. The study involved 266 kindergarten children from 16 classes in one school district, with 8 classes allocated to receive iPads with access to 22 types of apps for learning listening, phonemic awareness, phonics/writing mechanics, reading and writing. The most frequently used apps were Word Wizard, Spelling Magic and Montessori Crossword. The intervention lasted 9 weeks. Outcomes were measured using the Rigby, Children's Progress Academy Assessment (CPA) and the Observation of Early Literacy Achievement (OSELA) tests. The authors reported in the abstract and conclusion that iPads had a positive impact on literacy using the CPA and OSELA tests, but their Figures 2 and 4 (pp. 200–201) show that the differences are very small, sometimes negative, and might be disregarded in a study with only 8 clusters. A follow-up after three years no longer had a clean control group, and so the results were compared with different cohorts (i.e. no longer even a quasi-experiment). This aspect of the study reported large gains for literacy, but equally large negative 'impacts' on maths.

In summary, there is little evidence that the use of commercial software by itself during the transition period helps improve the literacy performance of those who used it compared to those who did not. Several studies of the use of computer software designed to improve literacy for students in the transition years have failed to show any positive impact. In fact, a number found the use of technology actually slowed down students' progress. In one study Brooks et al. (2006) found no beneficial effects of the use of computer on students' spelling and reading. If anything, the use of a computer had a negative impact on students' reading.

It is now routine for most schools to use technology-based products such as software packages and websites in teaching and learning – for literacy and other core subject skills. Part of the reason for this growth has been enhanced government funding for technology-based purchases and for staff development in the use of IT. However, solid evidence on the educational benefits of using software in the classroom is not clear.

Given that computers and associated software impose a cost, are frequently updated, and are in widespread use in schools, it is important to have evidence of their impact. The study described in Chapter 7 is a large RCT of a literacy software product.

The prior evidence on Response to Intervention (RTI)

Response to Intervention is a multi-tiered approach that involves initial screening to identify students' learning needs using research-based instructions with ongoing monitoring of progress, and different levels of intensity (or tiers) to meet pupils' learning needs. Much of the evidence so far has been weak (Table 6.11), although there are two higher quality studies both showing promise for RTI.

On balance, the evidence suggests that the small group and individualised approaches of RTI are effective both for literacy and maths. The two largest studies have substantial positive effect sizes, and the medium quality studies similarly offer promise at least for some forms of test outcomes (Table 6.12).

Piper and Korda (2011) looked at a combination of intensive teacher training, teacher support and regular information on student achievement to parents and communities. Three groups of schools serving the second and third grade in Liberia were randomly allocated to full treatment (59 schools, 934 pupils), light treatment (60, 1,065) and control group (57, 989). These groups were clustered within districts, such that several nearby schools were organised together. Attrition was at least 3%. In the 'full' treatment group, reading levels were assessed, teachers were trained on how to continually assess student performance focusing on reading instructional strategies, and teachers were provided with frequent school-based pedagogic support, resource materials and books. In addition, parents and communities were informed of student performance. In the 'light' treatment group, the community was informed about reading achievement using school report cards based on EGRA (Early Grade Reading Assessment) results or findings and student reading report cards prepared by teachers. Outcomes included early reading tasks (letter naming, reading fluency, phonemic awareness, reading comprehension and listening comprehension). These were assessed using the EGRA Plus: Liberia tool. The light intervention made no difference, but the full intervention pupils made bigger gains between baseline and final assessments on all seven tests of reading, with effect sizes ranging from ES = 0.39 (for reading comprehension) to ES = 1.23 (for unfamiliar word fluency). Overall impact was 0.79.

TABLE 6.11 Quality and impact summary: studies of RTI

	Effective	*Ineffective/unknown*
Higher quality 3* or better	2	0
Medium quality 2*	2	0
Low quality 1*	15	4

TABLE 6.12 Quality and impact detail: studies of RTI

Reference	Intervention	Smallest cell	Attrition	ES	NNTD-attrition	Quality
Piper and Korda 2011	**RTI**	**934 pupils**	**3%**	**0.79**	**709**	**3/4***
Al Otaiba et al. 2011	**RTI**	**251 pupils**	**Unknown**	**0.52**	–	**3***
Vadasy et al. 2013	RTI tier 2	92 pupils	45	Word reading 0.35 Early receptive vocabulary −0.09	0	2*
Jimenez et al. 2010	RTI	120 pupils	Not known	10 outcomes range from −0.04 to 0.68	–	2*

Al Otaiba et al. (2011) examined the use of assessment data to guide individualised instruction (RTI), in a teacher-level RCT, involving 14 schools, 23 treatment teachers (305 students) and 21 contrast teachers (251 students). The treatment used differentiated instruction in ongoing assessments of children's language and literacy skills. Teachers in the contrast condition received only baseline professional development that included a researcher-delivered summer day-long workshop on individualised instruction. Students in treatment classrooms outperformed students in the contrast classrooms on reading skills, comprised of letter-word reading, decoding, alphabetic knowledge and phonological awareness (ES = 0.52). Teachers in both conditions provided small group instruction, but teachers in the treatment condition provided significantly more individualised instruction.

Vadasy et al. (2013) looked at the longer term effectiveness of a standard protocol, Tier 2 supplemental vocabulary intervention for Kindergarten English learners (US Spanish speakers) for 20 minutes per day for 20 weeks in small groups. The intervention was designed to develop root word vocabulary knowledge, and reinforce beginning word reading skills. There were originally 93 pupils in the treatment group and 92 in the control but scores were only obtained for 74 and 66 pupils, respectively. The authors only computed ES for the positive outcomes – proximal reading vocabulary +0.23, distal reading vocabulary +0.29, and word reading +0.35.

Jimenez et al. (2010) undertook a study of a small group supplementary intervention based in the Canary Islands, involving 241 children aged 5 to 8 at risk in reading (121 in intervention, 120 control). Attrition was not reported, and there was some initial imbalance. The intervention included small group reading comprehension. For the 10 tests reported the ES were 0.04, 0.68, 0.52, −0.03, −0.04, 0.14, 0.02, 0.06, 0.49, 0.00.

A study by Graves et al. (2011) reported that RTI was particularly efficacious for pupils from disadvantaged backgrounds with learning difficulties, and was more effective for improving oral fluency than reading comprehension. All of the pupils involved were 'below' or 'far below' a basic level of literacy. This was a quasi-experimental study that compared small group intensive reading instruction (Tier 2) with a control group ('business as usual') involving sixth graders with and without learning disabilities. The duration was 30 hours over 10 weeks.

Faggella-Luby and Wardwell (2011) examined the effects of a Tier 2 intervention which randomly assigned 86 at-risk students in the fifth and sixth grades (age 10-12) to three treatments − Story Structure (SS), Typical Practice (TP) and Sustained Silent Reading (SSR). Only sixth-grade students on SS and TP outperformed those in SSR in all three tests (standardised curriculum-based test, Strategy-Use test and Gates-MacGinitie Reading Comprehension). The impact on fifth-grade students was not clear. The Strategy-Use test assessed strategies that were taught only to students in the SS group, and is not a test of general comprehension or reading, so using this test may not be valid for comparison. Also, the study compared only post-test results without establishing whether the three groups were similar to start with. The small sample divided into three treatment groups and two grade levels suggests that there were fewer than 20 in each group. This is too small for conclusive evidence.

Vaughn and Fletcher (2012) summarised a series of studies conducted over several years involving a total of 1,867 students (1,083 struggling readers and 784 typical readers) in grades 6–8 (age 11 to 14) from seven middle schools. The findings suggest that secondary school students who received both Tier 1 (enhanced whole class instruction) and Tier 2 (small or large group) interventions made greater improvements in decoding, fluency and reading comprehension compared to those who received only the Tier 1 intervention, but the effect was small (ES = 0.16). There was no difference between the small and large group intervention. Vaughn and Fletcher believed that the key feature of an effective RTI programme was the enhanced classroom instruction. Interestingly, the study showed that individualised attention had no particular advantage over the standardised approach for students with learning difficulties. In fact it did more harm than good.

Leroux et al. (2011) evaluated an intensive Tier 2 (small group) intervention and showed that there were 'significant' differences between treatment and comparison groups on two of three of the outcome measures. However, the differences were largely due to the continuing decline of the Tier 1 students in the comparison group, rather than real gains by the treatment group. The small sample of only

30 students across three grade levels (grade 6 to 8) from three middle schools is not large enough to provide convincing results.

The evidence on RTI so far is predominantly from the US, or has involved small samples or focused on those with learning disabilities. It is not yet clear whether RTI is suitable for 10 and 11 year olds struggling with literacy in the UK. There was therefore a case for an efficacy trial in the UK, as described in Chapter 7.

The prior evidence on summer schools

In September 2011, the Deputy Prime Minister of the UK announced that £50 million would be made available in England for a summer school programme every year. The scheme was intended to support disadvantaged pupils in the transition phase from primary to secondary school. By the summer of 2013 over 1,900 schools had participated in summer schools sponsored by the Department for Education. Such schools are now widespread, but are they effective?

Some of the literature on the effectiveness of summer schools for academic improvement looks promising. A research synthesis of 93 evaluations of summer schools suggested that they can be effective, especially with parental involvement, and perhaps with more promise in maths than literacy (Cooper et al. 2000). Schacter and Jo (2005) found a positive impact for literacy from a seven-week summer school for economically disadvantaged first-grade children in the US, randomised to the intervention. Matsudaira (2008) estimated the impact of summer school on both maths and reading as about +0.12, based on a form of regression discontinuity analysis.

Other studies suggest less promise. One study of around 2,000 pupils in transition from primary to secondary divided them non-randomly into two groups. It found no differential impact on literacy gain scores between the groups who attended a 50-hour summer literacy school compared to a control. Both groups demonstrated an equivalent decline in scores from pre- to post-test (Sainsbury et al. 1998). Therefore, it seems that the reason for any decline over that crucial summer does not have to do with whether literacy practice and teaching takes place. It could be due to anxiety about changing school, a change in school routine or a different curriculum emphasis. A smaller study from the US involved 331 pupils from grades 1 to 5 in one school (Kim 2006). Using stratification in terms of pre-test reading ability, pupils were randomly allocated to a treatment or delayed treatment in a waiting-list design. The treatment involved receiving 10 free books to read during the summer vacation, including postcards and letters to stimulate reading. Using self-report, the treatment group read three more books, on average, than the control. However, this did not convert to any difference in the literacy scores between the groups after the vacation. The number of pupils is quite small in the age range relevant to transition (grade 5), and 52 pupils moved away during the summer (proportionately for each group and stratum). Neither study means that a summer school intervention cannot work. But they do suggest that the decline in literacy over the summer of transition to senior school is not simply about lack of literacy practice or activity.

An evaluation of summer school impact in England was conducted by NFER in 2013, in which nearly 21,000 pupils participated (Marting et al. 2013). The study was conducted through a large scale survey in which the target group was pupils in schools that conducted a summer school programme and pupils in comparator schools that did not participate. The report mainly suggested a positive account of summer school programmes in terms of pupils' confidence, readiness to attend the secondary school and socialisation. The supposed 'evaluation' did not look at the impact on attainment, and was solely concerned with survey responses to items about pupils' confidence, social skill and readiness to attend their secondary school.

All of these studies on summer schools involve voluntary attendance. A problem with this is that those who turn up may be very different from those who do not. For example, Borman and Dowling (2006) compared 438 students randomised to summer school for three years with 248 receiving no intervention. The study reports success for the intervention, but as with almost all such studies the level of dropout is a concern. The study ended up comparing the post-test scores of the 'compliers' who continued to attend with all of the control students. This would tend to inflate considerably the perceived impact of the summer school.

The BELL approach has been reported as one of the few forms of summer schools with reasonable evidence of success (Terzian and Moore 2009). There have been several evaluations of the BELL summer schools in the US (BELL 2001, 2002, 2003). Unfortunately, their own 'evaluations' are often unclear, and reinforce the importance of having independent evaluations – where concern is more about finding the impact than in what that impact is. The BELL programme took place in several US cities, but the reports are not always clear which sites provided data for which analysis, nor how the students were allocated to the analytical groups. There appears to have been no benefit for writing (Harvard Family Research Project 2006). Gains are reported but no effect sizes were published. The gains were lower for low-income children and those in the age range relevant to school transition.

Impact evaluation of the BELL summer school programme in Boston and New York City by Chaplin and Cappizano (2006) suggests that the programme had no benefit on all measures (reading and academic self-concept). In fact, there was a negative impact on vocabulary score of being on the programme compared to the control group. The only statistically 'significant' impact reported was for increasing parental reading to children, but even then effect sizes were small. The overall 'effect' size for reading calculated here (not by the original authors) was +0.02 – which is negligible. Chaplin and Cappizano (2006) then claimed that because the post-test for the control group was taken 16 days later, they had a 16-day advantage and adjusted the results to account for this difference. If this was true then it means that 16 days in school is equally, if not more, effective than being on the summer programme. Nevertheless, Chaplin and Capizzano (2006) adjusted the test scores so that there was no difference between treatment and control schools in days at school. However, after adjustments the impact of the programme on academic outcomes was still negligible. The effect size for total score after adjustment was 0.08, and for vocabulary and comprehension 0.04 and 0.08, respectively.

The study reported that a total of 1,917 pupils applied to the programme, of which only 1,225 agreed to be part of the study, yet the random allocation to treatment or control was of the original 1,917. The report is not clear on the numbers finally appearing in the treatment and control groups. Of the 1,225 consenting, 138 were excluded from the study, leaving 1,087. But in their paper, data are only presented for 835 cases (44% of the original applicants). This means that the study can no longer be regarded as randomised in nature. The summer programme involved both maths and reading, but the results are only presented for reading. Despite finding no impact on most measures, negative effect on others, and small effects on academic outcomes, Chaplin and Cappizano concluded with the statement: 'Our results suggest that the BELL program has positive and substantively important impacts.' This is an example where the conclusions are not warranted by the findings, and highlights the need for critical evaluation of research reports and for policy-makers and potential funders to test these claims before putting money into such interventions.

Overall therefore, despite some claims to the contrary, there is no strong evidence that the BELL approach would work in England with disadvantaged pupils preparing for secondary school. The EEF has commissioned two other randomised control trials to assess the impact of summer schools on pupils' performance in reading and writing (Torgerson et al. 2014, Maxwell et al. 2014). In both studies common challenges were the initial recruitment of pupils to the summer schools and pupil dropout during the programme. Improvement in reading comprehension was reported by both studies. The new study described in Chapter 7 is larger and looks at both English and maths, as well as involving a full process evaluation.

Discussion

Despite the many interventions to improve literacy that have been proposed, those that specifically address literacy (or numeracy) for students in transition to secondary school in mainstream settings are a minority. The most relevant ones have mostly shown little or no positive effects, and in some cases, even negative effects. Some of the interventions were too complicated for easy implementation and some involved multiple strategies making it difficult to tease out the active ingredient, while some were too reliant on the competence of teachers and their ability to use the prescribed resources. Many involved a short-term and single application strategy. Those that reported positive effects had often only been evaluated once and on a small scale, or had no proper randomisation or no report of how assignment was carried out, high attrition or no report of attrition. There were also studies with a clear conflict of interest where the intervention was evaluated by the developers. There were some which reported positive effects using programme-developed tests, but not for standardised tests. Others targeted multiple components with mixed results, for example, showing impact for reading but not spelling. Consequently, there are no obvious interventions that can be recommended wholeheartedly without further evaluations of the kind described in Chapter 7.

7

WHAT WORKS FOR CATCH-UP LITERACY AND NUMERACY?

This chapter describes the six most promising or most popular interventions for which the existing evidence was presented in Chapter 6. In this chapter we describe how these interventions were implemented for the evaluations that follow, and the study designs and methods used to evaluate them. The chapter then summarises the ensuing results. We start by looking the overall approach used for all six studies.

Designs and methods used in the six catch-up trials

All of the studies that follow used the same basic design, involving only two groups – the treatment group receiving the intervention and a control group receiving standard practice (Gorard 2013a). In all studies, the cases were randomised to group by schools, classes or as individuals. All except the summer school programme were based on a waiting-list design in which the control group received the intervention once the trial was complete. This design is ethical since all pupils involved receive the intervention; this reduces the dangers from post-allocation demoralisation, avoids any bias caused by knowledge of grouping when taking the pre-test, and allows an unbiased estimate of the impact of the intervention. The major drawback is that it does not permit consideration of the longer term impact of the intervention, because there is no long-term control group.

The control group pupils in each study continued their usual classroom activities. All pupils were from year 6 (at the end of primary school) or the start of year 7 (in their new secondary schools), in state-funded schools from across England. All studies had both a pre- and post-intervention measure of literacy attainment (and sometimes in other subjects such as maths). The pre-tests were conducted before randomisation. Random allocation to treatment and control was conducted by the lead evaluator in the presence of another researcher. The pupils were young, so opt-out parental consent was obtained by the schools involved even though all of the interventions were exactly the kind of teaching that any school could have adopted anyway.

All analyses were based on intention to treat, meaning that cases were handled as being in the group they were randomised to, whatever happened subsequently, and pupils were followed up as far as possible even where they had moved schools. A sub-analysis of only those pupils eligible for free school meals (FSM) was conducted where possible. The analyses are based on an 'effect' size (the difference in means between the groups, divided by their overall standard deviation). The differences analysed where possible are the gain scores from pre- to post-test, in order to cater for any slight imbalances in the initial groups, and to aid comparison between trials. If the pre- and post-test scores have a different metric then they were standardised as z scores before analysis. Where possible, measures of attendance or completion of the intervention are used with the results for the treatment group to assess any impact of 'dosage'. All scores are presented as rounded, to eliminate decimal places and make comprehension easier. Further details can be found in Gorard et al. (2015a, 2015b, 2016b), Khan and Gorard (2012), See et al. (2015a), Siddiqui et al. (2014, 2015).

In order to help readers assess the security of the findings, the studies are rated between 0 and 4*, as described in Chapter 4. All are randomised control trials – which is a good design for an impact study. All use either standard assessments such as Key Stage results, or standardised tests of attainment. Those studies with individual randomisation of pupils to groups are, all other things being equal, intrinsically superior to those where classes or schools are randomised. Otherwise, the larger the trial, and the lower the dropout, the more trustworthy the results are. Trials in which the groups were reasonably well balanced at the outset are, all other things being equal, better than those where randomisation leads to imbalance. Other threats to the security of the findings are noted where relevant.

In order to help readers further, each result is compared to the number of counterfactual cases that would need to be added to the smallest group in order for the apparent 'effect' size to disappear (Gorard and Gorard 2016). This number needed to disturb the finding (NNTD) can be estimated by multiplying the 'effect' size by the number of cases in the smallest group. The larger this is, the stronger the finding. The NNTD can be compared directly to the number of cases missing (through dropout, missing values, or non-response). Where the number of cases missing is trivial in comparison to the NNTD, this shows that the result cannot be attributed solely to bias caused by missing data.

Each trial also had an integrated process evaluation to monitor progress, observe testing, consider unintended consequences, and assess fidelity to intervention. There is not enough space to describe these components in any detail for each trial, but the overall results and any key findings are outlined in the next section. Our general approach to process evaluations was described on Chapter 5.

Switch-on Reading intervention and methods

The model of Switch-on Reading being evaluated was provided for Year 7 pupils in mainstream secondary school settings in Nottinghamshire. The intervention is a short-term individual reading programme for pupils who have not achieved Level 4 English at Key Stage 2 (KS2). The intervention was delivered over 10 weeks and consisted of regular 20-minute one-to-one reading sessions with Switch-on trained staff members. The aim was for as many pupils as possible to achieve functional literacy, and so to close the reading achievement gap for vulnerable children working below the age-expected levels.

The intervention was conducted by staff including SENCOs, librarians, teachers and teaching assistants (who were the clear majority). Each member of staff was trained, and looked after no more than four pupils. Each pupil was given a schedule in which to come out of one standard class per day for 20 minutes at a time for the Switch-on session. The schedule was arranged so that parts of different lessons were missed.

In the first session, the materials used were selected to suit the reading age of the pupil as assessed by the pre-test and prior attainment. Switch-on Reading revolves around appropriately matched books that have been finely graded in bands and levels to provide small changes in challenge over time. These books had not been used with Year 7 pupils before and so one question was whether the pupils and staff found them suitable. Where there was a clear mismatch in the early sessions, the level was adjusted until the reading age required was just challenging enough. The books themselves included fiction and non-fiction with lots of visual images meant to encourage students' interest in reading as well as providing clues for comprehension.

Each Switch-on Reading session should have consisted of:

- Reading a familiar book (perhaps the first 100 words only)
- Discussion on the material, visuals and cover pages of the books
- Invoking interest of students by involving them in talking about visual content
- Reading the text and using the running record sheet for analysis of reading
- Feedback to the student
- Introduction to a new book

Therefore, each session incorporated revision of a familiar text, introducing new vocabulary, practicing phonics and also improving comprehension through questions and talking about the texts. In each session the student should read excerpts of text from four books.

At some point in the 20-minute reading session the member of staff recorded the reading assessment of the pupil on a sheet, and made an inventory of errors such as words missed, substituted with another, mispronounced or repeated, plus self-corrections and appeals for help. The form for recording these events and the rules for completion were standardised, and an integral part of the intervention.

Part of the intervention also involved analysis of errors. The average number of errors was calculated to determine which book set was followed next. After each book, the adult trainer praised the child when an effective reading strategy was observed, and prompted the student to use new strategies where behaviour had not been effective or advice had been ignored.

The evaluation of this intervention involved 19 primary schools in England, ranging in size from around 600 pupils to over 1,500. FSM eligibility ranged from 6% to 30%, pupils not speaking English as their first language ranged from 1% to 10%, and pupils with statements of special educational need or receiving School Action Plus ranged from 3% to 7%.

The schools identified 314 pupils eligible for reading support. Half were individually randomised to immediate support and the other half formed the control. This meant that each school was both a treatment and a control school. The Phase 1 intervention group of 157 pupils would be involved in reading every day, aiming for at least 40 sessions in the minimum of 10 weeks. The Phase 2 group of a further 157 pupils continued with normal lessons and any interventions or programmes that were also available to Phase 1 pupils and that would have been used anyway in the absence of this evaluation. After one term, the Phase 2 pupils received the intervention. The pre-test was conducted prior to the delivery of the intervention and before randomisation, and the post-test was conducted before Phase 2 pupils received the intervention. One pupil did not register a pre-test score, and five pupils did not take the post-test. The GL New Group Reading Test (versions A and B) was used for the pre- and post-tests. The evaluators observed the post-tests in operation, because the staff and pupils were no longer blind as to who was in which group. Both the pre- and post-tests were conducted online to encourage standard format and timing, to reduce the potential influence of staff, and to create instant results for the schools and evaluators. Overall, the two groups were reasonably well balanced in terms of these background characteristics.

This evaluation has a reasonable cell size of individually randomised pupils, initial balance between groups, and minimal attrition. The evidence from it is listed here as 4* in terms of its robustness.

Accelerated Reader intervention and methods

Accelerated Reader (AR) is a networked computer-based management programme intended to encourage pupils in independent book reading, and allow teachers to monitor pupils' reading levels and progress. The teacher's role is to support pupils in making an appropriate selection of books for reading, and to motivate them in achieving advanced reading levels. AR starts with a Standardised Test for Assessment of Reading (STAR) – a 20-minute screening test that determines each pupil's 'optimal' level of reading comprehension. The STAR scores pupil's reading ability and generates a diagnostic report that includes percentile rank, National Curriculum Level in reading, reading age, estimated oral reading fluency and Zone of Proximal Development (ZPD: maximum ability to read and understand a book of a certain difficulty level). The diagnostic report also gives recommendations to the teacher on how to support each pupil for further improvement in reading. STAR can be conducted periodically to monitor a pupil's progress. It is recommended on the Renaissance Learning Inc. website that teachers conduct STAR three to five times in a year to follow a pupil's gradual progress.

The readability of any book is calculated taking into account the word count, average sentence length, average word length and word difficulty. There are over 160,000 books (fiction and non-fiction) available in the AR programme, allotted to bands on the basis of the readability formula. Readability indicates the level of challenge in any book to be matched with a pupil's reading (ZPD) and their areas and levels of interest. Areas of interest based on pupil age are suggested along with book levels in order to help make an appropriate book selection.

Once an appropriate book selection has been made, pupils are given time in school to read independently. AR recommends teachers motivate pupils to read regularly, and finish reading the selected book promptly. It suggests 30 to 60 minutes of independent reading time every day. There are around 156,000 quizzes in AR. These reading practice quizzes assess pupils' comprehension of the specific books they select to read. The format is generally multiple choice with items that ask factual and inferential questions from the book. The quizzes are computer based. Each pupil gets an individual login and password to access AR and complete the quiz. It is recommended that pupils take the AR quiz within 48 hours of finishing the book.

As soon as the quiz is completed AR generates a report that is intended to be monitored by a teacher. If the pupil scores lower than 60% repeatedly then the teacher needs to recheck the book selection and make different choices according to the ZPD. Pupils achieve AR points every time a quiz is passed, calculated on the basis of the readability level and word count of the book (Paul et al. 1996).

The teacher can set AR point goals for each pupil or for the whole class. The computer programme flags issues if pupils are not attaining the set targets or are just selecting books to attain points rather than increasing the ZPD levels. Teachers are meant to be innovative in giving rewards for achieving the targets – such as certificates of achievement, gift vouchers, club memberships and announcements in school assemblies.

Four individual secondary schools proposed an intervention and evaluation of AR over a period of 20 weeks. The AR developers were not involved in any of these four proposals so the funders (EEF) decided that the schools should run the trial as a co-operative with advice from evaluators. All schools were urban, mixed schools, with a high proportion of disadvantaged pupils. A target group of 349 Year 7 pupils across the four secondary schools was identified by each school on the basis of their prior KS2 scores (pupils at Level 4c and below in English). Of these, 323 were individually randomised to groups (180 to treatment, 163 to control). See Siddiqui et al. (2015) for further details on this.

Pupils in the waiting list continued the usual school activities. There was no chance of contamination because pupils in the control group had no access to the

AR programme. No school dropped out from the trial. A total of 8 pupils (6 from the treatment group) did not provide a post-test score. The average KS2 scores of those who dropped out in treatment and control groups was about the same, and neither unusually high nor low, given the eligibility criteria. The findings are based on the post-test scores for the New Group Reading Test, developed by GL Assessment and the National Foundation for Education Research. There was no formal pre-test, and the initial balance of the groups was assessed in terms of their Key Stage 2 English scores.

This evaluation has a medium cell size of individually randomised pupils, initial balance between groups, and minimal attrition. The evidence from it is listed here as 4* in terms of its robustness.

Fresh Start intervention and methods

Fresh Start is a reading and writing programme. The aim of FS is to provide additional support to fill the learning gaps for children who have missed earlier opportunities, so that they can participate in mainstream literacy activities without falling further behind. The complete FS resource pack includes module sets, assessment charts, magnetic sound cards, speed sound cards, sound charts and a poster, lesson plans, a pronunciation DVD for teacher, teacher training books and handbooks to support the delivery of FS. The modules are graded according to reading age, and in this trial FS was conducted three times a week for one hour each over 22 weeks.

The programme begins with an initial assessment of pupil's phonics and word recognition. Pupils are assessed individually by teachers. The assessment involves pupils reading aloud or sounding out the letters and words to the teacher. Pupils are put into four groups according to the initial scores. This is to ensure homogeneity within the groups, which is believed to encourage progress. Depending on the individual pupil's progress, teachers may also provide additional 20-minute regular one-to-one sessions.

The ensuing phonic lessons involve the systematic teaching of 44 sounds in English. Using a sound chart and speed sound cards the teacher introduces the sounds and graphemes. Pupils practise blending the sounds through Sound Talk (sounding-out) by repeating the sounds after the teacher. This process is assisted using a number of learning aids such as picture cards, picture books, Fred puppet and talking fingers. Nonsense words are also used for pupils to practise independent blending of sounds. Pupils practise writing, although the letters are not mentioned by their names.

In the third week, pupils are withdrawn from the regular literacy class and put into groups for the phonics lessons. Pupils begin with an entry test to determine the starting lesson level. There are 33 modules altogether and pupils may start with different modules depending on their entry level. The modules are graded in six sets and each set consists of a pack of five booklets with different titles. Pupils are assessed after completion of each set to see if they are ready for the next module.

Inherent in the FS programme is a set of classroom management routines. These are used in each FS session and form the way teachers communicate with pupils. In addition to receiving the resource pack, teachers also took part in a two-day training workshop provided by Read Write Inc. The latter, along with the schools, decided on all aspects of the intervention, independently of the evaluators.

Three heads of school clusters in different regions of England had independently proposed conducting FS as an intervention. The funders (EEF) felt that each cluster was too small for a feasible efficacy trial. So they suggested that each cluster run their own intervention but that they should be constrained to use the same evaluation design, and the results should be aggregated by an independent evaluator. The independent evaluator would also train the school research leads, advise on design, oversee implementation and conduct a process evaluation from start to finish. This is therefore a school-led trial and, like AR, in addition to the substantive results it provided evidence on whether schools and teachers can conduct robust research, with advice.

At the start, as the independent evaluators, we held a one-day workshop for the heads and research leads in each of the 10 schools (and for those in the AR trial – above). This covered the craft of conducting a randomised control trial. A key issue was how to randomise the eligible pupils into the two groups, making the allocation fair and without bias. A second workshop was conducted by the evaluators with the cluster and school leads before the post-test phase. This explained the conduct of the test process (the need for 'blinding' or at least observation to prevent bias), and how to calculate and interpret the results for each cluster. The schools reported that the workshops were very useful. Attendance was high. And the evaluators also found them informative about the kinds of challenges teachers faced when conducting research projects in their schools.

A target group of 433 eligible pupils from the new Year 7 intake was identified by 10 secondary schools, based on them having KS2 scores at or below Level 4c in English (but six were not present at the outset). On the basis of the pre-test when in Year 7, all but 29 of the pupils were reading at National Curriculum Level 4c or below, and 237 were reading at Level 3c or below. By the end of the intervention, a total of 8 pupils provided no post-test. Reasons for absence included having left the country, long-term illness, suspension, or no longer attending the school with no information about their new destination. The average score of their pre-tests was 251, suggesting that the dropout was unremarkable and unbiased between groups. There were therefore 419 pupils in the final analyses, of which 215 were in the treatment and 204 in the control group. The main outcome measure was GL Assessment's New Group Reading Test, used as pre-test (version A) and post-test (B). As with all relevant evaluations described in this chapter, the headline findings are based on the 'overall reading score' provided by the software. This is used because our prior work has shown that there is a floor effect created by the minimum achievable score when using the 'standardised age scores' (Gorard et al. 2015a).

This evaluation has a reasonable cell size, randomised at individual level, some initial imbalance between groups, and low attrition. The evidence from it is listed here as a good 3* in terms of its robustness.

Literacy software intervention and methods

This intervention involved a piece of popular literacy software, widely used in schools to allow pupils to work at their own pace, provide regular progress updates, and permit the teacher to devote larger amounts of time to pupils most in need. We do not name the software used in the treatment (or its publisher). While regrettable, this is what was agreed at the outset, and it anyway makes little difference to the implications of this research. The publishers claimed that their reading software was 'award winning', and that if 11-year-olds worked on this program for one hour a day, spread over six weeks, it could improve their reading skills including single word reading, sentence reading and non-word reading. It also reportedly improved reading speed, reading fluency, vocabulary, comprehension and reading stamina. The software is multi-sensory in nature, combining vision, sound and touch. It allows pupils to progress at their own pace, with consistent and immediate feedback, and progress is measured. It was designed to be used in conjunction with standard reading exercises, based on the National Literacy Strategy in England. More than 100 starter texts are provided, including poems, tales, recipes, articles, descriptions, letters, points of view, instructions and official documents, and new content can be added via authoring tools. The standard of difficulty of each exercise, and the look and feel of the program, can be adapted to suit the pupil, making it suitable for all ages and abilities including children with learning challenges. It was aligned with National Curriculum standards, developed with guidance from some of the leading reading experts, and grounded in the most current research on literacy, using a carefully structured whole/part/whole approach to reading instruction. It has customised professional development ranging from CD-ROM and online courses to on-site workshops. A comprehensive Teacher's Guide with activities and lesson plans are included in the package. Free technical support is available during office hours.

The number of computers available for use, and access to them, were discussed with the ICT technicians in all participating schools. All of the schools in the trial had enough computers and headphones for the treatment group pupils to use during the trial. Trial orientation sessions were made available to all teachers, head-teachers, and school governors in the participating schools before the start of the study. A detailed description of the software and its learning activities, the timelines, study purpose, research questions, and expectations relating to participation were provided to all participating teachers. Teachers were given logbooks in which to keep records of implementation, and notes on progress of the trial.

Ongoing technical support was agreed with the software publisher for the period of the trial. All treatment teachers received training about how to use the software from consultants sent by the publisher. The training included a demonstration of the most effective ways of using the software. Teachers were provided with a copy of all materials. They were trained to view individual pupils' feedback, assigned a code for the software publisher's records, and given access to the consultant as well as a telephone number to use if they had any technical problems with the software or with any of the associated activities.

The sample consisted of Year 7 pupils in state-maintained schools in England agreeing to co-operate with the research and possessing a minimum level of technology access and support. Eight classes out of the total of 31 approached did not take part because at least one parent objected to their child taking part in the study. This left 23 classes containing 672 pupils at the outset. These were randomised to treatment (11 classes, 319 pupils) or control (12 classes, 346 pupils). No schools or classes dropped out. Four pupils moved to schools in another area before the pre-test, and a further three moved before the post-test. It was not possible to conduct an intention-to-treat analysis using these, since we could not follow the seven missing pupils. Nevertheless, their numbers are small and divided between both groups. A simple sensitivity analysis suggests that their inclusion could make no difference to the clear results of this trial.

The resulting 665 pupils were given a pre-test of their existing literacy levels in the first week and an equivalent post-test was given to both groups after 10 weeks of teaching. The assessment was the Lucid Assessment System for Schools (LASS secondary). This looked at eight related reading skills, forming a suite of three attainment tests (single-word reading, sentence reading and spelling), one ability test (reasoning) and four diagnostic tests (auditory memory, visual memory, phonic skills and phonological processing).

The intervention took place for 10 weeks, over a single term. The treatment group used the computer software for a designated time on three to four days each week. Headphones were supplied for every pupil to counter distraction, thereby maximising the pupils' attention. The software, the treatment schedule and the training all encouraged teachers to help pupils complete all of the learning activities provided by the software, over the ten weeks of implementation. The software itself automatically logged the records of each activity completed by each pupil and class. Most pupils in all classes completed the bulk of the activities. One class had some technical difficulties with their computer system early in the term.

The control group remained in routine teaching practice using a more traditional paper- and teacher-based format, with no specified ICT component.

This evaluation has a large cell size, and low attrition, but is randomised at class level, and has slight initial imbalance between groups. The evidence from it is listed here as 3* in terms of its robustness.

RTI intervention and methods

Response to Intervention is a personalised and targeted intervention developed in the United States as part of an inclusion policy to provide a differentiated programme of instruction for children with learning disabilities within regular school settings.

The theoretical and empirical framework of the approach was based on work by Clay (1991). According to Clay, children learn literacy skills by developing an inner control of strategies for processing text. If a piece of text is too difficult, the child cannot develop this control. So any text used should be pitched at the right level. With effective and explicit teaching, the teacher can help the child build a strategy to enable them to process the text. Based on their work on Reading Recovery, Fountas and Pinnell (2006) developed an approach called Guided Reading using books matched to children's abilities employing differentiated instruction in small groups, gradually building up the child's inner control. This was the basis for the differentiated levels or tiers of the RTI approach.

RTI is targeted at the specific needs of students in the form of a whole class approach as preventive teaching (Tier 1), followed by small group remediation (Tier 2) for those who needed more attention and one-to-one tutoring for those who did not respond to the small group instruction (Tier 3). It works in two ways. One is identifying the needs of the students via a case-by-case analysis and tailoring instruction based on these needs. Another way is the use of a standard treatment protocol to determine the most appropriate research-based practice to tackle these problems. RTI is delivered in three tiers of increasingly intensive instruction.

The RTI programme in this study was led by the Centre for the Use of Research and Evidence in Education (CUREE) who developed the specialist tools and resources, and delivered the training. Training was conducted prior to the implementation of the programme and after schools had been randomised. The training was a three-day event which included an introduction to the concept of RTI, and the range of tools and protocols. Teachers were shown how to use these in screening pupils for eligibility and assessing their needs, and how to select appropriate research-based approaches. In addition, treatment teachers also received ongoing support provided by another organisation known as AfA3As (Achievement for All 3As) through in-school coaching using their Achievement Coaches as part of the AfA programme. Teachers in the control schools, on the other hand, did not receive any special training. They continued teaching as normal, including any interventions that they might have already been undertaking.

The RTI programme used in this trial began with an initial screening to identify the individual needs of the pupils using the Close-Case Analysis Tool. The tool helps staff to determine the literacy areas to focus on for each pupil, such as phonics, fluency or comprehension. It also helps to determine the degree of intensity for the intervention – whether it would be Tier 1 (whole class) or Tier 2 (small group) intervention. The more intensive (Tier 3) is only recommended if the number of children with a particular issue in an area of literacy is small or if the pupils involved have already had interventions targeting this area, and the teachers do not think they are likely to make progress in a group setting.

Teachers then decide on the appropriate approaches to use with the targeted pupils using a set of 'Making Choices' information sheets. On these sheets is a menu of interventions or approaches, all of which are purportedly based on empirical research. For each intervention on the menu the appropriate levels of intensity or tiers is suggested. On the menu are strategies for promoting reading comprehension (for example, Peer-Assisted Learning Strategies or PALS), and for teaching paraphrasing and inference. There are also interventions for spelling, grammar, fluency, vocabulary and phonics.

For each aspect of literacy there is a Tracking Pupil Progress Tool to guide teachers in tracking pupils' progress and to assess how they are responding to the intervention, such as how well a child is doing in fluency, accuracy and speed. The tracking tool is in the form of a table where the teacher plots out the key features of the genre being taught. The teacher notes whether each pupil on the programme has included or used each of these features. Pupils' progress is monitored once in mid-intervention and once at the end of the intervention, based on teacher assessments and judgements. The mid-intervention monitoring is to enable teachers to decide whether to increase the intensity from small group to one-to-one for particular pupils.

Initially, 91 schools were approached through the AfA3As network of schools. Of these 85 indicated interest, but 24 subsequently declined to participate when they realised what was expected of them, leaving 61 schools. After schools were recruited, all Year 6 pupils in the 61 schools (N = 2,352) took the New Group Reading (NGRT) pre-test (a standardised test of literacy). Schools were then randomised, with 30 allocated to receive treatment and 31 to a waiting-list control.

All schools were then meant to identify and report to evaluators their eligible pupils (those who were at risk of not achieving Level 4 and likely to benefit from the intervention) using a combination of teacher's judgement about which child or group of children would benefit from the treatment and the NGRT data. In general, six to eight vulnerable target pupils were to be identified for each Year 6 class. Although not ideal, this sequence relative to school randomisation and testing was adopted at the request of the developers who wanted to use the pre-test results to identify eligible pupils, and with the permission of the funders, but against the advice of the evaluators. What happened in practice was that the list of eligible pupils provided by schools was neither complete nor clear. There were 79 pupils from the control schools and 37 from the treatment schools whose eligibility was unknown. This was partly a consequence of the sequence and partly due to the lack of direct communication between the evaluators and the schools – both insisted upon by CUREE. Therefore, the analysis presented later is based on all pupils known to evaluators to be at or below Level 4c from the outset, on the basis of the pre-test.

After randomisation, 11 schools (three treatment and eight control schools) dropped out, reportedly due to organisational issues as a result of changes in leadership. This is very high, and at a scale not encountered by the evaluators before. In addition, one other control school conducted the post-test on the wrong year group of pupils. So valid data was analysed from only 49 schools (27 treatment and 22 control). Overall attrition was in excess of 25% meaning that the results of the trial must be treated as indicative only. The findings are based on the gain scores from pre- to post-test for the New Group Reading Test.

This evaluation has a reasonable cell size, but randomised at school level, and initial balance between groups, but then high attrition. The attrition means that the evidence is listed here as only 1* in terms of its robustness.

Summer School 2013 intervention and methods

The EEF and Building Educated Leaders for Life (BELL), a major US summer-school provider, funded a pilot evaluation of a US-style academic summer school in England in 2012. The programme was targeted at primary pupils who had completed Years 5 and 6 from disadvantaged backgrounds, who were underperforming at their expected or potential levels, and likely to benefit from participation in the programme. The pilot was therefore designed to test the feasibility of organising a summer school in a relatively deprived area. In particular, it sought to assess whether there was demand for the programme, whether families would support and sustain the programme, and whether professional staff would be willing to work during their summer holidays. The report suggested that the approach was feasible, in a suburb of London (Siddiqui et al. 2014).

Therefore, a larger efficacy trial was set up in more varied locations to establish impact on attainment. The plan was to take 1,000 pupils at the end of Years 5 and 6 in three separate areas. The programme took place across three sites in London and the South East in the summer of 2013. It was targeted at pupils who were eligible for free school meals (considered to be disadvantaged by their school) and/or who were not expected to achieve Level 4 in English or maths at the end of Key Stage 2.

Over the four weeks of the summer school, all pupils participated in two 75-minute academic lessons each morning, one for literacy and one for numeracy. These were delivered in small tuition groups of a planned 10+ pupils by high-quality teachers, supported by two mentors (one of which was a sixth-former or other older student), using a scheme of work designed specifically for the programme. The lesson plans were designed by experts in each area in preparation for the summer, using formative feedback from the pilot study. Teachers were given details on the aims of each lesson, and the activities and resources they were supposed to conduct in the sessions.

In the afternoons, pupils took part in a diverse range of enrichment activities. These included drama performance, art and creativity, science challenges, cooking, dance, music and sports such as football, indoor cricket, fencing and gym exercises. There were also arrangements for outdoor activities such as raft building, swimming and theatre performance. To some extent these activities varied by site with London having a greater range of cultural and other resources within easy travelling distance. The programme closed with a special graduation ceremony for pupils and parents/carers at the end of the four weeks.

The teachers were generally recruited to work for only two of the four weeks. In the third week there was a teacher's transition phase and a new batch of teachers took over. The mentors and peer mentors remained the same. According to the developers this transition was necessary in order to get good teachers to work during the summer holidays and to ensure they would be able to give their full energy to the programme and return to school rested.

In total, only 435 pupils (and their parents) volunteered to take part in the study, suggesting perhaps that the treatment was not that attractive. The randomisation resulted in the allocation of 239 pupils to the treatment group to attend the summer school programme, and 196 pupils to the control which means they were simply followed to complete the post-test. The developers were successful in targeting pupils with various possible indicators of disadvantage, and these characteristics were proportionately very similar for both achieved groups.

The sample retained only 303 pupils – with 75 treatment and 30 control pupils not included in the final analysis. The former were largely those allocated to treatment but then not turning up to the summer school. The reasons given were that parents had work or holiday arrangements that clashed, or pupils were ill, changed their minds, or did not want to attend as their friend(s) had not been selected. The missing control pupils were largely those who moved away or whose subsequent secondary school would not conduct the test.

The prior attainment consisted of KS2 fine point scores from summer term 2013, and the post-test was GL Progress in English and Progress in Maths administered in groups in the secondary schools attended by both groups of pupils in the following autumn. Primary schools were generally co-operative in conducting the pencil and paper tests delivered to each of the schools by the GL Assessment team. It was harder to get agreement from secondary schools to test the original Year 6 pupils after they had begun Year 7. A great deal of effort was put in to reduce demoralisation and consequent dropout. This involved not revealing the groups until after the randomisation, use of a refundable deposit for registrants, and neutral administration of the post-test.

This evaluation has a reasonable cell size, randomised at individual level, and initial balance between groups, but attrition was high (31%). The evidence is listed as 2* in terms of its robustness.

The rest of this chapter presents summaries of the results of all six evaluations.

Results of the six catch-up trials

Switch-on results

Switch-on is considered first here, because its evaluation is the most robust. Overall, the effect size of the intervention was +0.24, suggesting a noticeable positive impact whether gain scores or only post-test scores are used (Table 7.1). Both randomised groups had very similar scores at the outset, which suggests that the randomisation was effective and so the test of the intervention was fair in that respect. The result based only on pupils eligible for free school meals was an 'effect' size of +0.36.

The number of counterfactual scores needed to disturb this finding would be 37, and there are 5 cases missing post-scores. This means that the level of attrition is low enough not to alter the results. The headline finding of this study is therefore that the intervention is effective. The estimated cost is £100 per pupil (for a school

TABLE 7.1 Difference in gain scores for Switch-on Reading Programme

Treatment group	N	Pre-test	Post-test	Gain	Standard deviation	'Effect' size
Switch-on	155	77	81	4	8	+0.24
Control	153	76	79	3	7	–

to set it up, including buying books), assuming that existing TAs are used. In future years the costs would be less.

The two-day training event for staff from all schools was professional and successful, followed by ongoing support and school visits from the developer. Once the intervention was underway, the evaluators observed that most members of staff conducted the sessions as they were trained to – using a variety of textbooks in a 20-minute session and talking about the texts, with comprehension questions by teaching staff and independent reading aloud of text by students. Sometimes the setting used was too public or otherwise inappropriate, or the teacher did not adhere to the protocol at all. Generally, this made the pupils less confident.

The evaluators observed most pupils making considerable progress both in terms of the band of books and their reported reading age. Most pupils appeared to enjoy the sessions. One pupil was enjoying them so much that he requested a member of staff to let him take the books home to read them with his mum. Another said that he preferred coming to the reading sessions as he enjoyed reading with 'Miss', and the other classes were boring for him.

A few intervention students who had to leave their classes on a regular basis reported that they felt conscious as their peers knew that they were the ones singled out for the intervention. For this reason, such sessions might have been better conducted during break times or after school, or when entire classes were broken up for different activities. In two schools observed, there was general apathy among the students. They did not seem particularly excited about the programme. When asked if they would like to continue the sessions the following term, many said they would not.

Members of staff were generally positive about the programme. Many were enthusiastic and excited about the progress they had observed among their students. In most cases they reported that students generally enjoyed the one-to-one attention, as something they would not otherwise have had. A number felt that the Switch-on sessions gave them the opportunity to get to know more about the students, including their attitudes and family background. Some staff commented that in an ideal world they would like to make this intervention permanent for their students.

However, some teachers raised concerns that the stories were 'too babyish' in style and content (not necessarily reading age) for their Year 7 students. It was assumed that introducing this kind of material to them in individualised settings would probably not adversely affect the confidence of the students. Most members of staff felt the second batch of Switch-on books were more appropriate for the age group of the students in terms of topics and level of difficulty. Children appeared to take more interest in the newer books. Some doubts were expressed about the validity of the running record as an assessment tool, since it does not record comprehension. One member of staff said that decoding itself was not the problem.

Accelerated Reader results

In terms of their prior KS2 English points, the randomisation was successful in creating balanced groups at the outset, which means that the analysis produces equivalent results whether it uses gain scores or post-test only (Table 7.2). Considered in terms of the NGRTA reading scores the treatment group is ahead of the control by about one quarter of a standard deviation at the end of the trial, suggesting that AR had a modest impact on the treatment group. An analysis using only those pupils listed as eligible for free school meals produced an 'effect' size of +0.38.

The number of counterfactual scores needed to disturb the finding would be 39, and there are 8 cases missing post-scores. The headline finding of this study is therefore that the intervention is effective. The costs include TA time (including for book banding and making book inventories), books, around £10 per pupil per year for the software licence, and any hardware needed. Total cost might be around £20 per pupil, excluding hardware. The cost of one day of teacher training is included in the subscription licence and the schools also have access to a free hotline telephone service for instant information.

The training included a tour of the Renaissance Learning Inc. website through which pupils and teachers could access AR resources. The training covered all aspects of STAR testing and reporting with an explanation on how to interpret the results. Teachers, TAs and literacy coordinators who were planning to implement AR attended the training. The majority of participating schools had no previous experience of using AR. The school leaders developed reward systems to encourage a culture of reading in their schools. This included setting up an after-school reading club, celebrating millionaire readers (those who had read one million words), using symbols/medals/badges for pupils who achieved the targets, a wall of fame for those who achieved 100% in quizzes, and Amazon gift vouchers to purchase books on completing the AR targets.

TABLE 7.2 Difference in outcomes for Accelerated Reader

Group	N	KS2 points	Standard deviation	NGRTA	Standard deviation	'Effect' size
Accelerated Reader	174	27	4	327	51	+0.24
Control	161	27	4	315	47	–

Overall, schools were observed to be implementing the intervention faithfully. Two of the schools purchased tablets to make the AR quiz time a more fun activity for pupils, with enough for each child in a small group to use one each. In one of the schools pupils were doing their independent reading every day for 40 minutes after school time. In two of the schools pupils were taken out of French and other language lessons, while in the other they were mainly taken out of English classes. The library space was used for independent reading time and for taking the AR quizzes. Pupils were also encouraged to take the books and read at home.

School leaders reported observing pupils gradually improving in their STAR performance. They thought that pupils having exposure to books of interest and appropriate readability, and monitoring and advising pupils, helped their confidence to take up a reading challenge. Several teachers felt that attaining AR points and setting targets was itself a motivation for the students, so external reward for achievement may not really have any deeper impact.

Pupils with low reading levels initially believed that finishing a book was almost impossible and that they would fail in the quiz. In some cases they were even reluctant to select a book for independent reading. However, teachers' advice and motivation strategies helped these pupils to achieve the reading targets. The teachers reported that the success of these pupils was very rewarding for themselves as well as for the pupils.

In terms of AR implementation during the transition from primary to secondary school one of the school leaders did not think that it was an the appropriate time for some of their pupils to be introduced to AR. Pupils coming from primary schools needed support from teachers to adjust to the new routine of secondary schooling. To be introduced to AR at such an early stage in the transition could pose a challenge to some pupils.

The AR attendance records showed that pupils were attending the sessions regularly. Although many had to come from regular classes and some even had to stay after school, the overall AR attendance record was very good. During observations and interviews, pupils reported that they liked coming for AR because there was no teaching and they would get a chance to do a quiz using the tablets. Some of them also reported that they preferred AR sessions to their regular classes, which they found boring.

Several teachers and literacy coordinators reported that conducting AR requires a lot of administrative work such as colour coding and banding of books, monitoring pupils and advising them on book selection, and following STAR reports for individual pupils and the whole class. It is not clear that this is more work than would be required for standard classes, or whether it was simply additional and new for this intervention.

It was also felt that the NGRT post-test is very similar to the AR quizzes and STAR test used in the programme. NGRT is a computerised screen test which adapts the level of challenge according to pupil's initial responses. AR quizzes and STAR test are also screen tests. This familiarity might conceivably have given a practice advantage in the post-test to the treatment group.

Fresh Start results

In Fresh Start, the control group was slightly ahead in terms of reading from the outset, making the gain scores a fairer test of impact here (Table 7.3). The control group had higher pre- and post-test scores than the treatment group (the pre-test 'effect' size was −0.36, and the post-test 'effect' size was −0.19). Using the gain scores, the intervention showed a small positive impact on reading comprehension (+0.24). The same 'effect' size occurred when only FSM-eligible pupils are considered.

Because of the initial imbalance between groups, we have to treat the results as more tentative than if the randomisation had led to more equal average scores. We repeated the analysis with only those pupils in either group whose pre-test score was below 262.7, the pre-test mean in Table 7.3. Although, as noted, more of the low-scoring pupils are in the intervention group, the reading scores of the two low-scoring groups are well balanced at the outset (Table 7.4). The results showed that the low-scoring pupils in the treatment group actually had a slightly lower average gain score than the low-scoring pupils in the control group. This suggests that overall the result could not be due to regression towards the mean.

The number of counterfactual scores needed to disturb the finding would be 49, and there are 8 cases missing post-scores. The headline finding of this study is therefore that the intervention shows promise of being effective as a programme for supporting pupils at risk of failing. The cost of running the programme for 22 weeks was largely the cost of the module booklets which is estimated at £100 per child, plus the cost of training the teachers, and the TA time.

To implement the intervention successfully requires training in the use of teacher–pupil communication routines and the strategies suggested in the teacher's handbook. In this study, teachers attended a two-day training workshop given by

TABLE 7.3 Difference in gain scores for Fresh Start reading

	N	NGRTA pre-test	Standard deviation	NGRTB post-test	Standard deviation	Gain score	Standard deviation	'Effect' size
Intervention	215	252	65	280	60	28	48	+0.24
Control	204	274	58	291	53	17	42	–

TABLE 7.4 Difference in gain scores for Fresh Start reading, low-scoring pupils

	N	NGRTA pre-test	Standard deviation	Gain score	Standard deviation	'Effect' size
Intervention	116	204.4	47.9	40.4	52.3	−0.04
Control	67	204.1	42.3	42.9	48.3	–
Total	183	204.3	45.8	41.0	50.7	–

experienced and professional trainers. In all, 65 teachers and teaching assistants attended the training, the majority of whom had no previous experience of using FS. The classroom management strategies are inspired by reception years and primary school teaching. FS teachers are expected to use body language, praise and dramatisation to get pupils' attention. As such, several secondary school teachers found these strategies and management styles difficult to adopt.

Similarly, one school leader reported that parents expressed initial concern that the intervention was too low level for secondary school pupils. Consequently a meeting was organised to explain to parents the purpose of the intervention. There was also some initial resistance from some pupils who felt that the activities were too patronising. Private discussions with a few individual pupils eventually convinced them of the purpose of the activities. There was also resistance from some of the more experienced teachers. In fact a head of English in one school refused to take part, and a substitute was found.

Classroom observations suggested that the FS teaching strategy was quite effective in keeping pupils engaged. In each session the trained teacher was supported by one trained TA. The pupils received a lot of help and individual attention which they would not otherwise have had. The records showed that pupils were attending the sessions very regularly. Many pupils reported that they preferred coming for these sessions rather than attending regular classes.

One of the other aspects commonly reported by teachers was that FS provided positive results for pupils who have learning difficulties (although the results of the impact evaluation did not support this). A number of teachers reported that pupils who were usually quiet or disruptive in class were more focused and confident in the small group FS sessions.

Response to Intervention results

In terms of the reading test, RTI appears to have had a positive impact (+0.20). The two groups were reasonably well balanced at the outset, and so a post-test only analysis produces a similar result (Table 7.5). An analysis using only those pupils listed as eligible for free school meals produced an 'effect' size of +0.48.

However, all of the results have to be taken as indicative only, because of the level of school dropout after allocation (over 25%), the number of schools in the control group which did not carry out post-testing, and the uncertainty over which pupils were eligible for the intervention. This suggests that the difference

TABLE 7.5 Difference in gain scores for Response to Intervention

	N	NGRTA pre-test	Standard deviation	NGRTB post-test	Standard deviation	Gain score	Standard deviation	'Effect' size
Intervention	171	264	54	288	51	24	50	+0.20
Control	180	261	60	270	56	9	42	–

between the means is insecure, and could easily have arisen even if only some of the missing cases would have been counterfactual to the overall finding. Slightly different assumptions about initial eligibility would produce a different (but still positive ES).

The number of counterfactual scores needed to disturb the finding would be 34, and there are 132 cases missing post-scores. The headline finding of this study is therefore that the intervention shows only weak evidence of being effective. Nevertheless, there is some promise here for a bigger and better controlled trial, taking into account the problems that arose during this study. The cost is hard to estimate but could be around £100 per pupil.

Although only the outcomes of pupils identified as eligible to receive the intervention were supposed to be compared, in reality it was not clear who these pupils were. Some schools did not provide this information, and some of the pupils who were not identified as eligible also took the post-test. It was not clear if any of these pupils did in fact receive the intervention despite being reported as ineligible. Further, some pupils who were identified as 'eligible' had the highest pre-test scores in their schools, and even across all schools. According to the published criteria of eligibility they would not be deemed eligible for RTI, yet schools considered them as suitable for the intervention. So the analysis ignored the incomplete list of reported eligibility provided by the developer, and considered only those pupils who were graded at Level 4c and below at pre-test (and should thus be deemed eligible for the intervention). However, this means that we cannot be sure that those in the labelled 'treatment' group did in fact receive the intervention, which might dampen the impact.

The process evaluation revealed wide variations in the intensity and frequency with which schools implemented RTI. Some schools were able to deliver all three tiers (whole class, small group and one-to-one) while others decided to deliver only one level of RTI. Some schools managed only five sessions of 20 to 30 minutes each in total, and most schools struggled to fit in only two to three sessions instead of five a week. This was too short for proper monitoring, tracking and adjustments to intensity, and would not be deemed sufficient in the protocol for impact to be realised. This was largely due to the timing of the programme, being introduced in the last few weeks of the final term after the Key Stage assessment, which was in turn a result of political timing behind the extra funding.

As the intervention was implemented in the last few weeks of term, there were several distractions – such as end-of-term activities like sports days, prize-giving and rehearsals for end-of-year productions. A number of other transition programmes were also arranged for Year 6 pupils, such as visits to secondary schools, school camps and secondary school integration programmes. In one primary school the pupils spent a whole week in their secondary school, thus losing a week of RTI.

Another challenge for teachers was planning multiple lessons for each session where there was more than one tier of intervention. Even with only one tier, teachers still had to prepare one lesson for the intervention children and one for those not targeted for the intervention. In one school the teacher had three preparations: one for the whole class, one for the RTI pupils and one for the weaker pupils. Finding space to accommodate different groups of children receiving different intensities of treatment within one period could also be a potential barrier to effective implementation.

Accounts from teachers, pupils and Achievement Coaches suggested that RTI has beneficial effects as a catch-up literacy programme. One school claimed that the data they collected showed that their pupils had made an equivalent of five months' progress in comprehension and spelling in the four weeks, and in some cases as much as a year's progress. The teacher reported how two pupils improved their reading fluency from reading 200 words in three minutes to nearly half of that time. Dramatic improvements in reading were also observed. At a later assessment, all of their targeted pupils achieved Level 4. According to the teacher:

'This has never happened in the history of the school before.'
Pupils also remarked on how the activities had helped them.
'I remember things that I learn now.'
'I can do a lot more – better with spelling, reading and writing.'

One pupil told us how she used to hate reading but since the programme was introduced she was enjoying it. Some pupils said they now preferred books to films as books allowed them to use their imagination and there was also an element of suspense. They explained how they were excited to find out what happened in the books. Some claimed that they were reading more books than in previous years and were enjoying reading more now than before. Of course, this could be the result of maturation, or even of coaching.

Other pupils explained how the use of mirrors also helped them with their spelling as they could see all the letters when mouthing the words. They could see how their mouths shaped the words and how seeing the shape of the word had added 'texture' so when they read they could feel the word.

'With a tricky word, now I say it and I write the sounds down.'

One school perceived the intervention as such a success that they were considering a home version of the programme to monitor further results at Year 7. The headteacher of another school was so confident in the intervention, having seen the results it had produced among their Year 6 pupils, that she planned to roll out part of the RTI programme to other year groups. In another school, the teacher was so encouraged by the impact she saw that she was already preparing to introduce the intervention to her new Year 6 class. Schools were generally so confident in the effectiveness of the intervention that they had asked for a similar programme for numeracy. When asked if they would continue with the programme after the trial, almost all the teachers interviewed said they definitely would.

Literacy software results

At the outset of the literacy software trial, the pre-test scores show that the treatment group was slightly superior (Table 7.6). After 10 weeks of software use the treatment group improved their standardised mean score substantially, just as the software publishers had claimed. Therefore, a simple before and after design with no control could easily, but falsely, conclude that the use of commercial software was an especially effective approach to literacy teaching and learning. This illustrates the danger for education research of conclusions drawn from what constitutes the majority of published work, conducted without suitable comparators. By the end of the trial the control group had caught up and overtaken the literacy software group, with an overall 'effect' size of −0.29. This suggests that the intervention was actually harmful to pupils' reading compared to normal teaching. There is no evidence here that the improvement for the treatment group was due to the software used.

The number of counterfactual scores needed to disturb the finding would be 93, and there are about 60 cases missing post-scores. The headline finding of this study is therefore that the intervention shows no promise of being effective, and is likely to be harmful. It cost around £20 per pupil.

Intriguingly, the in-depth data collected routinely as part of the trial suggested a high level of satisfaction with the treatment. The technology-based instruction reportedly provided teaching groups with a range of information, links and activities in an accessible and entertaining way. The teachers involved in the treatment said that the software had an encouraging focus on language for early Key Stage 3 and that the activities were stimulating for pupils and teachers alike. They believed that it offered a reliable way to help pupils improve their reading skills. The pupils were satisfied with the technology-based reading materials, and were observed getting heavily involved in the activities. When asked, all teachers indicated that they would use the same or similar software in the future, and almost all of them said that they would recommend it to other teachers.

One class had extended difficulty with their computer system and a low gain score which contributed in part to the poor showing of the treatment group. However, this does not explain all of the difference. It certainly does not suggest that the treatment was more effective than the control. And in a pragmatic trial we expect these differences. Such technical difficulties are a real consideration for technology-based instruction and should not be 'cleaned' away to enhance the apparent

TABLE 7.6 Difference in gain scores for literacy software

	N	Pre-test mean	SD	Post-test mean	SD	Gain score	SD	'Effect' size
Treatment	319	823	68	863	88	40	79	−0.29
Control	346	817	72	886	78	69	131	

effect of the treatment, any more than poor teaching of the control would be ignored on the basis that it 'should not happen'.

The results of this study add to the body of research that shows concerns about the effectiveness of technology-based instruction. Several prior studies have shown limited or no beneficial impact of generic ICT-based approaches on pupil learning in reading skills. But in isolation these studies do not reveal the scale of wasted opportunities and possible harm done to pupils. In general, marketing teams in the UK offer software to schools on a trial basis. During the trial they show how pupils are making progress by using the in-built assessment process (without appropriate comparator). Teachers can then see pupil progress over learning activities and may be persuaded to purchase. Once teachers have bought the software they tend to use the convenient in-built assessment process regularly. This makes all involved part of a reinforcing cycle. The software publishers make money. Teachers have a record of progress made by pupils, for their own and others' satisfaction. Pupils generally enjoy working on computers and playing with different technology applications. Parents will be pleased to see a record of their child's progress. Local and national government is content that their funding of technology initiatives is justified, and schools are persuaded to spend that funding on technology products, making money for the companies to develop new products. This should cease and a more sceptical and ethical approach should prevail.

Summer School 2013 results

For the summer school evaluation, the two randomised groups were reasonably well balanced in terms of the available prior performance from the outset, despite the high level of dropout. Whether considered as post-test only or gain scores, the 'effect' size in English (reading) is around +0.17 (Table 7.7).

The effect size for gain scores in maths is zero, suggesting that the summer school made no difference at all (Table 7.8). The intervention group were marginally ahead at pre-test and remained marginally ahead by the end.

The results based on only FSM-eligible pupils are about the same for both subjects. The number of counterfactual scores needed to disturb the finding for English would be 25, and for maths it would be zero, and there are up to 132 cases missing post-scores. The headline finding of this study is therefore that the intervention shows little evidence of being effective.

TABLE 7.7 Difference in gain scores for Summer School 2013, English

	N	KS2 reading	Standard deviation	PiE score	Standard deviation	Gain score	Standard deviation	'Effect' size
Treatment	169	23.66	4.86	39.06	16.08	3.71	13.24	+0.17
Control	144	23.42	5.76	36.36	15.41	1.46	12.79	–

TABLE 7.8 Difference in gain scores for Summer School 2013, maths

	N	KS2 maths	Standard deviation	PiM score	Standard deviation	Gain score	Standard deviation	'Effect' size
Treatment	169	23.32	6.40	20.87	10.07	7.51	8.43	0
Control	144	22.89	8.12	20.39	11.02	7.53	9.24	–

The achieved pupil to teacher ratio was around 5.5, and each teacher class also had a peer-mentor and a mentor. The total cost of provision was between £500,000 and £550,000 for 193 pupils (not all of whom participated in this evaluation) across three sites. Therefore, the programme cost over £2,000 per pupil. This is a very expensive intervention, even if the improvement in English is considered trustworthy. As this chapter demonstrates there are much cheaper and more effective approaches to catch-up.

Training was conducted for all teachers, mentors and peer-mentors who were planned to be employed at three different sites. Ultimately, not all of them could be employed due to low recruitment of pupils. The training was well conducted and structured, with many examples of activities which teachers could use. Teachers were generally motivated and eager to try something new. The role of mentors was defined in terms of academic support to pupils in the classroom rather than just assisting teachers in executing the lessons. During our observations, mentors were seen supporting pupils in the classrooms, specifically those who regularly needed the individualised attention of an adult.

The literacy and numeracy sessions were delivered following the lesson plans closely. However, numeracy sessions were observed to change with time into individualised tutoring sessions. One of the reasons was because of the wide range of abilities in some class groups, so teachers with the help of mentors broke numeracy classes into further small groups or one-to-one sessions to cater for the different abilities of pupils.

The number of pupils in each classroom was fewer than expected. There were usually three or even four adults in each classroom of 10+ pupils, and every child was seen receiving extra attention and time from the adults. On some occasions there were more adults than pupils in each classroom. This was partly due to low recruitment, and partly due to pupil absences. Once class observed was at half strength. The results of the programme need to be interpreted in the light of these high ratios.

Several lessons observed by the evaluators were poorly taught – especially for maths. Basic pedagogical and factual errors were observed, and in one case pupils' written responses were marked incorrectly. In literacy especially, more sessions were seen to be fun and enjoyable for all. Despite the pupil ratios, class control was sometimes poor.

Interviews with parents suggested that the free summer programme kept their children engaged in reading and maths. Parents reported their satisfaction concerning the quality and overall management of the programme. Some of them also stated that they could not afford expensive holiday trips for their children so such an arrangement provided opportunities to their children which they could not have managed otherwise.

Pupils were generally enthusiastic about attending the summer schools. Many of them also reported that it was the afternoon activities they enjoyed more than the teaching sessions. They said that the teachers and mentors were very supportive and several pupils wanted to come back to the programme in the next summer.

Regular attendance at summer school was also perceived to be an indicator of success by parents, teachers and mentors. Most pupils, on all three sites, were reportedly attending the school regularly, and they had enjoyed coming despite it being during the holidays. Because the programme was in a secondary school, pupils could gain a different type of school experience, and a different approach to teaching and learning. This could help them with the transition to secondary school. Also, through being out of their usual roles as possible 'naughty' or 'silly' kids they could have a fresh start with all-new teaching and management staff members. Mixing the Year 5 and 6 groups was perceived by some pupils as a fun experience and a positive influence on their learning.

This was a well-run intervention, generally supported by teaching staff and pupils. To achieve this level of co-ordination and support required considerable energy and monitoring. Despite the efforts of the developers, a significantly smaller number of pupils attended the school than they had hoped for, with less than half of the target number of students signing up for the programme. These challenges were particularly apparent in the numbers recruited outside of London, suggesting that there may be problems if the programme was to be rolled out, particularly to less densely populated areas.

Conclusions from the six catch-up trials

Table 7.9 provides a simple summary of the new results from this chapter. The costs per pupil can only be estimated from information provided by the intervention developers, and are based on direct costs such as resources, equipment, licences and training. In some cases these are start-up costs that would reduce as a proportion over time. Some figures are dependent upon the number of pupils and the costs would reduce with more pupils. Some would also involve the use of staff time, such as the involvement of teaching assistants, but staff costs are only included for the summer school (as these are clearly additional).

Several conclusions are immediately obvious. The security of any finding does not depend only on the research design – or put more simply, a randomised control trial is not a 'magic bullet', and its results are not necessarily a 'gold standard'. Here six studies with very similar designs range from excellent (4*) to weak (1*), largely due to variation in attrition, and factors such as errors in identifying eligible pupils that were beyond the control of the researchers. Nor, assessed correctly, is the security of a finding linked to its 'effect' size. Robust studies can have negative or neutral findings, in the same way that weaker studies can have larger 'effect' sizes.

TABLE 7.9 Summary of findings from six catch-up trials

	Effect size	Effect size FSM-only	Quality of evidence	NNTD-attrition	Cost per pupil (rounded)
Switch-on	+0.24	+0.36	4*	69	£100
Accelerated Reader	+0.24	+0.38	4*	31	£20
Fresh Start	+0.24	+0.24	3*	41	£100
Literacy software	−0.29	–	3*	0	£20
Summer School 2013 English	+0.17	+0.17	2*	0	£2,000
Summer School 2013 maths	0	0	2*	0	£2,000
RTI	+0.20	+0.48	1*	0	£100

On the basis of these findings, and the prior evidence citied in Chapter 6, a school looking to assist pupils with literacy at the transition period, and reduce the attainment gap between disadvantaged pupils and their peers, would be advised to select Switch-on Reading, Accelerated Reader, or perhaps Fresh Start, from these six. This is justified by a combination of the impact, cost and security of the findings. However, all three findings should still be replicated by other researchers where possible. EEF is now funding larger effectiveness trials of some of these.

It is clear that simply using commercial software to teach literacy does not work, and this should be avoided.

Response to Intervention holds enough promise of impact and of being effective for poorer children that it should be assessed again, with individual randomisation and a different developer. Until then the evidence here is not sufficient to suggest that it should be preferred to the alternatives above.

The summer schools did a lot more than teach literacy. But assessed purely in terms of impact for reading or maths, they were very expensive and hold little or no promise of reducing the poverty gradient.

The way in which the evidence is assessed here suggests a way forward for practitioners and policy-makers navigating the evidence in their areas of interest. The overall results reinforce the importance of having appropriate comparator groups, and suggest that 'soft' evaluations and pre/post-comparisons may actually be worse than useless, and that theoretical explanations might appear satisfying but are unnecessary when assessing 'what works'. These implications are discussed further in Chapter 10.

8

MORE OF THE SAME OR RADICAL CHANGES TO THE WAY WE TEACH?

This chapter goes beyond compensatory or catch-up interventions focused on low-attaining pupils in literacy or maths to consider some whole school approaches to improving learning. Some are quite radical, some are not. It also addresses a key current question for the curriculum – what is the right balance between thinking skills and subject knowledge? There are tensions within formal education between imparting wide knowledge and the development of skills for handling that knowledge. In the primary school sector, both can be squeezed out of the curriculum by a focus on basic skills such as literacy and numeracy. State-mandated programmes and interventions in the UK, such as synthetic phonics, are generally concerned with structure and skills. However, a number of ministers and advisers across administrations have sought to expand the explicit teaching of world knowledge – in terms of culture, geography, history and science. We assess the evidence for this in this chapter. Other commentators, such as Mitra (2012), have argued that information is now freely and easily available to all and that educators should focus on how to find and process information rather than learning the information itself. The chapter therefore also describes an explicit attempt to develop young children's reasoning, and the results both in terms of pupils' apparent cognitive abilities and their basic skills. A third approach, represented by encouraging teachers to give enhanced formative feedback, is to keep the curriculum as it is but to improve the quality of teaching more generally. Which of these three general approaches is the more promsing?

What does the existing literature say?

Prior evidence on Core Knowledge

There are attempts in the US and now the UK to teach wider and greater content knowledge to primary age children. A theory behind this movement is that children, especially those from disadvantaged backgrounds, do not read well because they do not possess the necessary background knowledge to make sense of what they read. One programme addressing this is the Core Knowledge Language Arts curriculum, whose aim is to expose children to new words and concepts so that the new words stay in their long-term memory and thus facilitate future learning. And if children understand the words they read they can understand the text. In cases where children have less exposure to a wide range of vocabulary, they do not have the background knowledge to build on, or a context in which to place what they are trying to read. Core Knowledge Language Arts (CKLA) is a US-imported programme that has received much attention in England. It first gained popularity in the US after the publication of the book *Cultural Literacy* (Hirsch 1987). Core Knowledge is now being used in classrooms in thousands of schools across the US.

Several influential commentators in England including a Minister of State for Education (Nick Gibb) and an Education Secretary (Michael Gove) have spoken openly of their admiration for Hirsch's philosophy (The Guardian 2012). In 2013 Gove set out to reform the curriculum to emphasize the teaching of Core Knowledge (Coughlan 2013). Following this, two primary schools were set up in London specifically using a curriculum that is built on the philosophy of CKLA. The journalist Toby Young also opened a secondary free school in West London basing its curriculum on the Core Knowledge Sequence. The teacher Daisy Christodoulou (2014) wrote an influential book, *Seven Myths about Education*, based on her arguments from research in cognitive science. It championed this philosophy about learning facts and acquiring knowledge as a necessary step towards general literacy.

Although the Core Knowledge curriculum has been widely implemented in the US, the programme has not been as widely (or rigorously) evaluated. Where it has been evaluated, the evaluations have often been conducted by or directly for the CKLA foundation, and results so far have been mixed and unimpressive (Table 8.1).

Whitehurst-Hall (1999) reported mixed results from a longitudinal study following 301 seventh- and eighth-grade children over three years using a matched comparison design. Impact was measured using the Iowa Test of Basic Skills (ITBS) subtests on reading, language and maths. Positive 'impacts' were noted for some measures but not others. There were no clear differences between CK and control pupils in terms of grade retention and grade failure.

An evaluation of CKLA conducted by Stringfield et al. (2000) also showed mixed effects, using four matched pairs of CK and comparator schools across the US with norm-referenced tests. The overall impact of CK on reading was

TABLE 8.1 Quality and impact summary: studies of Core Knowledge

	Effective	*Ineffective/unknown*
Higher quality 3* or better	0	0
Medium quality 2*	0	0
Lower quality 1*	4	1

negative for children who had CK for three years starting when they were aged six (effect size of −0.06) as well as for older children who received the programme from age 8 to 11 (effect size of −0.08). The programme appeared to be more beneficial for low-achieving younger pupils (effect size of +0.25), but not older pupils (effect size = −0.53). Schools in each state (Washington, Maryland and Texas) apart from Florida registered a negative impact on reading. The authors explained that the exceptionally poor performance of CK pupils in one low implementing school in Maryland had skewed the overall results. The overall impact is therefore unclear despite the authors' claims of success.

Dartnow et al. (2000) reported that schools implementing the programme successfully showed greater improvements in standardised test scores (Comprehensive Test of Basic Skills). But on page 179 the paper said 'There was considerable variability in the overall mean effect sizes across sites, ranging from −0.56 to +0.51. Mean effect sizes across all schools were close to zero, averaging −0.05 for math and −0.06 for reading.' The CK results are actually slightly worse overall. The paper went on to say that when the children were assessed on Core Knowledge content, CK pupils performed significantly better than their non-CK counterparts, but this is to be expected. The study did not take account of the fact that not all the pupils were retained in the final analysis. Only 59% of the first-grade children and 70% of the third-grade children took the basic skills test three years later. For the Core Knowledge content test, the dropout rate was even higher. Only 44% of first-grade and 52% of third-grade pupils took the test three years later. The results are therefore largely meaningless. There is a sense across the prior evidence we have read that authors want to report success.

An independent evaluation of the Core Knowledge curriculum across schools in Oklahama City reported on the Core Knowledge website (Core Knowledge Foundation 2000) suggested promising results. On both the ITBS Norm-Referenced test and the Oklahoma Criterion-Referenced Tests, CK pupils performed, on average, better than those in the comparison group on reading comprehension, vocabulary and social studies. However, pupils were not randomly assigned to the intervention, and although the author claimed that pupils were precisely matched, matching is never perfect, especially when there is attrition.

The Core Knowledge curriculum may be more promising for younger children. A study of an early literacy pilot in New York City in 2012 (NYC Core Knowledge Literacy Pilot 2012) reported gains in reading tests (Woodcock-Johnson III) especially in kindergarten, although the differences decreased by the third year. Using the standardised TerraNova test, however, no differences were detected in oral reading comprehension and vocabulary. Although the summary report suggested that children who were on the programme for the longest had the highest post-test scores compared to those with only one and two years of exposure, these children had higher pre-test scores too. In other words, they started from a higher base score. The only reference to this study is on the Core Knowledge website.

In summary the evidence base for the impact of CK on literacy is very mixed. Positive effects have been reported for only some year groups, in some states and for only some sub-tests. The largest study found no benefit from CK. When taken together the overall results appeared to be negative or neutral in almost all but one study conducted in one city in the US. However, since this approach is so widely used and heavily promoted by some of those in power it was worth evaluating further.

Prior evidence on Philosophy for Children

Turning instead to learning about how to use information and ideas effectively, the focus here is on learning critique, reasoning and argumentation. As with other areas such as behaviour there is some research on how to improve reasoning that does not test improved attainment or progression (e.g. Bottino et al. 2009, Shayer and Adhami 2010). This can be valuable because any successful intervention must address something malleable, but does not in itself show that it works.

Philosophy for Children (P4C) was developed in 1970 with the establishment of the Institute for the Advancement of Philosophy for Children (IAPC). P4C has since become a worldwide educational approach, and something like it has been adopted by schools in 60 countries across the world, although the nature of the practice varies (Mercer et al. 1999). In the UK, the Society for the Advancement of Philosophical Enquiry and Reflection in Education (SAPERE) was established in 1992 to promote the use of P4C in schools.

The evidence base so far has been weak or mixed. Several of the studies so far have used a matched comparison design (e.g. Tok and Mazi 2015), and most have measured cognitive abilities, reasoning skills or other affective outcomes rather than school attainment directly. Moreover, while there have been several studies in the UK, they have tended to be small scale. There are some unsystematic observations of beneficial impact from OFSTED reports. It is therefore difficult to say if philosophical enquiry can lead to enhanced performance in academic domains and whether it would have the same impact in UK schools with British children.

An initial evaluation of the original scheme was conducted using a matched comparison design involving only 40 pupils from two schools (Lipman et al. 1980). The study reported gains in logical reasoning and reading, measured using the California Test of Mental Maturity (CTMM).

One of the earliest studies in the UK was conducted by Williams (1993). This small study examined the effects of 27 one-hour P4C lessons (using Lipman's materials) on reading comprehension, reasoning skills and intellectual confidence. Participants were 42 pupils from two Year 7 classes in one school in Derbyshire, UK. Results were obtained for only 32 children. Children were randomised to receive P4C lessons (n = 15) or extra English (n = 17). Pre- and post-test comparison of reading comprehension using the London Reading Test showed that the P4C group made bigger gains than control pupils. Gains were also reported for reasoning skills and intellectual confidence. These were measured using bespoke evaluation tools and video recordings of pupils' interactions during lessons which the evaluators had to make subjective judgements about.

A systematic review of evidence for P4C was conducted by Trickey and Topping (2004) suggesting consistent moderate effects on a range of outcome measures. The mean 'effect' size for the studies included was 0.43. However, these studies were not always fully comparable because of the different outcomes measured and the different instruments used for measuring them. For example, Institute for the Advancement of Philosophy for Children (IAPC) (2002) used the New Jersey Test of Reasoning Skills (NJTRS), while Doherr (2000) assessed emotional intelligence using a Cognitive Behavioural Therapy Assessment. Campbell (2002) evaluated listening and talking skills using questionnaires, focus groups, interviews and observations. It has to be noted that the NJTRS was specially developed for Lipman and the IAPC to measure reasoning skills taught in the P4C curriculum. This is likely to bias the results against the control group of pupils not exposed to the P4C curriculum. Moriyon and Tudela (2004) noted that studies using NJTRS showed larger effect sizes than when using more generic tests of literacy and numeracy.

The longer-term impact of P4C was assessed by Topping and Trickey (2007). They followed pupils over two years. A total of 177 pupils (105 experimental and 72 comparator) from eight schools were matched and tracked from the penultimate year of primary school to the first year of secondary school. Pupils' cognitive abilities were measured using the Cognitive Attainment Test (CAT). Complete data were available for only 115 pupils. After 16 months of intervention (with one hour of P4C per week) the treatment pupils made substantial improvements in test scores whereas control pupils performed worse than when they started (ES = 0.7). Results two years later indicated that treatment pupils maintained their advantage in follow-up test scores.

A more recent longitudinal study of the long-term impact of P4C was conducted in Madrid (Colom et al. 2014). This was intended to track children from two private schools over 20 years. Four hundred fifty-five children aged 6 (first year of primary school) to 18 (final year of high school) from one school were trained in the P4C programme. Another 321 pupils from another school matched on demographic characteristics formed the control group. Data on children's cognitive, non-cognitive and academic achievements were collected at three time points when children were aged 8, 11/12 and 16. Preliminary analyses of 281 treatment children and 146 control children showed that the programme had positive impacts on general cognitive ability (ES = 0.44), but results on academic achievement were not yet available. The authors implied that the programme was particularly beneficial to lower ability pupils, but this was not clear from their presentation of the analysis. Moreover, although large scale and long term, the students were not randomised in terms of receiving P4C instruction, and the study may not be generalizable as pupils came from relatively prosperous families in private schools. In short, the results from this preliminary analysis should be treated with caution.

A randomised control trial was conducted with 540 pupils in Years 7 and 8 (Fair et al. 2015). The study found positive relative gains in the CAT scores for Year 7 pupils who received the treatment, compared to control pupils who were taking language arts classes. The equivalent gains for Year 8 pupils were much lower.

This could be because pupils in Year 7 were exposed for 26 weeks and pupils in Year 8 were given a P4C session for only 10 weeks. The study does not clarify the baseline equivalence of pupils who were allocated to the two groups and there is an indication that pupils were not equally balanced as pupils in the treatment group were ahead of their counterparts in CAT pre-test scores.

Our review identified 16 studies of at least minimal quality on teaching thinking skills more generally (Table 8.2). Two higher quality studies reported positive effects (Table 8.3).

Reznitskaya (2012) examined the impact of dialogic discussion in a P4C tradition on writing and reading comprehension, with random assignment of fifth-grade classes in five schools to P4C (138 pupils) or normal classes (125). It appears that there are no follow-up scores for 63 pupils (31%). There were no benefits in terms of post-intervention assessments including essay, recall and interview. The small number of cases (n = 6 classes in each group), the high attrition (31%) and the subjective measures of outcomes all weaken the security of the findings.

Worth et al. (2015) compared the use of mathematics and reasoning, with literacy and morphemes and a control, with Year 2 pupils in 55 schools in England. There were 517 pupils in the smallest group, with 13% attrition. The authors reported 'significant' success for maths (ES = 0.2) but not literacy.

Hanley et al. (2015) considered a programme to make science lessons in primary schools more practical, creative and challenging. Teachers were trained in a repertoire of strategies to encourage pupils to use higher order thinking skills.

TABLE 8.2 Quality and impact summary: studies of teaching thinking

	Effective	*Ineffective/unknown*
Higher quality 3* or better	2	0
Medium quality 2*	0	1
Lower quality 1*	10	3

TABLE 8.3 Quality and impact detail: studies of teaching thinking

Reference	*Intervention*	*Smallest cell*	*Attrition*	*ES*	*NNTD-attrition*	*Quality*
Reznitskaya 2012	P4C	125	31%	0	0	2*
Worth et al. 2015	**Maths and reasoning**	**517 pupils**	**13%**	**0.2**	**36**	**3***
Hanley et al. 2015	**Higher order thinking in science**	**1513 pupils**	**16%**	**0.22**	**60**	**3***

For example, pupils are posed 'Big Questions', such as 'How do you know that the earth is a sphere?' that are used to stimulate discussion about scientific topics and the principles of scientific enquiry. There were 41 schools, of which 21 (with 655 Year 5 pupils) were randomised to treatment. Attrition was 16%, and the advantage for the treatment schools on average was 0.22.

Other less robust studies uncovered in our review provided some insight into the pedagogical aspects of teaching critical thinking that could support learning. For example, Larrain et al. (2014) demonstrated that whole class teaching of critical thinking did not yield much benefit (ES = 0.09), and that it was learning to provide justifications and contradictions among peers that prompted learning. This was a weak study because of the high attrition for both pupils (83%) and teachers (36%). Also assessments of learning were based on researcher-developed instruments. Tseng (2014) confirmed the findings of Larrain et al. in that teaching children to question, argue and reason could be beneficial in science learning. Children taught an inquiry-based approach made bigger progress than children taught using the traditional didactic approach.

Overall, the evidence here is promising. It suggests that critical thinking can be improved and is generally associated with improved outcomes, perhaps especially in science, maths and reading.

Prior evidence on enhancing feedback

A third whole-school approach to improvement considered here is improved formative feedback. Many reports on effective pedagogy identify feedback as a characteristic of effective teaching and learning (Harris and Ratcliffe 2005, Creemers 1994, Scheerens 1992, 1999, Siraj-Blatchford and Taggart 2014, Coe et al. 2014, DfEE 2000). However, this work does not, in itself, establish clearly that enhanced 'feedback' is generally effective. It is widely agreed that good teachers tend to use more and stronger feedback naturally. But what is not so clear from these passive correlational and longitudinal designs is how easy it is to enhance the use of such feedback by other, perhaps more reluctant, teachers, and whether this would make any difference to pupils' attainment

Assessment for learning (AfL) is a kind of formative assessment (defined as an activity that provides rapid feedback to inform teaching and learning) and one of the strategies advocated for use in the classroom. An early experimental study called 'Inside the Blackbox' indicated a substantial impact for AfL on learning for all age groups (from pre-school to undergraduate level), and claimed that formative assessment was especially effective for low achievers (Black and Wiliam 1998). Black (2000) cited research where the use of formative assessment techniques produced learning gains with effect sizes of between 0.4 and 0.7, larger than those produced by some other significant educational interventions. Fuchs and Fuchs (1986) reported benefits for children with special needs. White and Frederiksen (1998) also reported that feedback was more effective for low achieving students (effect size of 1.0) than for high achieving students (effect size of 0.27).

The EEF Teaching and Learning Toolkit recorded feedback strategy as having an impact equivalent of +9 months progress and assessment for learning with an impact of +3 months progress (Education Endowment Foundation 2015).

A meta-review by Hattie and Timperley (2007) was based on an impressive number of meta-analyses (n = 74) of studies relating to feedback, involving a large number of studies (n = 4,157) and 5,755 effect sizes. However, as noted elsewhere in this book, such meta-meta-analyses often synthesize results from several small and flawed studies. The large effect sizes cited were often those involved in assessments of outcomes using researcher-developed tests. Hattie and Timperley reported wide variations in effect sizes depending on the types of feedback used, but there was no comment on the quality of these studies nor the reliability of the evidence. A synthesis that heavily informed their model was by Kluger and DeNisi (1996) because it was 'the most systematic' and 'included studies that had at least a control group, measured performance, and included at least 10 participants'. This suggests that other studies in the 73 other meta-analyses were not particularly systematic, had no control group, had fewer than 10 participants or did not even measure performance. How many of such studies were in these meta-analyses was not known. Therefore, the number of studies whose evidence we can rely on is unknown. Hattie and Timperley added that many of these studies were not classroom based. Presumably these studies were undertaken in laboratory conditions, which may be less relevant. Kluger and DeNisi then went on to say that their evidence based on 131 studies (conducted largely in controlled conditions) included 470 effect sizes and involving 12,652 participants showed an average effect size of 0.38 (SE = 0.09). Of these 32% showed negative effects or decreased performance. This cannot be explained by the scale of the studies or even by theories of feedback use. But an explanation might involve the kinds of feedback such as praise, reward and punishment, the nature of the pupils or students involved, or the quality of implementation which is often not very helpful. Hattie and Timperley reported that the 'average sample size per effect was 39 participants'. This is a very small sample per study.

Of the studies that Hattie and Timperley (2007) cited, we could not locate all of the effect sizes listed in the summary table (Table 1, p. 83). For example, the review states that the effect size of 54 studies in Lysakowski and Walberg (1982) was +1.13 whereas the original paper reports it at 0.97 (study-weighted). The figure 1.13 appears nowhere in their paper. In Hattie (1992) and repeated subsequently, it is said that 'Skiba, Casey and Center (1986) used 315 effect-sizes (35 studies) to investigate the effects of some form of reinforcement or feedback and found an effect-size of 1.88', but the later 2007 paper reports this review as having 35 effect sizes not studies, and an effect size of +1.24. While none of this undoes the work that has been done or eliminates the evidence for the impact of enhanced feedback it ought to lead to caution. Overall, the evidence is not as clear as some commentators have suggested.

Most of the studies cited did not use random allocation of subjects and yet quoted p-values, which must therefore be meaningless. If Hattie used meta-analyses based on p-values but did not eliminate the majority where it was used incorrectly then the results will be incorrect. For example, one study synthesised had used MANOVA based on those students who agreed to participate compared to those who refused, and then ridiculously presented this as evidence of the impact of the intervention.

What these meta-meta-analyses appear to do is aggregate scores from a wide variety of research designs, practical approaches and educational settings and taking no account of the bias introduced by attrition, treating a study with full response as equivalent to one with high dropout or missing data. Some include both passive designs along with randomised control trials (RCTs), some only the former, and no distinction seems to be made between them.

Some research reports cited in the meta-analyses went back as far as 1960. These meta-analyses used different calculations of effect sizes, for different measures of the same parameters (e.g. different types of reinforcement and a range of feedbacks) for different groups of children at different phases of schooling (even university and postgraduate study). Some studies were specifically for SEN children, or children with behavioural, emotional and disruptive behaviour. Some were based on very young children, and some used undergraduates at university. How Hattie and Timperley arrived at the summary effect sizes in the paper was not explained.

There are other problems with this array of evidence. Some of it is not particularly robust, and little of it sheds light on what happens when feedback practices are implemented across a wide variety of schools and teachers. Other studies are not directly about the impact of enhanced feedback on attainment. For example, some are about how possible it is to implement an intervention such as AfL (Jonsson et al. 2015), while others are about the nature and perception of the feedback generated by teachers (Carvalho et al. 2014).

Many of the studies conducted so far have been small scale. For example, most of the 1,387 studies in a recent review by Hopfenbeck and Stobart (2015) on AfL were small case studies (with one or two schools), while very few were large-scale or well-designed evaluations. White and Frederiksen (1998) was based on only three teachers in two schools. Truckenmiller et al. (2014) had only 39 cases in the smallest group, and Lipko-Speed (2014) involved only 65 fifth-grade students (10- to 11-year-olds) altogether. The original Black Box experiment involved six volunteer schools, and it is evident that the approach does not always lead to equivalent success in less propitious circumstances (e.g. Smith and Gorard 2005). These small studies generally reported positive effects. For example, Truckenmiller et al. (2014) reported an effect size of 0.66, while Lipko-Speed (2014) confirmed that the use of enhanced feedback was better than using additional study or summative testing only.

In our own review we found four large-scale studies of at least moderate quality (Tables 8.1 and 8.2), and these were equally balanced in terms of feedback working or not. The most promising was Lang et al. (2014) which suggests that feedback may be beneficial in raising the academic attainment of very young children. It was the best in terms of quality with a large sample size (over 4,000 pupils) and low attrition. One of the others reported positive effects, but the tests were developed by the researchers, and teachers were trained to teach the topics tested (Decristan et al. 2015). This poses a threat to validity and reliability. Torgerson et al. (2014b) evaluated self-regulation and writing in England using 261 pupils in Years 6 and 7 allocated by school. The ES was +0.74, with at least 11% attrition but the reporting is unclear on this.

TABLE 8.4 Quality and impact summary: studies of feedback

	Effective	Ineffective/unknown
Higher quality 3* or better	1	1
Medium quality 2*	1	1
Lower quality 1*	11	3

TABLE 8.5 Quality and impact detail: studies of feedback

Reference	Intervention	Smallest cell	Attrition	ES	NNTD-attrition	Quality
Lang et al. 2014	Formative assessment	15 schools, 2,000+ pupils	1 school, unknown pupils	0.20	500+	3*
Phelan et al. 2011	Feedback (Year 7)	2,045 pupils		0.03	0	3*
Decristan et al. 2015	Formative assessment in science	11 teachers (232 pupils)	10%	Unknown	0	2*
Torgerson and Torgerson 2014b	Self-regulation and writing	130 pupils	11%+	0.74	Unclear	2*

Lang et al. (2014) evaluated the Formative Assessment System in 31 US elementary schools involving 2,317 kindergarten and 2,515 first-grade children and 301 teachers, after randomisation at school level. The formative assessment process provides feedback to teachers to adjust ongoing teaching and learning to address gaps in children's knowledge related to the instructional objectives. In lessons teachers ask students to perform tasks, explain their reasoning, and prove their solutions. The evidence collected enables teachers to differentiate instruction based on students' mathematical thinking and reasoning rather than solely on incorrect answers. The programme was designed to provide teachers with tasks and rubrics to employ the following five key strategies: (1) assess the student's level of understanding during instruction, (2) identify the student's specific misconceptions and errors, (3) examine samples of student work for further evidence of student understanding, (4) pose additional questions to elicit student thinking, and (5) obtain guidance on next steps for instruction.. The result showed a positive effect on children's maths outcomes (ES = 0.2 for kindergarten and ES = 0.24 in first grade).

Another large-scale but slightly weaker study evaluated the impact of embedding formative assessment as teaching practice on children's academic outcomes (Decristan et al. 2015). 551 third-grade German children (age 8-9) and 28 teachers and their classes were randomly assigned to receive professional development training on embedded formative assessment (17 teachers, 319 pupils) or to control (11, 232). Treatment teachers were also taught how to teach the target topics. Control teachers received training in parental counselling. Treatment students showed higher levels of science understanding than control. However, the test instruments were developed by researchers – so there is a possibility of bias such as teaching to the test, or teacher and researcher expectations since teachers were not blind to the intervention. Researchers claimed that the test items had been judged as valid by experts in science education. Teachers were trained to teach the topics that were tested. The question is whether the same results can be produced if teachers taught just using embedded formative assessment without the CPD that makes it impossible to decide of the feedback was a causal element.

One large-scale study involving 4,091 pupils from 25 schools tested the use of a toolkit made up of a list of formative assessment items for teachers to use to check their pupils' understanding of mathematical concepts so that they can tailor their instruction and feedback to their pupils (Phelan et al. 2011). Experimental teachers received CPD and instructional resources. Control teachers had no access to the resources. Negligible differences were detected (ES = 0.03). The authors reported that higher ability pupils benefitted more from the intervention than lower ability pupils. The participants were grade 6 children (age 11-12).

Another study for older children (Meyer et al. 2010) reported that children receiving elaborated feedback made substantial progress in reading comprehension (d = 0.55) compared to those receiving simple feedback (d = 0.15). Weaker students also made greater progress between pre- and post-tests (d = 0.73) compared to more competent readers (d = 0.27), although this could be result of regression to the mean. The participants were 111 fifth- and seventh-grade students. The results of this study have to be taken with caution because of the small sample size in proportion to the large number of groups, meaning that there were on average only four students per grade and treatment condition. There was also no pure control group.

The remainder of the chapter focuses on large-scale evaluations of each of the three main generic approaches to raising attainment described so far – enhancing curriculum content, improving reasoning and better teaching through feedback. The next section describes the specific interventions and the common methods used to evaluate them.

Generic methods for the three trials

As in Chapter 7, all of these new studies used the same basic design, with one group receiving the intervention and a control group receiving standard practice. All were based in primary schools across England, involved all year groups, and had both a pre- and post-intervention measure of attainment. All use either standard assessments such as Key Stage results, or standardised tests of attainment. Randomisation was undertaken after the pre-test to ensure blinding because knowledge of group allocation could affect pupils' performance in the test and teachers' attitude towards the test. For the same reason, the administration of the post-test was monitored or conducted by the evaluators since schools would now know which group pupils are in. All analyses were based on intention to treat, meaning that cases were handled as being in the group they were randomised to, whatever happened subsequently, and pupils were followed up as far as possible even where they had moved schools. We also conducted a sub-analysis of only those pupils eligible for free school meals (FSM). The analyses are based on 'effect' sizes. The differences analysed where possible are the gain scores from pre- to post-test, in order to cater for any imbalances in the initial groups, and to aid comparison between trials. The trials are rated 0-4* in terms of robustness, and each result is compared to the number of counterfactual cases that would need to be added to the smallest group in order for the apparent 'effect' size to disappear, as described in Chapter 4. Each trial had an integrated process evaluation to monitor progress, observe testing, consider unintended consequences, and assess fidelity to intervention, as described in Chapter 5. Further details can be found in Gorard et al. (2017), See et al. (2016) and See et al. (2017).

Specific methods for each trial

Core Knowledge intervention and methods

We conducted a pilot evaluation of an adaptation of the Core Knowledge approach, called the 'Word and World Reading programme' (WWR), developed by The Curriculum Centre. It was used in 17 primary schools in England, representing a diverse range of schools of differing sizes and levels of disadvantage. Schools were randomised to either receive the intervention (9 schools) or wait for one year (8). The core curriculum being taught in this study involved knowledge of world history and geography.

The outcomes were assessed for the 1,628 Year 3 and 4 pupils. Over the course of the trial, nine pupils in Year 3 and 4 were withdrawn across all schools. These were pupils identified with special educational needs and were receiving another intervention which was deemed more appropriate for them. In addition, a large number of pupils from one treatment school did not take the post-test. This accounted for 43% of the overall attrition. The teachers mistakenly thought that since they did not intend to continue with the programme the following year, they did not have to do the post-test. Schools also routinely excluded pupils with special educational needs (SEN) from tests because teachers did not want to put them under undue stress. This explained why there were proportionately more boys and SEN pupils who did not take the post-test. A total of 287 post-test results were missing (206 from the treatment schools, and 81 from control schools), representing an overall attrition rate of 18%.

The impact of the intervention was measured by comparing the gain scores between the pre- and post-test of both groups using the long version of the Progress in English (PiE) test. PiE is a standardised test of reading and comprehension. Presumably because of the small number of cases randomised (17 schools), the groups were not well balanced at the outset in terms of their characteristics. The treatment group had substantially more FSM-eligible and ethnic 'minority' pupils and those for whom English is not their first language. The control group, on the other hand, had markedly more pupils listed as having a special educational need.

This evaluation has a large cell size at pupil level, but was randomised at school level, with initial balance between groups (in terms of their pre-test scores, but not all of their background characteristics), and just under 18% attrition. The evidence from it is listed here as 3* in terms of its robustness.

The Word and World Reading programme is a whole class intervention, carried out twice per week over one school year. Each lesson lasts around 45 minutes. It includes 34 planned geography and 35 history lessons. The lessons are very structured, following a set sequence. Every lesson begins with a reading passage, no more than a page long. The teacher reads the passage aloud and then pauses and asks questions about the text. A few new words are introduced explicitly in every session. There is a lot of repetition of keywords/concepts. To reinforce the learning of these keywords pupils answer a few short mastery questions in their workbook followed by a keyword exercise. One aspect of the intervention is instant feedback. Teachers are expected to go round to check pupils' answers and mark their workbook, giving immediate feedback or to pencil in some suggestions for improvement. As part of the methodology pupils are required to use full sentences. The emphasis is on the acquisition of knowledge and using the keywords correctly.

The teaching resources include textbooks for pupils, teacher handbooks, globes and atlases. The pupil textbook is organised in units and each unit consists of a sequence of linked passages, allowing pupils to build their conceptual understanding and vocabulary. The texts are written in a simple language appropriate for the age group. The textbook is also the bound pupil workbook. The teacher handbook is similar to the pupil textbook, but with guidance notes for teachers and prompts indicating where to stop and repeat the information for students or engage them in discussion, and suggested questions.

Philosophy for Children intervention and methods

To assess the impact of improving reasoning rather than knowledge, a total of 48 primary schools were recruited in England, with no prior experience of using Philosophy for Children. All schools had at least 25% of their pupils known to be eligible for free school meals. At least 10 of the schools had fewer than 60% of pupils achieving Level 4+ in English and maths, and with pupils making below-average progress in English and maths. Twenty-two of these schools were randomised to receive the intervention, with the control schools funded to receive P4C after the trial. There was no school dropout. The two groups were well balanced in terms of sex, FSM eligibility and SEN status.

The evaluation was a randomised control trial with schools allocated to one of two arms receiving the P4C intervention over one year or not. Pupils involved in the intervention were in Key Stage 2, and impact outcomes were assessed for 3,159 pupils who were in Years 4 and 5 at the beginning of the intervention. A total of 3,159 pupils in Years 4 and 5 (entire year groups) were in schools taking part in the trial at the outset (1,550 in the treatment group and 1,609 in the control). The main outcomes of interest were the English and maths Key Stage 2 scores of pupils who were in Year 5 when the schools were randomised and Year 6 by the end of the trial, and the Cognitive Abilities Test (CAT) scores of all initial year 4 and 5 pupils. The individual results for reading, writing and maths were provided by the National Pupil Database (NPD) linked to unique pupil numbers (UPNs) supplied by all participating schools. There was very little missing attainment data. Because the KS1 pre-scores and KS2 post-scores used different metrics both were converted to z-scores to assist comparability.

This evaluation has a large cell size, but randomised at school level, some initial imbalance between groups, very little attrition for the attainment scores, and around 11% attrition for the CAT scores. The evidence from it is listed here as 4* in terms of its robustness.

The P4C intervention aims to help pupils to think logically, voice their opinion, use appropriate language in argumentation, and listen to the views and opinions of others. P4C, as promoted by SAPERE, is a template to practice, and to organising a classroom session for philosophical enquiry. It does not have any specified materials or stimuli that must be used; there are only examples and suggestions. It may involve standard material for teaching such as a projector, board, pens or sheets of papers. The steps outlined in training are a guide to organising the classroom dialogue and can be used flexibly as the teacher's expertise grows. For example, the stages do not all need to be completed in one session. Choosing a question in one session and discussing it in another is a popular option. There is also the expectation for teachers to use existing curriculum material in their lessons when they judge it to have the potential to stimulate philosophical discussion and clarify key concepts in subject areas such as democracy, justice, nation, history, truth, cause, evidence, beauty, art, real, belief, knowledge, tolerance and theory.

Usually, pupils and teacher sit in a circle so everyone can see and hear one another. The teacher negotiates with pupils on guidelines for the conduct of sessions and the purpose is to set some basic rules of communication agreed by all the pupils. The teacher then introduces the planned material they have chosen in order to provoke pupils' interest, puzzle them or prompt their sense of what is important. A minute of silence is followed by pupils in pairs sharing interesting issues and themes, or jotting down key words. The teacher often records some of the key words and ideas that emerge.

Children present their group's question so that everyone can see and hear it. When all of the questions have been collected children are invited to clarify, link, appreciate or evaluate the questions prior to choosing one for discussion. The selection of one question as a dialogue starter is made by pupils using one of a range of voting methods. The discussion is then open for all to share their views.

Pupils participate in the discussion, building on other pupils' contributions, clarifying them, questioning them and stating their own opinions. Whether agreeing or disagreeing with others the rule is to justify opinions with reasons. Teachers may prompt pupils to imagine alternatives and consequences, seek evidence, quantify with expressions like 'all', 'some' or 'most', offer examples and counterexamples, and question assumptions.

The session ends with last words from all pupils. Pupils might have the same opinion as in the beginning or it could have changed as a result of dialogue. Pupils are invited to sum up their views concisely and without contradiction from others. This activity could either be a verbal statement or a detailed reflection whereby a teacher could ask pupils to write a summary of their views.

The teacher invites reflective and evaluative comments about the enquiry with reference to broad criteria such as the guidelines the group has adopted. For example, the teacher asks 'What went well?' 'What could we improve on?' or 'What do we need to do next?' The teacher could point to issues of pupils' behaviour and turn-taking in the session and ask them to reflect on their progress. The review could include suggestions on what needs to be focused on in the next P4C session.

Enhanced feedback intervention and methods

A partnership of nine primary schools in Bexley proposed a whole-school intervention to enhance their teachers' use of feedback in class. All of these schools wanted to try out this whole-school intervention, involving enhanced feedback for all Year 2 to Year 6 pupils over one academic year, and so it was evaluated as a quasi-experiment. The comparators achieved were a set of five neighbouring schools not in the partnership (compared in terms of data collected specifically for the evaluation), and all other state-funded schools in the same local authority (compared in terms of official Key Stage 2 results, and of their published value-added scores).

For the Year 6 pupils in the nine treatment schools, attainment was compared to the national test scores of the 49 other state-funded primary schools in the borough, based on progress measured by national test scores, and to improvements since the year preceding the intervention. Because the treatment and control schools were not randomly assigned or matched, it was necessary to compare the treatment schools with all other schools in the area, to get a better picture of how well the treatment schools actually did in comparison. For other year groups it was necessary to use the end of year teacher assessments since no official national test scores were available for those age groups. A total of 1,677 pupils in Years 2 to 6 were involved in the intervention. A total of 2,187 Year 6 pupils in the 49 comparator schools, and 1,177 pupils in Years 2 to 6 in the five local schools, had assessment scores for comparison.

There was no chance of contamination because pupils in the comparator group had no access to the programme. No school dropped out. The findings are based both on teacher assessment and official Key Stage results at both pre- and post-test stage.

This evaluation has a large cell size of pupils allocated at school level, initial balance between groups, and minimal attrition. The evidence from it is listed here as 2* in terms of its robustness (largely because of the inherent weakness of the design).

The feedback intervention was developed by the schools themselves, based on the model presented in Hattie and Timperley (2007), using an action research cycle approach. The schools wanted their teachers to use the paper itself as a basis for devising improved classroom practices. It is important to note that the research article was not a teaching manual, so few examples were given. Teachers had to make their own interpretation of what each level and process involved. Pupils completed an online Learner Effectiveness survey to establish their 'learning styles' and had to set their own goals for the period ahead ('Success Criteria'). Teachers had to identify the gap between what the learner knows and what they need to know, as well as how they could reach that goal, or target, using feedback strategies to guide them towards self-regulatory proficiency. They collected examples of the three types of feedback:

1. Feed Up   *Where am I going (the goals)?*
2. Feed Back   *How am I doing?*
3. Feed Forward   *Where to next?*

According to the model described in the paper, each of these feedback questions can be directed at four levels: (1) Personal (Self), (2) Task, (3) Process and (4) Self-regulation. The aim is to guide pupils towards the level of self-regulation. Feedback at the personal level is about giving feedback about the person. At the task level, the teacher gives feedback about the task, such as whether the task is completed correctly or not; this may include directions to achieve the correct answer. At the process level, the feedback is about the learning process needed to complete a task. Feedback can also be directed giving feedback on the skills needed for self-evaluation. The most effective feedback is considered to be the one that moves pupils from task to processing and from processing to self-regulation.

A pack of training materials (the starter pack) was prepared by the school project leads. Working in pairs on a school training day, schools initially received training using these packs. The training involved the school leads reading and discussing the research article. A moderation meeting was convened with project leaders and school leads, to help them agree on examples of the types of feedback. School leads then delivered feedback moderation training to staff. This was followed by a moderation staff meeting to establish starting points. Each school lead was given three days of temporary teacher cover so that participants could collect examples of the proposed types of feedback.

Teachers audited each other's lessons to assess the prevalence of the 12 combinations of feedback. They then created an action plan aiming for a new balance of feedback, making it 'proportionate' to its value, looking for more self-regulatory feedback and fewer personal comments. Periodically, each teacher audited pupils' skills in terms of the Hattie and Timperley (2007) model of being an effective learner, using the results of the initial and subsequent Pupil Learner Effectiveness survey delivered by the schools. Teachers then reflected on their current practice and monitored pupils' understanding and application of the concept of being an effective learner. The schools identified areas for improvement and strategies to achieve these. School leads then met to discuss issues and challenges, and report on progress made.

Findings from the three evaluations

This section summarises the results from the three new evaluations of whole-school approaches.

Core Knowledge results

The 'effect' size (−0.03) based on Progress in English (PiE) gain scores showed that the WWR programme had no discernible benefit for reading comprehension (Table 8.6). The groups were well balanced at the outset, and so the same conclusion of no benefit would have been drawn from a post-test only analysis. And the same result emerges if standardised age scores from the PiE test are used instead of raw scores.

One control school did not take the pre-test, but their post-test score was 50.6, which was slightly higher than the overall average of 47.7 (Table 8.6). So using the post-test scores for this school may artificially reduce the apparent effect size of the intervention. Excluding this school from analysis, we found the overall finding remained the same (Table 8.7). This means that including this school in the analysis made no difference to the substantive outcome.

The results were substantially the same for all year groups analysed separately. However, when we analysed the results separately for only those children eligible for free school meals, the result (+0.06) was slightly positive (Table 8.8). Although this might suggest some promise for disadvantaged children, we have to be careful about reading much into this, considering that the number of FSM pupils is small and also because these children were not randomised as such.

TABLE 8.6 Difference in gain scores for Core Knowledge

	N	PiE pre-test	Standard deviation	PiE post-test	Standard deviation	Gain score	Standard deviation	'Effect' size
Treatment	659	22.9	8.4	47.5	15.7	24.7	12.6	−0.03
Control	678	22.2	8.9	47.8	16.3	25.1	12.9	–
Total	1337	22.6	8.6	47.7	16.0	24.9	12.7	–

Note: One control school provided only post-test scores. Therefore the gain scores have an N of 565 in the control group.

TABLE 8.7 Analysis using raw scores for all schools, excluding the school without pre-test scores

	N	PiE pre-test	Standard deviation	PiE post-test	Standard deviation	Gain score	Standard deviation	'Effect' size
Treatment	659	22.9	8.4	47.5	15.7	24.7	12.6	-0.03
Control	565	22.2	8.9	47.3	16.6	25.1	12.9	-
Total	1224	22.6	8.6	47.4	16.1	24.9	12.7	-

TABLE 8.8 Raw score results, all schools, FSM-eligible pupils only

	N	PiE pre-test	Standard deviation	PiE post-test	Standard deviation	Gain score	Standard deviation	'Effect' size
Treatment	237	22.9	8.6	46.2	15.9	23.3	12.5	+0.06
Control	157	20.4	9.0	42.8	16.3	22.5	14.2	-
Total	394	21.9	8.9	44.7	16.1	23.0	13.2	-

The number of counterfactual scores needed to disturb the finding would be 0 regardless of the missing cases, because there is no clear positive impact. There was relatively high attrition (just under 18% of 1,628 pupils, mostly from one treatment school), which means that all results must be treated with caution. Taking this large pilot trial and prior evidence into account, the conclusion is that there is no good evidence a wide liberal curriculum has any benefit for basic skills learning (whatever value it may have in its own right). We do not know from this evaluation how successful the attempt to increase knowledge itself actually was.

As with so many interventions, and in contradiction to the actual impact results, the developers and many teachers and pupils appeared to believe that the intervention was having a perceptible impact on children's writing composition. They said that the practice of answering in full sentences was useful in tests, and that the habit had also filtered into other work. Teachers reported students using sentence starters, which they applied in other subjects, becoming more confident in using technical terms, and improving their comprehension skills. There was some observational evidence that pupils were thinking about the vocabulary they learnt during the lessons. For example, one pupil asked one of the evaluators whether it was proper to use 'death' or 'died', such as 'after his death' or 'after he died'. Others were using the words associated with the compass points, seasons, cities, farming, invention and the environment in their writing. Further evidence of learning could be seen in pupils' workbook exercises. Pupils demonstrated their grasp of quite abstract concepts such as 'democracy' and 'government' in their sentences.

Although the programme and its resources were attractive to teachers, there were some barriers to effective implementation. The syllabus developed for this pilot trial did not sufficiently differentiate between year groups, or higher and lower attaining pupils. Some pupils, particularly those with special educational needs and those for whom English was an additional language, found the topics challenging, while in a number of lessons we observed that the higher ability pupils had completed the writing activities with ease and had to wait.

Some teachers found it hard to adapt the rigid structure of the curriculum to their teaching style. Consequently, some lessons appeared forced and contrived. There was little attempt to develop the theme further. Part of this could be a lack of confidence on the part of the teacher to venture beyond the set text. The high staff turnover in a few schools also made it difficult for them to implement the programme fully. In one school almost all of the originally trained teachers, including the lead, left. The trainers went to schools to deliver catch-up training for new staff. However, we still found untrained teachers and supply cover in our final visits, who generally did not follow the protocol.

The biggest hindrance to the successful implementation of the programme was teachers' lack of background knowledge. A number of teachers found it difficult to handle quite thought-provoking questions from children. There were also instances where teachers made elementary factual errors – such as consistently confusing latitude with longitude in a session designed specifically to teach the difference, describing a rocky coastline as a sand dune, confusing pupils with the same definition of tides and waves at sea, defining tropical as hot and wet before talking about the tropical savannah, telling the pupils about the 'Marina Trench' and a whale's 'sprout', mis-describing any trench as the deepest part of the ocean, describing reefs (as opposed to corals) as living, and asking what the bottom of the 'ocean floor' was called. There were many further examples. It is essential for a fact-based curriculum that teachers either know more, or are at least aware that they do not know such basic facts. In each case, pupils (especially the more alert ones) were confused, their attempted corrections were ignored, and opportunities to learn were missed. The training provided in this study emphasised the theory underpinning the WWR programme and the practical applications of this theory. What many teachers appear to need instead is a lot more knowledge about elementary history and geography.

Because of the prescriptive nature of the programme, there was little scope for discussion. According to Hirsch, teaching facts to pupils gives them the foundation to think critically and opportunities to apply the knowledge and to question the facts. Hirsch's original idea for the sequential curriculum was a curriculum that is 50% content and 50% wider discussions of the topics covered. The curriculum should be designed to allow for such discussions (Core Knowledge 2014). One recommendation, therefore, is to scale down the number of topics to allow teachers more time to cover each one in greater depth. These topics could be developed as the child moves up each level, progressing from simple concepts to more complex ideas. Interestingly, this was what the children proposed in the focus groups.

Philosophy for Children results

At the outset, the control group had slightly better KS1 scores in each of reading, writing and maths (Tables 8.9 to 8.11). By the end, the treatment group had narrowed this gap in all three subjects, especially reading (+0.12) and maths (+0.10), suggesting a small relative gain for the treatment group. There is no benefit for writing in the overall results, which is perhaps not surprising since there is little or no writing element in P4C.

In terms of CAT scores at the outset, the control group was again slightly ahead (Table 8.12). Again, the treatment group made a slightly larger gain in CAT scores

TABLE 8.9 Difference in gain scores for Philosophy for Children, reading

	N	Mean KS1 points z-score	SD	Mean KS2 fine points z-score	SD	Gain z-score	SD	'Effect' size
Treatment	772	-0.08	1.01	-0.02	1.01	+0.06	0.88	+0.12
Control	757	+0.08	0.98	+0.02	0.99	-0.05	0.91	-
Total	1529	0	1	0	1	0	0.90	-

TABLE 8.10 Difference in gain scores for Philosophy for Children, writing

	N	Mean KS1 points z-score	SD	Mean KS2 fine points z-score	SD	Gain z-score	SD	'Effect' size
Treatment	772	−0.07	1.03	−0.05	1.00	+0.01	0.77	+0.03
Control	757	+0.07	0.96	+0.06	1.00	-0.02	0.90	-
Total	1529	0	1	0	1	0	0.84	-

TABLE 8.11 Difference in gain scores for Philosophy for Children, maths

	N	Mean KS1 points z-score	SD	Mean KS2 fine points z-score	SD	Gain z-score	SD	'Effect' size
Treatment	772	−0.09	1.04	−0.04	1.01	+0.04	0.74	+0.10
Control	757	+0.08	0.95	+0.04	0.99	-0.04	0.82	-
Total	1529	0	1	0	1	0	0.78	-

TABLE 8.12 Difference in gain scores for Philosophy for Children, CAT score

	N	Pre-CAT4	Standard deviation	Post-CAT4	Standard deviation	Gain score	Standard deviation	'Effect' size
P4C	1366	94.37	11.24	96.59	12.26	2.22	7.59	+0.07
Control	1455	95.20	11.19	96.90	11.90	1.70	7.32	–
Total	2821	94.80	11.22	96.75	12.07	1.95	7.46	–

than the control (+0.07), but the difference is too small to be convincing especially considering that over 10% of the initial pupils are missing post-test scores due to changing schools. The P4C group showed the biggest 'impact', on average, in terms of the verbal sub-scale (+0.08). This is both to be expected and ties in with the greater gain for the treatment group in KS2 reading.

The results for the most disadvantaged (FSM-eligible) pupils were larger for attainment (+0.29 in reading, +0.17 writing and +0.20 maths), but not for CATs (−0.02). This suggests that if the intervention is deemed effective, it is more so for the most disadvantaged pupils and so would tend to reduce the poverty gradient in schools.

As discussed in Chapter 4, when there is initial imbalance after randomisation there is sometimes a concern about 'regression towards the mean'. This was unlikely here because none of the scores were extreme. However, it is worth checking. For each test outcome, the pupils were divided into those at or below a middling pre-score and those above that pre-score, regardless of their treatment group. The effect size for the intervention was then computed for high and low pre-attainers separately. In each result, it was the higher attaining pupils at the outset that showed the greatest gains from the treatment, and because it was the control group ahead at the outset, this means that the results cannot possibly be due to regression to the mean. For example dividing the pupils into those obtaining 15 or more KS1 points for reading and those below 15, the first group had an effect size from being in P4C of +0.17, whereas the second group had ES of −0.03 (the equivalent for maths was +0.07 and 0). Similarly for the CAT scores, those pupils with scores at or above average at the outset had a treatment 'effect' of +0.14 whereas the lower scores had an ES of −0.02.

The number of counterfactual scores needed to disturb the headline literacy finding would be 91, with very few cases missing post-scores (administrative data from NPD was available even where students moved schools). The number of counterfactual scores needed to disturb the headline CAT finding would be 96, with 168 cases missing post-scores. Our conclusion is that, for those wishing to improve attainment outcomes in the short term, an emphasis on developing reasoning is promising, especially for the poorest students, but the evidence is not yet convincing. However, for those who value reasoning for its own sake, this evaluation clearly demonstrates that using curriculum time in this way does not damage attainment (and may well enhance it and reduce the poverty gradient in attainment), and so suggests that something like P4C is an appropriate educational approach. The P4C foundation course is the initial training for teachers and teaching assistants after which they can implement the intervention at a whole school level. This would typically cost £25 to £30 per pupil.

Observations and interviews suggest that the intervention was generally enjoyable and thought to be beneficial for pupil confidence. It was up to schools how often they conducted SAPERE's P4C lessons. Many schools implemented one P4C lesson per week in place of a literacy session. A few faith-based schools used religious studies sessions instead, and some schools had more than one session per week. P4C does not directly teach elements of the National Curriculum as measured through SATs, and it was sometimes reported as a challenge to make space for P4C in the regular teaching schedules. Teachers used classrooms, assembly halls and libraries as venues for conducting P4C sessions.

The intervention is appealing to many schools as a way of raising and debating pupil–school discipline problems in an enquiry group. The school leads reported that they discussed the concepts of bullying, racism, lying and cheating, equality and fairness which are core issues of school discipline and ethos. P4C was reported by the teachers to be very helpful in thinking critically about these issues, raising questions, reflecting on experiences and coming to fair conclusions. P4C creates an opportunity for school leads to engage with pupils and develop a whole school culture of thinking, listening, speaking and arguing. Some of the examples of questions discussed in P4C observed sessions were as follows:

- Is it acceptable for people to wear their religious symbols at workplaces?
- Are people's physical looks more important than their actions?
- What is kindness?
- Can you and should you stop free thought?
- Is it OK to deprive someone of their freedom?

This list of questions, and many others, was created by pupils themselves from a given stimulus such as a story or short video, using a blind voting system. The substance of these questions is clearly relevant to the broader purpose of schools.

There were some clear challenges to the delivery and implementation of P4C. The main challenge reported by teachers and school leaders was the difficulty of embedding P4C in the fully-packed timetable and with targets for literacy and numeracy from the National Curriculum. Teachers reported that there is often not enough time to be regularly devoted to P4C when there are so many other activities going on. P4C is particularly focused on underlying key concepts such as 'knowledge' and 'belief'. Deep discussion of these kinds of foundational concepts is often not seen by teachers as so important a part of subject teaching as the learning of subject content.

P4C is a practice of dialogic teaching. There is no complete syllabus or unyielding methodology for the SAPERE approach to P4C. Without clear guidance or set discussion topics, there is a danger that this approach may be open to the influence of teachers' biases, beliefs and ideologies, and examples of this were noted in our fieldwork.

A few pupils in some of the necessarily large enquiry groups were sometimes neglected by the teachers and their peers. It was observed in the sessions and was also reported by the pupils that they wanted to contribute at certain points and put their hand forward but teachers just moved on or gave the opportunity to another pupil. Where, as is desirable, the speaker decides who speaks next there is a fine line between a genuine back and forth between two pupils necessary for sustained argument, and abuse of the system by groups of friends.

It was observed by the evaluators that a complete P4C session should usually cover the ten steps of enquiry; otherwise pupils would not gain the sense and purpose of the whole activity. For example, in one of the sessions the discussions initiated were not summed up and sufficiently reviewed. The session was rushed to the end as the time for the session was passing quickly. As an observer it was felt that the pupils did not really understood the sense and purpose of the discussion because there was no proper conclusion. Sometimes pupils said that the questions were not fairly selected and pupils cheated and voted for their friends' questions. In one of the sessions the pupils were not given enough thinking time, and this was possibly the reason that they could not reflect on the issues for developing interesting questions.

Enhancing feedback results

Comparing the nine Partnership schools trying out enhanced feedback in the classroom with the five neighbouring comparator schools, the analysis for all-year groups combined shows small and mixed results (Tables 8.13 to 8.15). Intervention pupils made no gains in teacher assessments for reading (effect size of −0.04) or writing (−0.05) but were slightly ahead in maths (+0.05). Overall, this suggests that teachers' use of research to enhance feedback had no discernible benefit for core skills after one year of implementation.

In terms of gains for Year 6 (age 10 to 11) pupils only (the only year group where such data was available) from the end of the school phase Key Stage 1 (pupil ages 6 to 7) to the end of the school phase Key Stage 2 (pupil ages 10 to 11), results show that intervention pupils in the nine Partnership schools made slightly bigger gains in reading, maths and writing compared with the 49 other state-funded primary schools in Bexley, with an effect size of +0.06 (Table 8.16). However, it is important to note that using the value-added scores, intervention pupils did not show any greater progress when compared to the schools in the Bexley area.

TABLE 8.13 Difference in gain scores for enhancing feedback, reading

	N	Gain	Standard deviation	Effect size
Intervention	1676	4.16	2.97	−0.04
Comparison	1173	4.27	3.16	–
Overall	2849	4.20	3.05	–

TABLE 8.14 Difference in gain scores for enhancing feedback, writing

	N	Gain	Standard deviation	Effect size
Intervention	1649	3.95	2.82	−0.05
Comparison	1177	4.08	2.99	-
Overall	2826	4.01	2.89	-

TABLE 8.15 Difference in gain scores for enhancing feedback, maths

	N	Gain	Standard deviation	Effect size
Intervention	1677	4.17	4.17	+0.05
Comparison	1174	4.02	4.02	-
Overall	2851	4.11	4.11	-

TABLE 8.16 Comparison between Year 6 pupils in intervention schools and all other primary schools in Bexley, progress 2012 to 2013, and value-added (VA) scores 2013

	% Level 4+ in reading, writing and maths, 2012	% Level 4+ in reading, writing and maths, 2013	Gain in Level 4+ 2012-13	KS1 to KS2 1VA score, 2013
Treatment schools	78.2	83.0	6.1%	100.0
Bexley (other schools)	77.5	81.6	5.3%	100.2

Source: compiled from DfE School Performance Tables

There is no convincing evidence of a beneficial impact on pupil outcomes from this intervention, although sub-group analysis shows that the intervention may be beneficial for FSM-eligible pupils. For example, the gain score 'effect' sizes were positive for FSM-eligible pupils in all three subjects – reading (+0.17), writing (+0.12) and maths (+0.41). However, the number of cases was small (360), and volatility and differences in reporting cannot be ruled out.

Although the use of feedback may seem like a natural part of practitioner activity, for *all* teachers to be able to use higher levels of feedback to encourage learning appears to require guidance and practice. Our process evaluation showed that some teachers do not recognise what higher levels of feedback look like, and so are unable to use them effectively. Practitioners need to be given more examples, resources and direction at the outset of any change in practice. In the case of feedback, ample examples of 'Success Criteria' and different types of feedback should be made available in a resource pack or on a website which teachers have easy access to. Video recordings of effective lessons could be used as a training resource so that teachers can model these lessons. Teachers need to be clear about what 'Success Criteria' are, what the different processes and levels of feedback look like, and how to use feedback strategies to guide pupils to achieve their Success Criteria. Success Criteria need to be phrased in specific or measurable terms so that pupils know when they have achieved them or not.

There should be a conscious effort to use higher levels of feedback to guide pupils to self-regulation, and to minimise the use of self-feedback, which previous research has suggested as the least effective – such as 'you are a superstar' and 'this is a clever idea'. In fact, such fatuous praise can be damaging (Brummelman et al. 2014). All feedback should be clear, simple, specific and directed appropriately to specific learners. Greater differentiation in the use of feedback is needed, including more use of 'feed up' and 'feed forward' for the more able pupils.

Effective classroom instruction must be used in concert with feedback. Feedback should not be a substitute for classroom instruction, nor for teacher content-pedagogical and assessment knowledge. For example, telling pupils that they need to use more interesting vocabulary is not helpful if pupils have not learnt the vocabulary. Neither is saying to pupils, 'check your answers again', if pupils cannot see what is wrong with their answers. Good classroom instruction can be more effective than feedback because feedback has to be built on something.

Conclusions

Table 8.17 provides a simple summary of the new results in this chapter, based on the same approach as in Chapter 7. On the basis of this evidence and the prior work described at the start of the chapter, the generic whole-school approach of these three that is worth most consideration by practitioners is Philosophy for Children. Put simply, learning to reason beats learning facts at present. All outcomes assessed in four different ways are slightly positive, and the results for the poorest children are better. P4C may also be worth pursuing for other reasons not assessed here (but see Chapter 9). Enhancing feedback alone is not promising, but the weight of prior evidence suggests that it may have some value. It is also very cheap to implement. The use of a wider liberal curriculum to enhance literacy does not seem to work. However, as with P4C, it may have a considerable or longer-term benefit in its own right.

All of these studies were tested for impact after about one year – which is a short time. If there are wider or longer term benefits to studying philosophy at primary school then this could make the intervention more cost-effective. However, we do not yet know about these benefits. KS2 tests may not be the most appropriate way to assess improved reasoning. On the other hand, children's learning of factual knowledge probably needs to be built up over time, so the one-year implementation may not be long enough for any effects of Core Knowledge to be apparent either. A knowledge-based curriculum may also need more specialist primary school

TABLE 8.17 Summary of findings from the three trials

	Effect size	Effect size FSM-only	Quality of evidence	NNTD-attrition	Cost per pupil
Core Knowledge	−0.03	+0.06	2*	0	£50
P4C reading	+0.12	+0.29	4*	53	£30
P4C writing	+0.03	+0.17	4*	0	£30
P4C maths	+0.10	+0.20	4*	38	£30
P4C CAT	+0.07	−0.02	3*	0	£30
Feedback reading	−0.04	+0.17	2*	0	£22
Feedback writing	−0.05	+0.12	2*	0	£22
Feedback maths	+0.05	+0.41	2*	0	£22

teachers (Young 2012). Having a ready-made curriculum alone is not enough. Teachers have to be passionate about the subjects and willing to engage pupils in discussions and explore beyond what is in the text. Many teachers would need to be shown how this can be achieved. For all three interventions, the teachers themselves must have the knowledge or access to the knowledge and skills necessary, or at least be willing to engage in learned discussions. Good teaching of whatever may be more important than anything else. So the issue for policy-makers is whether to search for approaches and interventions that can be successfully conducted by existing teachers, or even teaching assistants, such as those in Chapter 7. Or whether the more radical whole-school approaches described here are more promising but require a different kind of teacher or at least a different kind of teacher development.

9

EDUCATING THE WHOLE PERSON OR JUST A CHEAP WAY TO IMPROVE RESULTS?

Wider outcomes of schooling

The previous chapters have all focussed on pupil attainment as the outcome used to indicate any improvement. However, schools are about a lot more than this. They are where pupils learn how to interact with a wide range of peers and with the formal adult world. They are where pupils begin to see what society is like, who they can trust and what they can contribute. Policy-makers have traditionally emphasised the economic benefits of education – for society and individuals. But education is also about the happiness of individuals, their preparedness for life other than work and their general 'flourishing' (Brighouse 2008). Some studies have considered these wider outcomes as merely stepping-stones to higher attainment. So, for example, the happiness of students is considered to matter because happier students might perform better in tests. Schuepbach (2014) reports that access to extra-curricular activities at school is linked to improved maths outcomes. But despite previous promise from work in the US, a large study of the impact of raising self-esteem found no benefit for overcoming achievement gaps (Dee 2014). However, this chapter is primarily about taking these enrichment activities and wider outcomes as valuable in their own right (whether they lead to better test outcomes or not).

Why concern with wider outcomes?

While academic achievements may facilitate access to pathways of success in life, some commentators suggest that there are underlying attitudes and behaviours also influenced by education, which may be important in their own right (Heckman and Rubenstein 2001, Brunello and Schlotter 2011, Gupta and Simonsen 2010). The list of such personal qualities is long and could include social and communication skills, resilience, determination, motivation, confidence, self-esteem and self-efficacy. Various collective terms are used in the literature such as non-cognitive skills, soft skills, personal characteristics, personality traits, life skills and social and emotional skills. For consistency and clarity we have used the term non-cognitive outcomes (of education). We are especially concerned with:

- Social and communication skills
- Resilience
- Empathy
- Fairness and justice
- Happiness and life at school

Schools can help pupils foster skills for effective communication and socially accepted behaviours. OFSTED inspections judge pupils' social skills as one of the school effectiveness criteria (OFSTED 2015). Pupils who struggle to communicate effectively are likely to be at risk of social isolation, rejection and even bullying (Botting and Conti-Ramsden 2000, Clegg et al. 1999, Knox and Conti-Ramsden 2003, Hartshorne 2007). In an international comparison, children in England were the most likely to report being bullied by other pupils (Gorard and Smith 2010). Studies have shown that children bullied in schools have low self-esteem, poor confidence and suicidal/self-harming behaviour (Winsper et al. 2012).

Poor communication and social skills can also lead to behavioural and social emotional difficulties. Studies have shown that these children are more likely to be given detentions and excluded from school (DfE 2016, DfE 2012b). In the year 2015 nearly 6,000 pupils were given permanent exclusion in England. Verbal abuse, threatening behaviour, persistent disruptive behaviour and physical assaults to other pupils/adults are the most common reasons of school exclusions (according to our analysis of the National Pupil Database 2015). These reasons are categorised broadly as anti-social behaviours and have long-term impact on pupils' life (and often the life of their peers).

Longitudinal studies have shown that children having social emotional and behavioural problems at primary school age are also less likely to achieve good results in school (Patalay et al. 2016), less likely to attain higher education qualifications, more likely to be involved in crime and are at higher risk of poor health, drug addiction, depression and other mental health problems (Carneiro et al. 2007). Children with good social skills, on the other hand, are more engaged in schools and have positive friendship clusters (Gutman and Vorhaus 2012), and these are correlated with later life outcomes such as employment status and hourly wages, and well-being in adult life (Olsson et al. 2013).

The role of the school

To study children's social and emotional skills, it is necessary to understand children's early life experiences. In 2015 close to 70,000 children in England were reported to be living in public care (DfE 2015). This group of young people is highly vulnerable to neglect and abuse and most likely to be the victim of sexual exploitation, peer violence, bullying and unfair discrimination in schools (Morgan 2008, Wood et al. 2011, Rahilly and Hendry 2014). They are deemed to be more likely to have conduct disorders, mental health problems and self-harming behaviour (Department of Health 2012), and to have worse attainment at school (Seba et al. 2015).

However, some disadvantaged children appear to have higher resilience to the challenges of poverty and abuse and can break through the mould associated with their social disadvantage (Schoon 2006, Goodman et al. 2015). Consistent and positive parenting is believed to help develop resilience among children (Malmberg and Flouri 2011, Hill et al. 2007). However, not all socially disadvantaged children have permanent homes and positive relationships with parents, foster parents or carers (Farmer and Lutman 2009). Therefore, the role of school could be more important for children who lack such permanence. Schools could provide the care and warmth that might be lacking in the homes of some vulnerable young children.

There is evidence that social skills are malleable at school age level (Gutman and Schoon 2013). Supportive peers, school environment and community develop characteristics that are associated with nurturing good social skills and effective communication behaviours. In particular, active engagement with school (or school connectedness) is thought to be inversely linked with risk-taking behaviours. Schools are a micro-society for children where they learn about trust, mutual respect and expectations from a wider society (Gorard and Smith 2010).

One of the challenges for schools is to foster an overall ethos of understanding and valuing individual differences (Humphrey et al. 2010). Children surveyed in England have more often reported 'being deliberately hurt by another pupil' (12%) or 'being left out by other pupils' (22%) when compared with other OECD countries (Gorard and Smith 2010). A more recent survey of about 30,000 children aged 8 to 17 also reported bullying and inconsiderate behaviour of peers as a key issue affecting the subjective well-being of young people (The Good Childhood Report 2015). Bullied children have reported that appearance, behaviour/personality and disability are the common reasons for bullying (Benton 2011). This does not only apply to minority ethnic groups or children with reported disabilities.

The hallmark of state-funded mainstream schools in the UK is heterogeneity. A comprehensive school, as the name suggests, is where children of different social classes, ethnicities, languages, family backgrounds and religions mix (DEMOS 2015). While heterogeneity in schools can cause diversity, dissension and conflicts, it also provides opportunities for children to learn important social skills like empathy, social cohesion, tolerance, acceptance and even critical thinking skills (Braster and Dronkers 2013, Roksa et al. 2017). Following the Special Education Needs and Disability Act 2001, mainstream schools now include children with a range of disabilities. Schools provide an ideal situation for children of different abilities or disabilities and social backgrounds to interact (Ajegbo et al. 2007).

School is also a place where teachers can be role models of acceptable behaviour. Unfortunately, this is often not the case. Under half of the pupils surveyed in The Good Child Report fully agreed that their teachers treat them fairly (The Good

Child Report 2015). The school, as a micro-society, is a place where children can learn acceptable social behaviour. The role of the teacher when interacting with young people is therefore paramount in this. Programmes to sensitise children's attitudes towards emotions, feelings and the situation of others might play an important role in overcoming the common challenges of children's disruptive behaviour, bullying, racism, aggression and violence towards peers and teachers. However, teachers' attitudes and sense of empathy towards pupils often gets ignored.

Enhancing the enjoyment of school for young people, not only for the disadvantaged, should be a part of the policy agenda for education. Poverty is not the only cause of low life satisfaction although children living in relative poverty are likely to report low scores on satisfaction with life in general and specifically life at school (Goodman and Gregg 2010, Chowdry et al. 2010, Statham and Chase 2010, Tomlinson et al. 2008). Enjoyment of school, unlike academic attainment, is much less stratified by young people's background characteristics (Gorard and See 2011).

There is a general trend towards lower satisfaction levels for children as they get older. This means that younger children tend to report more positively about life in general, life at school and health as compared to older children (Ho and Ip 2016, Rees et al. 2011). A possible explanation could be that children's general awareness, language and experiences develop with time and they become capable of reflecting on life and expressing feelings and emotions (Chanfreau et al. 2008). The transition from primary to secondary school is also a factor (Lester and Cross 2015). Possibly, they become more sceptical and less idealistic.

We have previously looked at how young people's views on trust, civic participation and their role in society are strongly linked to the way they are treated at school, and to a lesser extent to the kinds of school they attend (Gorard and Smith 2010). Schools can make inequalities worse by providing differential opportunities to learn (Schmidt et al. 2015). This applies to youth social action opportunities as much as the traditional curriculum. This might produce differences in political tolerance, volunteering, and intended political participation (Fleming et al. 2014). School systems with tracked or selective pathways or where there is high segregation by SES (social economic status) between schools produce young people who, on average, have lower civic engagement (Hoskins et al. 2014), weaker civic knowledge (Collado et al. 2014), or poorer social skills (Gottfried 2014). The 2009 International Civic and Citizenship Education Study showed that intended participation in elections and other civic activities was linked to prior experiences at school (Quintelier and Hooghe 2013). In particular, a participatory democratic climate at school was beneficial in this respect.

But all of this work, including our own up until now, was passive in design and some of the differences could be due to the self-selecting nature of students in some schools and the activities therein. Can such wider outcomes from schooling be improved through interventions?

Development of young people's citizenship

It is believed that developing young people's citizenship can help in their social development and enable them to relate to others. It also promotes understanding and care for the society and communities they live in.

In the 1990s a number of initiatives and programmes were introduced to promote citizenship among young people. Apparently these came about as a consequence of a very public debate which portrayed young people in UK as disproportionately alienated, disaffected and apathetic (Fogelman 1995, Haste 1996). This led to the establishment of the Youth Parliament campaigns by the British Youth Council, as well as activities by Community Service Volunteers and the Carnegie Young People Initiative. Citizenship lessons were also introduced in schools in response to these concerns, and these now form a part of the standard curriculum in most schools in England.

In recent years there was concern that young people in the UK were not sufficiently engaged in civic activities, such as volunteering and social action, because opportunities for such activities are rarely available in schools (Birdwell et al. 2012). The Home Office Children and Young Person boosts to the Home Office Citizenship survey showed that about half (49%) of young people aged 11–15 were engaged in some civic activities (Birdwell 2012; Ockenden and Stuart 2014). Some studies suggest that young people were put off volunteering and social action by the negative perception associated with such activities and the perception by some young people that social action activities were not sufficiently inclusive or open to people from different backgrounds (Bradbury and Kay 2005). Birdwell et al. (2015) reported that pupils from fee-paying schools were more likely than those in state secondary schools to have the opportunity to take part in non-formal learning like uniformed group activities.

In 2012, the UK Prime Minister approached Demos to develop strategic actions to support young people between the ages of 10 and 20 to engage in social action. This resulted in the launch in 2013 of a cross-party, cross-sector and collaborative campaign to increase the level of participation in youth social action. As a consequence of this, the Cabinet Office provided a grant of £5million to 28 organisations working with young people across England to deliver a range of youth social action projects in diverse settings (Kirkman et al. 2015).

There is a growing number of youth social action programmes in the UK today. Several studies have been conducted suggesting positive effects on a range of young people's outcomes, such as employability, self-esteem, and confidence. However, the evidence on such wider outcomes remains very mixed. Self-esteem is not related to student dropout from school, once other factors are accounted for (Parr and Bonitz 2015). In a systematic review of civic education, no evidence was found that civic education itself has an impact on voting behaviour or voter registration (Manning and Edwards 2014). Few actual interventions have been evaluated, and where they have, the evaluations have often not been rigorous enough to assess the impact convincingly.

For example, almost all of the studies in the review conducted by the Institute for Volunteering Research (Ockenden and Stuart 2014), looking at the impact of volunteering, youth leadership and youth social action, were based on surveys of young people who volunteered to take part in these activities and made no comparisons with those who did not. A number of the studies were cited in the review as providing evidence of 'impact' even though there were no comparison groups or counterfactuals and no random allocation of participants in order to control for other factors. Two studies, one looking at the impact of Co-operative StreetGames Volunteers (Co-operative StreetGames Volunteers 2014) and one on the impact of the Youth Action Network and Centre for Social Action (Boeck et al. 2009), also did not have comparison groups, but reported that youth volunteering and social action helped develop 'social connectedness' and foster positive behaviours such as empathy, cooperation, tolerance and better understanding of other people. These are strong but completely unjustified causal claims. The findings were based on a survey of the volunteers and case studies of these volunteers.

Even where experimental studies have been conducted, the evidence is unclear because of the high attrition and mixed results. One example is a large-scale randomised control study conducted by seven research teams across the US (Social and Character Development Research Consortium 2010). The study tracked 6,600 pupils in the third grade (age 8–9) over 2 years. Attrition was high, and 31% of the pupils were lost over the 2 years. The study evaluated the impact of school-based Social and Character Development programmes on 20 school and pupil outcomes including self-efficacy, problem behaviour, altruistic behaviour, engagement in learning, academic competence and perceptions of school climate. Data was collected from a combination of surveys from pupils, teachers and primary caregivers. The results were mixed; some programmes reported beneficial results and some were shown to be detrimental. Any effects were seen in only one year group and not replicated in others. The year-by-year analysis showed no evidence of impact of the seven programmes (both individually and combined) on pupils' social and character development. Growth curve analysis used to estimate impact over time also reported no 'significant' effects of the combined programmes on pupil outcomes. Six of the individual programme effects were deemed 'significant', of which two were positive and four were detrimental. There are several limitations to this study. There was a large number of missing cases. Close to 40% of pupil data were not collected either because the caregiver did not give consent for participation or because pupils were absent. These pupils may be systematically different to those for whom data was collected.

A large-scale experimental study by the Cabinet Office in the UK evaluated the impact of Youth Social Action (YSA) programmes on young people aged 10 to 20 in 73 schools (Kirkman et al. 2016). The evaluation consisted of three RCTs and one matched trial of youth social activities from four providers. All of the programmes included an element of citizenship. Using validated questionnaire items as outcomes, the RCTs suggested positive effects from youth participation on young peoples' work and life skills, such as empathy, problem solving, cooperation, grit and resilience, sense of community and educational attitudes. In addition to the survey, the study also measured observable behaviours. One involved an interview task where pupils' performance was assessed by experienced hirers and the other was a task where pupils were given four 50 pence pieces to decide whether they would keep the money or how much to donate to charity. The study found that compared to their non-participating counterparts, young people who participated in youth social action expressed greater interest in volunteering activities, but were less willing to donate money to charity. Pupils who participated in YSA were more likely to be judged as employable compared to control pupils.

Although promising in some respects, it is hard to judge how reliable this evidence is because there was no clear reporting of attrition and school selection criteria. There were also few details on the targeted and achieved samples. Four organisations were involved: Citizenship Foundation (CF), Community Service Volunteers (CSV), Envision and IMAGO. The report suggested that Envision worked with 130 schools and included 2,000 young people in their social action initiatives, but only 364 were surveyed. IMAGO was reported to be operating in 25 schools engaging 5,000 young people, but only 2,190 were included in the study. It seemed that the analysis included only those with pre- and post-test scores, thus discounting any missing cases and dropouts despite claiming intention-to-treat analysis. The report does not clarify if young people were assigned to the treatment or control groups or if they were asked to take part first and then volunteers were assigned to treatment and control groups. It is not even clear whether randomisation was at school level or individual level. The explanation on page 35 says 'The sample of control students was composed of students in a classroom randomly selected by the school'. In other words, comparisons were not made with similar pupils who indicated interest in both control and treatment schools.

The report of the Cabinet Office initiative of National Citizen Service for 15–17-year-olds by Booth et al. (2015) similarly claims success but there is very high attrition (with over 91% of pre-test students missing from the treatment groups at post-test). This makes the results untrustworthy, and the authors' use of significance testing absurd.

Other than concerns about the designs used in prior studies of the wider outcomes of schools there are also widespread doubts about the nature and value of some of these reported outcomes, and about how to assess them. For example, is autonomy necessarily a good thing if it means ignoring expert advice? For gratitude to mean something it has to be freely given, in which case how can it be improved via an education intervention (Carr 2015)? Despite its use in policy documents, it is not clear what resilience or even 'grit' is. Is it asking others to accept failure (O'Brien 2014)? The same queries arise when considering a whole range of mental and personal constructs from self-esteem to aspiration (Gorard et al. 2011). On examination they may be considered by some to be rather sinister, or simply bland and unimpressive (Hyland 2015). In addition, it is hard to envisage how best to assess any of these constructs for an individual. In education, we might approach teachers to ask for their judgements of pupils, or we might observe pupils in action and over time, provide them with tasks to perform or games to play, or ask for their self-reports (Duckworth et al. 2015). All of these approaches have some relative advantages and several disadvantages, and none is satisfactory. While accepting these limitations, in the evaluations described later in this chapter we relied largely on repeated self-reports from pupils as being the only feasible way to obtain relevant data at the required scale. However, our instrument contained some vignettes that acted as a kind of practical 'moral' task, in which the socially desirable responses were less obvious, and we also observed and spoke to as many pupils and their teachers as possible.

It is clear that there is variation in the wider outcomes of schools, and also importantly that this variation is not nearly as stratified by socio-economic status (SES) and other pupil characteristics as attainment outcomes are (Gorard and Smith 2010). If ideas like trust, citizenship and self-confidence are malleable (and we believe that they are) then it should be possible to provide more convincing evidence than above. The remainder of the chapter looks at the evidence on the impact of uniformed groups, social action modules and Philosophy for Children (P4C) on non-cognitive results.

What is the prior evidence on the approaches we tried?

Prior evidence on Youth United

One of the approaches we tested, to look at the impact of participation in uniformed group activities on young people's wider outcomes and citizenship, is the Youth United (YU) youth social action programme. Youth United is an umbrella organisation for uniformed groups, who developed new groups in secondary schools in England for Scouts, Sea Cadets, Fire Cadets and St John Ambulance Brigade.

An evaluation of Youth United projects reported positive effects of participation in uniformed group activities on communication, empathy, grit and resilience (Family, Kids and Youth 2015). These findings were based on interview data and case study reports. Questionnaire surveys collected responses from young people aged 11 to 18 about their character outcomes. A limitation of this study was that treatment and control pupils were not randomly allocated and there was attrition of 40% for the treatment group and 67% for control pupils between pre- and post-surveys.

Evaluation of the impact of Girlguiding (Girlguiding 2012–2013) and the Duke of Edinburgh award suggests that participation increased young people's resilience and promoted responsible behaviour (Duke of Edinburgh 2010). Almost all of the girls in Girlguiding said that participation in the uniformed activity had increased their confidence and leadership skills. Young people's attitudes and changes in behaviour were compared over time, but no comparisons were made with similar children not involved in these activities.

One study looked specifically at the impact of participation in the fire and rescue services on young people identified as having a range of anti-social and behavioural problems (Ward et al. 2009). The study concluded that the structured, disciplined environment and close group work often associated with uniformed group activities did have benefits. Although not all pupils completed the course, there were reported positive outcomes in terms of behaviour and attitudes from pupils, school, home and peers. A decline in the number of offences such as hoax calls or deliberate fires committed by young people in the community was noted, and the number of permanent exclusions from school also dropped.

Surveys of the Combined Cadet Force (CCF) in two Welsh state schools suggested perceived improvements in attendance, behaviour and attitudes and social relations (Glover and Sparks 2009). Teachers reported that pupils were better organised, and had better communication and thinking skills. Again, this study did not compare similar pupils who were not in the CCF so it is difficult to say if the pupils would have made similar improvements if they had not been in the CCF.

An evaluation of cadet forces across the UK involving 5,100 cadets from the Combined Cadet Force (CCF), Sea Cadet Corps/Royal Marine Cadets, Army Cadet Force (ACF) and Air Training Corps (ATC) reported positive effects across a range of outcomes, such as leadership skills, teamwork, self-esteem, confidence and positive attitude (Moon et al. 2010). A similar evaluation was carried out in 2014 looking into the impact of volunteering in uniformed organisations such as The Boys' Brigade, Catholic Guides, The Girls Brigade, and Girl Guides and Scouts in Northern Ireland (Volunteer Now 2014). Some of the positive benefits reported were learning new skills, gaining qualifications, leadership skills, teamwork and better communication skills. The findings of these studies were based largely on reports by participants, volunteers, parents and teachers. Again, no comparisons were made with those who were not involved in the cadet forces so we cannot be sure if they would have made similar improvements if they had not been in the cadet force. It is possible that pupils who participated in these cadet forces were already likely to have high self-esteem, or be more academically able and confident. Or the changes observed could have occurred anyway. Without proper randomisations it is hard to say if this was the case.

There are overall signs of promise but currently there is a lack of robust evaluation of the impact of organised uniformed youth groups, and so the time was right for a large-scale robust evaluation of the wider outcomes of providing such opportunities to schools and pupils.

Prior evidence on Children's University

Children's University (CU) is a charity trust in the UK and worldwide. CU works with children in schools, and the activities they offer are intended to impact on pupils' learning and attainment, a range of wider non-attainment outcomes such as aspiration, motivation and self-confidence, and some longer-term outcomes such as enhanced opportunities for subsequent employment.

The feasibility of the Children's University programme is suggested by various self-evaluations by CU (MacBeath and Waterhouse 2008, MacBeath 2012). Volunteers with parents able to pay for the programme who attended previous CU programmes reported high levels of satisfaction, higher levels of attendance at school than average, and higher levels of subsequent attainment (literacy and numeracy) than those who did not volunteer, or otherwise could not attend (MacBeath 2012). However, pre-post-test differences were only included for those who attended CU activities.

Chanfreau et al. (2016) suggested benefits from out-of-school activities (breakfast clubs, after-school clubs, sports activities, music and art lessons, tuition, religious services) on children's KS2 attainment. These results are based on a national longitudinal birth cohort study (Millennium Cohort). The study included the sample of 11,762 pupils and systematically recorded details of their home and school life. Records on children's out-of-school activities were taken at three instances during their primary school stage. The out-of-school activities participation rate increased from age 5 to age 11. However, the findings confirm a big social income gap in the take up of after-school activities. The KS2 results showed a positive association with attending out-of-school activities, but was not related to any non-cognitive outcomes.

As with the CU-sponsored evaluations, this difference is only indicative and does not suggest any causal relationship between after-school activities and outcomes. A more robust evaluation is clearly indicated.

Prior evidence on Philosophy for Children

Philosophy for Children (P4C) is an educational approach to teach children critical thinking skills through engaging children in philosophical dialogue. The prior evidence of its effectiveness is described in Chapter 8. The focus in this chapter is on non-cognitive outcomes rather than the attainment outcomes already covered.

P4C can be seen as part of a worldwide critical thinking movement in education that has brought changes to teaching approaches and the overall purpose of school education (Higgins 2015). There are various versions of the P4C approach and different names but all share the core ideas of promoting critical thinking, nurturing young people's curiosity, supporting them in using language of reasoning and argumentation and sharing views for better understanding.

Some studies of P4C have looked at non-cognitive outcomes as well, such as self-esteem (Sasseville 1994, Trickey and Topping 2004), self-concept and confidence (Williams 1993), and pupils' participation level in the classroom (Topping and Trickey 2007, Swain et al. 2013). However, most of these studies are small scale with non-random selection and allocation of pupils to treatment groups or they involved unclear pupil matching criteria, unaccounted-for pupil age differences, and they rarely report pupil or school dropout rates. The impact of P4C on non-cognitive outcomes is therefore unclear.

A study conducted in Québec assessed the impact of P4C on pupils' self-esteem (Sasseville 1994). The study involved 124 pupils and was conducted over a period of nearly five months. Details of the initial sample are not presented in the report. The reported effects of P4C in the post-test were more pronounced for pupils with low self-esteem. The study also mentions that pupils receiving P4C who had high self-esteem at the pre-test stage declined relative to the other group. There was no explanation about how the grouped were selected or allocated to treatment conditions. Nor was there any report of pupil dropout rate, the timing of the testing events, and the average difference in pupils' age in months. All these could be relevant to pupils' self-esteem outcomes.

A study in Madrid presented some preliminary findings on the longitudinal outcomes of P4C on pupils' social emotional behaviour (Colom et al. 2014). The sample included 455 treatment pupils in the first year of primary school who were tracked thorough to completion of secondary school. These were matched with a comparison group of 321 pupils recruited in 2005 on socio-demographic variables but the recruitment of these schools is years apart from those who were introduced to P4C in 2002. The details of socioeconomic variables and pre-test scores were not reported. The initial report included 427 pupils with results for standardised tests of cognitive ability conducted when they were in Grade 2 and Grade 6. Pupils in the P4C treatment (N = 281) outperformed those in the matched comparison group (N = 146) in social interactions and extraversion (ES = +0.13) and honesty (0.15). However, P4C pupils also showed positive signs on anxiety and emotional instability (0.13). It is not clear if these results are gain scores over a period of five years or post-test differences between the two matched groups.

A randomised control trial conducted in Tehran reported a positive impact for P4C on pupils' interpersonal skills (Hedayati et al. 2009). This study included 190 pupils in primary school, of whom 88 were allocated to the P4C group. Pupils were balanced on the pre-test. However, the randomisation and group allocation was carried out before the pre-test was administered. There is a chance that group allocation before the pre-test administration could influence the pre-test scores if allocation was known to participants. The impact was assessed after four months of intervention on a questionnaire of social skills and problem solving. There is no report of attrition at the final stage of the study. The lack of information about initial and final sample and timeline of events makes it difficult to judge the trustworthiness of the findings.

A number of small-scale studies were conducted in the UK, and all reported positive effects on some measures of non-cognitive outcomes.

A quasi-experimental study conducted in primary schools in the UK suggested a positive impact from P4C on pupils' self-esteem and social skills (Trickey and Topping 2006). The study included eight primary schools, of which five participated in the intervention. The schools were non-randomly allocated to treatment conditions. Twenty teachers from the intervention group were trained to deliver P4C to Year groups 5 and 6. Two instrument measures were selected to assess pupils' social and emotional effects at pre and post stages of the intervention. Myself as a Learner Survey (MALS) is a pupil survey measuring pupils' self-esteem as a learner and Taxonomy of Problematic Social Situations (TOPS) is a teacher-reported survey of pupils' social behaviour assessment. 171 pupils completed the MALS and 47 pupils were assessed on TOPS, but it is not clear how pupils were selected for TOPS assessment by teachers. The results are reported in probabilities, and the use of significance test for a non-random sample is meaningless. The study claimed improvement in pupils' self-esteem as a result of P4C and no clear gains in pupils' social behaviour.

A study conducted by the Liverpool Primary Care Trust in England (Meir and McCann 2016) in four primary and four secondary schools reported increases in pupils' reflection skills, respect for others, increased pupil participation, pupil attendance, improvement in pupils' confidence and self-esteem. Such findings cannot be taken seriously as there was no comparison group, so it is not possible to attribute any improvements to the intervention alone. Moreover, the perceived outcomes of P4C were estimated from teachers' reports of children's behaviour. Teacher observations can be subjective and biased especially if they somehow believe that the programme should deliver change.

The Wiser Wales study by the Council for Education in World Citizenship tracked the impact of P4C across seven schools from 2009 to 2012 (Dyfed County Council 1994). The study reported improvements in pupils' social skills, concentration, their ability to question and relationships as a result of increased confidence in self-expression. These outcomes were based on pupils' and teachers' self-reports.

In one study, the Northumberland Education Directorate, in collaboration with Newcastle University, compared the effectiveness of teaching thinking strategies and P4C in primary, middle and secondary schools (Williams and Wegerif 2004). The majority of teachers surveyed reported a range of positive effects of P4C on their pupils, including pupil motivation and cognitive, social and affective benefits. These 'soft' evaluations are useful in testing the feasibility of P4C programmes, reporting in-depth details on the success and barriers of programme implementation, but are not useful as impact evaluations. In the absence of an appropriate comparator, self-report measures of outcomes are not reliable as test of impact.

In summary, while there are signs of promise, not that much is really known about the impact of P4C on non-cognitive outcomes and so a large pilot trial of the kind we describe below was indicated.

Generic methods

The three new evaluations described in detail in this chapter have several similarities in terms of their design and the methods used. Each involved a comparison between a large group of pupils who received the intervention and another group who did not but continued with 'business as usual'. Schools across England were allocated to one or another of the groups. To assess the impact on non-cognitive outcomes the pupils in all three evaluations completed the same self-report questionnaires at the outset and the end of the evaluation.

The instrument was developed by the evaluators especially for use in these trials, in co-operation with the UK Cabinet Office. The instrument comprised basic questions about whether respondents had participated in any youth social action activities similar to those offered by Youth United or Children's University, and how keen they were to undertake such activities. A pre-test was given before randomisation, and for YU and CU the results from these items were used to help identify 'volunteers' in all schools, regardless of whether those schools were going to be offered any intervention.

In addition, the instrument contained a set of single-item questions on a range of wider outcomes covering concepts including teamwork, communication, motivation, self-esteem, confidence, resilience, civic mindedness and future intentions. These items were taken from validated instruments, provided by ONS (Office for National Statistics), the Cabinet Office, reviews of the literature, prior studies by the evaluators, and professional advice. All have clear audit trails leading to their derivation. For example, the item on self-esteem is the one recommended for single-item use by Rosenberg (1965). The key consideration was that the items were measurable, malleable in individuals, and deemed important by stakeholders either in their own right or because they are linked to behavioural outcomes including attendance and participation at school. It was piloted in schools from areas not participating in the trials. The instrument was also tested for suitability for all pupils being able to respond with minimal assistance, and as appropriate for the reading age of Year 5 (age 9–10) pupils (the youngest group of children in the three trials). The questionnaire was designed with mostly pre-coded tick-boxes for ease of completion. Some items were reverse-coded to try and encourage pupils to focus on the meaning of each one. Two items were based on short stories (vignettes) in which the socially desirable responses were not as clear as in the scaled tick-box questions. The questionnaire took approximately 10 minutes to complete. It was designed for ease and speed of completion to encourage full responses and to prevent dropout or non-response caused by fatigue and frustration. Schools are also more likely to agree on their pupils taking the survey if it does not take up too much of their curriculum time.

The administration of the post-test survey was monitored by the evaluators in case knowledge of group allocation could affect pupils' performance in the test or teachers' attitude towards the test. All analyses were based on intention to treat, meaning that cases were handled as being in the group they were randomised to, whatever happened subsequently, and pupils were followed up as far as possible even where they had moved schools. A sub-analysis of only those pupils eligible for free school meals (FSM) was also conducted where possible. The methods of analysis presented depend upon the nature of the data. Differences between mean scores are based on 'effect' sizes. The relevant data is presented for pre-intervention (to check for initial balance between groups), post-intervention and gain scores.

The differences analysed where possible are the gain scores from pre- to post-test, in order to cater for any imbalances in the initial groups, and to aid comparison between trials (but see below for a problem relating to the P4C trial). Some of the questionnaire responses are categorical in nature and the results for these are presented as pre- and post-odds ratios. An 'odds ratio' is the proportion of two 'odds' or percentages to each other. The odds ratio of 20% to 10% is 2, whereas the odds ratio of 20% to 80% is 0.25. In this chapter an odds ratio represents how much more likely a pupil in the treatment group was to respond positively to any question than a pupil in the control group. An odds ratio of less than one means that the treatment group is less likely to respond positively compared to the control or comparison group.

The trials are rated 0–4* in terms of robustness, and each result is compared to the number of counterfactual cases that would need to be added to the smallest group in order for the apparent 'effect' size to disappear, as described in Chapter 4. Each intervention involved a comprehensive process evaluation collecting information about the programme, mode of delivery, consistency and fidelity of implementation, and feedback from developers, teachers, pupils and parents via lesson/session observations, focus groups and interviews. Further details can be found in Gorard et al. (2016c), Siddiqui et al. (2017a), and Siddiqui et al. (2017b).

The three interventions and specific methods used to evaluate them

Youth United intervention and methods

The 'treatment' in this trial is not a single intervention as such, but a programme of activities provided by four uniformed youth organisations supported by the Youth United Foundation (YUF). YUF is a charity supporting a network of voluntary organisations which offer established long-term uniformed youth programmes. In this trial YUF acted as a broker arranging for their regional uniformed organisations to set up units in schools in England. The uniformed organisations in this trial included the St John Ambulance, Scouts, Sea Cadets and Fire Cadets. Although these organisations have separate missions, activities, format and delivery, they share the core aims of promoting volunteering, inspiring young people to do community work, to learn new skills such as life-saving, and to be active citizens. The role of YUF was largely in the recruitment of schools. They wrote to schools in the six regions to offer the uniformed group programme, and put them in touch with the uniformed organisation in the region (if available). The schools then ran their recruitment drive to get pupils. Pupils were therefore not given a choice of uniformed group.

The uniformed groups were managed and run by different organisations, and so the method of delivery, the instruction and training, and the number of sessions delivered varied between schools and uniformed groups. The Scouts units, in particular, had fewer sessions than the other uniformed groups, due to a delay in starting up because they relied on identifying teacher/parent volunteers. The average number of weekly sessions across all units was 24, with most sessions lasting two hours. Offsite activities were occasionally conducted after school and tended to last the whole afternoon. These were for practical training where special equipment was needed. For example, canoeing, kayaking and sailing activities took place in a local boating area and fire training was taken in the local firehouse.

Fire Cadet sessions aimed to equip young people with life skills to interact and respond to potentially risky situations in their community. All sessions were conducted by specially trained instructors from the local Fire and Rescue Service, in line with the delivery of the Level 2 BTEC Award in the Fire and Rescue Service in the community. This included a mixture of operational firefighting activities, such as hose running, shipping a standpipe, foam drill and search and rescue techniques. The cadets also learnt and practised the standard drills, safety words of command, fire and water safety, first aid and concepts related to the structure and role of the Fire and Rescue Service, as well as activities to develop teamwork, leadership and communication skills. Visits were arranged for cadets to the Fire Control room and the Marine Rescue Unit. Fire cadets also had the opportunity to attend a three-day residential camp. At the end of their training cadets received a completion certificate and a first aid awareness certificate. Upon successful completion, cadets received an externally and internally verified BTEC Level 2 award in Fire and Rescue Services in the Community. Awards were also given for the most improved fire cadet and the most outstanding cadet as encouragement for their participation. These awards were presented at a graduation ceremony.

Sea Cadets provided training on a naval theme in which young people were given an opportunity to learn and practise new life skills needed in water, led by trained personnel from the Marine Society and Sea Cadets. The usual sessions consisted of 45 minutes of recreational or fun activities (e.g. football, tennis, balloon stampede, tunnel race and softball) followed by 45 minutes of Sea Cadet activity. The latter included basic drills, semaphore (using Sea Cadet flags), first aid, orienteering, seamanship, meteorology and camping skills (using the stove, pitching tents), and boating sessions – canoeing, sailing, kayaking and rowing. All Sea Cadets worked towards the BCU (British Canoeing Union) and the RYA (Royal Yachting Association) Stage 1 qualification. They also took part in a weekend outward bound where they tried zipwire, campfires, abseiling, problem solving, bushcraft, laserzone, caving and Jacob's ladder. Visits were organised for the cadets to the local Sea Cadet Unit where students got to witness the full range of Sea Cadet activities. They also had the opportunity to attend taster lessons on Marine Engineering. At the end of the course, trophies were awarded for the Best Cadet, Most Improved Cadet and for all round commitment.

The St John Ambulance (SJA) course consisted of a combination of theory and practical sessions as well as physical activities. The course included a mandatory 12 one-and-a-half hour sessions on first aid skills to qualify for the first aid qualification. These sessions were conducted outside school hours by trained SJA officers. All participating pupils were enrolled as cadets of SJA, and were given a polo shirt as a uniform to wear during the weekly sessions. They were also issued with a personal first aid kit which they could keep. All pupils completed the Cadet First

Aider programme to qualify as Trainee Cadet First Aiders. This enabled them to support their school at events such as sports day. The weekly sessions followed a scheme-of-work where cadets learnt how to treat a range of injuries and conditions including recognising heart attacks and asthma, supporting an unconscious breathing casualty, CPR, choking, minor and severe bleeding and bandaging, making emergency phone calls, casualty communication and care and fainting. At the end of the course, pupils' first aid skills were assessed. Upon successful completion of the assessment, pupils received a certificate which states that they are first aid qualified. This certificate is valid for three years, after which they are required to renew it.

The aim of the Scouts programme is to provide an opportunity for learning new skills and teamwork, in units conducted by teacher volunteers and instructors from the Scouts association. In one of the schools we monitored, the sessions were delivered by four/five Scouts trainers once a month, with a teacher committed to overseeing the programme throughout. These monthly Scouts-led sessions were practical sessions where pupils learnt navigation (map reading), cooking (including what food was suitable for expeditions), team-building activities, tent building, and first aid. Otherwise the weekly sessions were about one to one and a half hours long. In one school the programme was developed by the teacher to tailor the activities to feed into the Duke of Edinburgh award. Most of the sessions were conducted within the school, for example, in the school hall and library. The Scouts programme also included outdoor activities. For example, one unit went to Matlock to visit a local mountain biking centre (Great Tower Windermere Activity Centre). At the centre, the Scouts learnt a range of skills, such as climbing and raft building.

A number of the uniformed groups incorporated volunteering activities. The Fire Cadets, for example, took part in a number of social action events, which included fundraising activities (bag packing at local supermarkets) and events to help the local community (supplying food and helping out at the local foodbank and facilitating bingo events at local old people's homes). They also helped raise money from cakes donated by local businesses to buy games for a local children's hospital. Some cadets organised and ran afternoon activity sessions for pupils at a special school. In one school the cadets represented their schools in the Remembrance Parade supported by the Fire Service staff. The Sea Cadets picked their own charity projects to work with. The St John Ambulance cadets volunteered as first aiders at their individual schools' sports days as well as becoming involved with a range of SJA promotional activities in their local areas. Some units also volunteered their services coaching children and adults to play cricket and netball.

The one-year trial involved 71 secondary schools in six areas in the north of England. Opt-out consent forms were sent to parents by participating schools. Thirty-eight of the schools were randomised to treatment and 33 to control. To help reduce post-allocation demoralisation, and thus dropout, the control schools were offered an incentive payment of £1,500 on completion of the post-test. This was to encourage them to remain in the trial in terms of providing the necessary data. A total of 7,781 Year 9 (age 13–14) pupils from these schools were involved in the project, of which 4,012 were in the treatment schools and 3,769 were in the control schools. Of these 3,377 (1,733 treatment and 1,644 control) reported in the initial survey that they would like to take part in the kinds of activities offered by YUF. In the treatment schools, 633 pupils are known to have participated in the uniformed group activities. As each uniformed group could only offer a limited number of places subject to availability of the uniformed group capacity to provide trainers, only a certain number (average of around 20 to 30 per group) actually took part in the activities.

Five treatment schools were not able to open their Scouts unit because of a combination of poor uptake by pupils, lack of teacher volunteers and change of management. Two SJA schools could not get a teacher volunteer to run the unit. One school allocated to treatment indicated after randomisation but before the programme started that they would like to offer the Duke of Edinburgh award instead. They received no YUF intervention, but agreed to remain in the trial. Nonetheless, they were all analysed as being in the intervention group.

Data on the non-attainment outcomes were collected using the bespoke questionnaire survey (see above). The pre-intervention survey was conducted prior to randomisation of schools. The main analyses involved comparing the 3,377 pupils from the pre-intervention survey who reported that they would like to take part in a youth social action activity like the ones offered by YUF (these are known as 'the volunteers') across treatment groups. This is deemed the fairest comparison, because only a subset of pupils in the treatment schools could actually receive the intervention, and it is not clear otherwise who their counterparts would be in the control schools. In addition, we compared those in treatment schools who actually participated with those who did not (with a measure of attendance used to assess 'dosage').

No school dropped out from the trial. A total of 27 'volunteer' pupils (and 64 from all pupils) were missing data from the post-test (14 treatment and 13 control), which represents attrition of around 1%. In addition, some pupils did not provide a valid response to all items in the survey. The trial is rated as 4* (in terms of these non-cognitive measures).

Children's University intervention and methods

Children's University organise out-of-school hours learning activities for pupils aged 5 to 14. The purpose of CU activities is to encourage learning through pupils' participation and acquiring new skills and experiences which are different from learning in a regular classroom environment, aiming to raise pupils' aspirations, interests and motivation towards learning and higher achievement goals. For this trial, CU developed social action modules including volunteering as part of the programme.

Pupils participating in CU must complete 30 hours of activities in order to achieve initial certification level and to graduate. Fifteen hours are non-specified learning activities and 15 hours are for activities that involve some kind of positive social action. Each child gets a 'CU passport' (a small booklet) in which their teacher gives point stamps after completing specified hours of the activities. The concept of keeping a passport book is to increase pupils' motivation through a point-rewards system.

CU has included a set of social action modules where the idea is to promote volunteering and networking within and across communities. In 30 hours of learning pupils are expected to devote 15 hours in social action activities where the focus is volunteering, participation in active citizenship or community service. The social action activities are aligned with the aims of CU that target pupils' improvement in raising aspiration, self-esteem and confidence, resilience and social skills development. The CU centres provide support and ideas to schools in planning social action activities. Pupils' participation is monitored, guided and credited in the learning passports by teachers and CU staff members. There are several social action activities and projects validated by CU, including charity and fund raising, community work, and volunteering.

CU maintains a database of all activities, learning destinations and pupils' participation. Schools need to get CU staff endorsement on any new activity or learning destination which is not in the existing database. The purpose is to endorse only those out-of-school activities which have learning aims and opportunities for pupils. In partnership with schools, CU manages after-school clubs (e.g. clubs for reading, cooking, gardening, cleaning, health and first aid, charity and fund raising), visits to local libraries, museums and learning sites, after-school community days, swimming and music lessons and games learned through coaching and practice.

Our two-year trial of Children's University (CU) was based on a waiting-list design, in which all of the 68 primary schools recruited were offered the intervention. Thirty-six of the schools (2,166 pupils) were randomised to receive the intervention (including the new social action modules) immediately, with 32 schools (and 1,677 pupils) in the control. The evaluation is based on children initially in Years 4 and 5 (age 8–10). Other than the intervention and the age range, much of the evaluation is the same as for YUF (above). The same questionnaire was used pre- and post-intervention, and it was analysed in the same way – focussing on the children in the pre-intervention survey who expressed a wish to participate in CU or similar. As with YUF there was no school dropout in terms of data. However, six of the treatment schools withdrew from the intervention itself after receiving the training, which may be an indication of the perceived appeal of the intervention. All of these schools still provided the post-intervention data. The pre-survey of attitudes and aspirations collected 3,701 responses. Of these, 371 pupils did not complete the post-survey, leading to 3,330 maximum usable results after one year (around 10% attrition, balanced between the two groups). After two years the original Year 5 pupils had left school, and 1,720 of the original Year 4 pupils completed the second round of the survey. The trial is rated as 4* (in terms of these non-cognitive measures).

Philosophy for Children intervention and methods

The impact of P4C on attainment at primary school is described in Chapter 8. It was based on a waiting-list design meaning that the 26 control schools were funded to receive the intervention once the trial was complete. We used 16 of these control schools (1,099 Year 4 and 5 pupils), committed to the introduction of P4C and agreeing to continue the evaluation, to form the 'treatment' group for a further evaluation – this time of the non-cognitive outcomes such as possible social, emotional and behavioural impacts, using the same instrument as above. SAPERE provided teacher training to these 16 schools and gave login and passwords to the teachers to access teaching ideas and resources from their website. In addition SAPERE provided extra support days where SAPERE staff conducted P4C sessions in the classrooms and the teachers observed for their own practice and knowledge. An online teacher's feedback survey was used to judge the implementation quality and dosage of the sessions.

For this quasi-experiment, 26 of the control schools (1,623 pupils) from the CU evaluation (above) formed a ready comparator. The CU control schools introduced neither P4C nor CU. The children were of the same age as the P4C group when they completed the post-intervention survey at the end of Years 5 and 6. The pupils in both groups also took a pre-intervention survey in the same school year as each other, and this provides a kind of baseline for the comparison. However, the P4C group took the early survey in December near the start of the school year, whereas the CU group took it in June towards the end of the year. Because the attitudes of young children change a lot over six months, we use the post-intervention survey only for the headline results.

Overall attrition form pre- to post-intervention was 10%, with 154 pupils lost to follow-up in the control, and 131 in the treatment group. Because of the intrinsically weaker design of this study this evaluation is rated as only 2*.

Findings from the three wider outcomes trials

Youth United results

There are several items using a similar 1–10 scale on the questionnaire and so they are summarised here in terms of their effect sizes for gains or changes over time from pre- to post-test (Table 9.1). Because the groups were generally balanced at the outset on all items it makes little difference whether the 'effect' sizes are calculated for the post-test only or for these gain scores. The results suggest that being in the treatment schools for YU (regardless of participation) may have had

TABLE 9.1 The 'effect' sizes for all attitude scale items, Youth United

Item	'Volunteer' pupils	FSM-eligible
I am good at explaining my ideas	+0.06	−0.03
I like meeting new people	**+0.04**	**+0.07**
I can work with someone who has different opinions	+0.07	−0.04
I can do most things if I try	**+0.10**	**+0.04**
Once I have started a task I like to complete it	+0.09	−0.09
I want to try and make my local area a better place	+0.07	+0.17
I like to be told exactly what to do	*+0.04*	*+0.12*
I am often afraid to try new things	*+0.01*	*0*
I feel happy most days	+0.04	+0.11
I try to understand other people's problems	+0.06	+0.10
I know where to go for help with a problem	+0.08	+0.11

Note: the items in bold were pre-specified by YU as the ones which the uniformed groups are most likely to have an impact on and so were deemed the headline findings. The items in italics could be deemed negative.

a small positive effect on pupils' wider outcomes. The impact was always likely to be muted because not all volunteers in the treatment schools were able to participate in a uniformed group for a number of reasons (above). However, nearly all of the differences are in favour of the intervention schools, with the largest differences in the self-confidence and resilience items, and the smallest (negligible) concerning trying new things. The same results appeared when the responses of all pupils were analysed, except that the differences are even more muted. The results for the smaller sub-set of pupils eligible for FSM are more extreme. Unlike the volunteer pupils, these figures do not have the force of a trial but they suggest that in many respects FSM pupils gain more from the intervention – in terms of happiness, civic-mindedness and empathy. It is intriguing that the desirability of 'being told what to do' has also increased, and this could be a factor stemming from the nature of the intervention and the health and safety and other instructions described above.

Similarly, the items with categorical responses including the two vignettes portray an increase in the desirable (for youth social action) outcomes for the volunteers in the treatment schools. Young people with the chance to take part in these uniformed activities end up with considerably increased 'professional' aspirations compared to volunteers in control schools (Table 9.2).

TABLE 9.2 Change in professional aspiration odds ratio from pre- to post-survey, Youth United 'volunteers'

	Pre-professional	Pre-not professional	Pre-odds ratio	Post-professional	Post-not professional	Post-odds ratio
Treatment	1014	695	0.87	994	927	1.04
Control	1007	600	–	727	706	

Note: this table compares those listing a professional occupation with all others.

TABLE 9.3 Change in social responsibility odds ratio from pre- to post-survey, Youth United 'volunteers'

	Pre-'responsible'	Pre-'non-responsible'	Pre-odds ratio	Post-'responsible'	Post-'non-responsible'	Post-odds ratio
Treatment	1436	276	0.99	1459	265	1.02
Control	1360	260	–	1376	256	–

TABLE 9.4 Change in generosity odds ratio from pre- to post-survey, Youth United 'volunteers'

	Pre-generous	Pre-not generous	Pre-odds ratio	Post-generous	Post-not generous	Post-odds ratio
Treatment	576	1142	0.94	473	417	1.09
Control	571	1065	–	1247	1200	–

TABLE 9.5 Change in charitable activity odds ratio from pre- to post-survey, Youth United 'volunteers'

	Pre-charity	Pre-not charity	Pre-odds ratio	Post-charity	Post-not charity	Post-odds ratio
Treatment	916	790	0.94	833	737	1.14
Control	900	733	–	896	904	

They are slightly more likely to report being socially responsible about clearing up a mess rather than wanting others to, or simply ignoring it (Table 9.3).

They became considerably more generous or empathetic in reporting allowing a teacher to spend more time with a struggling pupil even if it meant less help for themselves (Table 9.4).

And they are naturally more likely to report having been involved in charitable or other volunteering activities over the last year (Table 9.5).

The headline indicators selected before the trial by YUF (for self-confidence and teamwork) suggest a small differential improvement for the volunteers in the treatment schools. This is backed up by the same kind of improvements for all pupils in the treatment schools (i.e. if there is an effect it is not caused solely by motivation or self-selection), and for all other indicators of youth social action, aspiration and well-being. The same improvements appear in the responses to the social action vignettes as in the self-report scales. Given that the intervention itself was received by only a minority of pupils per year, only a small average result was to be expected. Therefore, it is possible to conclude that there is some evidence that YUF works to some extent for youth social action and civic engagement.

Generally, the uniformed activities were well received by pupils, teachers and trainers. Overall, the Youth United Foundation programme of activities can be considered a success to the extent that it was shown to be feasible. Feedback from stakeholders (parents, teachers, trainers and pupils) suggests that pupils have benefited from these experiences and their lives have been enriched. Of particular benefit were the weekend residential stays, organised by the Fire Cadets, the Sea Cadets and SJA. These were described by trainers as providing the best experience for pupils who would otherwise not have such opportunities. Teachers and trainers observed positive changes in pupils' behaviour as a result of the experiences. The pupils' views were often positive and included the following unprompted comments:

> When this course is finished I was saying to my mum that I don't want to stop here. I want to go on, like learning more, to help myself improve.
>
> I think I may fail my GCSEs so I need something else for the future on my CV and thought the Sea Cadets would help me gain qualifications.
>
> I have got a lot stronger at working in a team and delegating. I enjoyed building a shelter with a small team at . . ., and I have a great partnership with Jermain at our weekly boating sessions.

The process evaluation also highlights some possible barriers to successful implementation of such a programme. One of these relates to young people's motivation to participate. Some children attended the first few sessions and found that uniformed group activities were not for them. A few dropped out due to reported peer pressure. Some were excluded for bad behavior, or because the activities were not considered appropriate for them for health and safety reasons.

The other barriers to implementation are to some extent all related to the lack of managerial and leadership support. Recruiting staff volunteers to oversee the uniformed group was found to be quite challenging in a number of schools, and in some cases schools struggled to start a unit. Where there was no dedicated teacher in charge of the programme, communications between trainers and the school was more difficult. Because some units were run within standard school time, this made it difficult to plan for off-site activities like water sports or firehouse training – leading to an impoverished version of the intervention. Several pupils said they felt overwhelmed by the amount of work they had to cover, but would be happy to stay longer after school to finish some of the activities. However, school bureaucracy with health and safety requirements meant that planning offsite activities took longer than anticipated, and so fewer such sessions could be conducted. A detailed rundown of the activities and a risk assessment report had to be submitted weeks in advance before such activities could be carried out. This made it difficult to plan outside school activities for the cadets. A visit to the fire station, for example, was cancelled because the risk assessment report could not be produced in time. The Sea Cadets were also unable to conduct as many sessions of water sports as they wanted because every activity had to be carefully coordinated with the school. Trainers explained that since they were dealing with issues like fire or water they had to take safety seriously. Discipline is therefore an important element in the training, but many trainers complained about poor pupil behaviour. Support from the school leadership is important to ensure successful implementation.

Children's University results

As with YU, the headline results for this study are based on a comparison between the two groups only involving those pupils who had said from the outset that they would like to take part in some kind of social action. There were 1,451 of these children in CU schools, and 1,150 in the control schools.

In terms of the 11 items in the attitude scales, there is only a small overall difference between the two groups – represented as gain scores after one year of intervention (Table 9.6). This is so whether the results are considered for all pupils or only those who reported wanting to take part in some form of youth social action in the pre-survey. Of course, the results only for FSM-eligible pupils tend to be more volatile because of the smaller number of cases involved. The figures for all volunteers after two years are all positive, but this includes the two items that are reverse-coded – I like to be told exactly what to do, and I am often afraid to try new things. There are larger 'effect' sizes for communication, determination and happiness. The two items pre-selected as suitable for the kind of thing that CU promotes – teamwork and social responsibility – only have small 'effect' sizes which must be treated as near equivalent to zero given the initial loss of 10% of the cases. Overall then, the indications are good but the results are not yet secure.

Over time, more of the primary pupils in both groups in this study selected a professional occupation as their aspiration. However, this trend is more marked for the treatment group. The two groups started fairly level (0.96), but the odds ratio rose to 1.12 (Table 9.7). This could be evidence of the impact of the intervention.

Similarly, both groups were slightly more likely to report being socially responsible about clearing up a mess rather than wanting others to or simply ignoring it

TABLE 9.6 The 'effect' sizes for all attitude scale items, Children's University

Item	'Volunteer' pupils, after one year	FSM 'volunteers', after one year	'Volunteer' pupils, after two years	FSM 'volunteers', after two years
I am good at explaining my ideas	0.16	0.02	0.18	0
I like meeting new people	0	−0.21	0.01	−0.10
I can work with someone who has different opinions	**−0.05**	**−0.16**	**0.03**	**0.02**
I can do most things if I try	0.10	−0.08	0.06	−0.02
Once I have started a task I like to complete it	−0.07	−0.06	0.14	−0.04
I want to try and make my local area a better place	**−0.03**	**0.01**	**0.07**	**+0.39**
I like to be told exactly what to do	*−0.01*	*−0.10*	*0.15*	*−0.07*
I am often afraid to try new things	*0.03*	*0.01*	*0.10*	*0.11*
I feel happy most days	0.02	−0.10	0.14	−0.14
I try to understand other people's problems	0	−0.03	0.01	0.09
I know where to go for help with a problem	0.10	−0.10	0.04	0.10

TABLE 9.7 Change in professional aspiration odds ratio from pre- to post-survey, Children's University, all pupils

	Pre-professional	Pre-not professional	Pre-odds ratio	Interim professional	Interim not professional	Interim odds ratio	Post-professional	Post-not professional	Post-odds ratio
Treatment	907	1259	0.96	1098	824	1.13	580	347	1.12
Control	720	957	–	763	648	–	457	316	–

Note: this table compares those listing a professional occupation with all others.

TABLE 9.8 Change in social responsibility odds ratio from pre- to post-survey, Children's University, all pupils

	Pre-responsible	Pre-not responsible	Pre-odds ratio	Interim responsible	Interim not responsible	Interim odds ratio	Post-responsible	Post-not responsible	Post-odds ratio
Treatment	1948	206	0.93	1741	121	1.11	874	52	1.01
Control	1519	149	–	1366	105	–	729	44	–

(Table 9.8). And as with aspiration, the treatment group made more 'progress' in terms of this choice. However, the responses to this item are so skewed towards that one response that it is difficult to be sure of any of the changes over time.

Pupils generally became more generous over time reporting that they would allow a teacher to spend more time with a struggling pupil even if it meant less help for themselves (Table 9.9). And again this was slightly more marked for pupils in the treatment group, who had been 'ahead' from the start (odds ratio of 1.18).

Having started out relatively balanced in terms of whether they wanted to take part in some kind of social action or charitable activity, pupils in the treatment group are naturally more likely to report having been involved in charitable or other volunteering activities over the last year (Table 9.10). But the progress on this self-report is again greater for the treatment group.

In summary, the responses to the social action vignettes suggest a small social benefit from the intervention. Given that the intervention itself was received by only a minority of pupils per year, only a small average result would be expected, if it was effective. Therefore, it is possible to conclude that there is some evidence that CU works to some extent for youth social action and civic engagement.

The participation level in CU varied across schools and seemed to be dependent on school leadership and challenges or targets faced by schools. The school participation rate was lower than the CU prediction given that schools would not pay the full cost of the programme. CU could recruit 68 schools, and some showed early signs of losing enthusiasm and interest when the CU introduction workshops were conducted. Six schools from the treatment group dropped out immediately after the first training session. They had signed the Memorandum of Understanding (MoU), so they continued to cooperate with the evaluation itself.

Some teachers also questioned the lack of financial support or other benefits to schools for organising after-school activities, visits to Learning Destinations and exploring the ideas and opportunities of social actions. Some of the schools also showed mild resentment at the increased amount of workload that involved monitoring pupils' participation and logging individual pupil's activities and hours spent on each activity. One teacher said:

> If all children got was a 'graduation ceremony' at the end of the year, what would be the benefit for the schools and teachers to complete all the paperwork and 'force' the creation of new clubs?

TABLE 9.9 Change in generosity odds ratio from pre- to post-survey, Children's University, all pupils

	Pre-generous	Pre-not generous	Pre-odds ratio	Interim generous	Interim not generous	Interim odds ratio	Post-generous	Post-not generous	Post-odds ratio
Treatment	837	1319	1.18	875	987	1.28	450	476	1.24
Control	656	1218	–	602	868	–	333	438	–

TABLE 9.10 Change in charitable activity odds ratio from pre- to post-survey, Children's University, all pupils

	Pre-charity	Pre-not charity	Pre-odds ratio	Interim charity	Interim not charity	Interim odds ratio	Post-charity	Post-not charity	Post-odds ratio
Treatment	1585	630	1.23	1521	694	1.47	753	174	1.41
Control	1191	584	–	1061	714	–	583	190	–

Some school leads also raised a point that their schools are already engaged in social action activities and school visits to museums, libraries and historic places. Participation in CU was not considered essential, but rather an additional cost on staff time and engagement. Several of the participating schools already had OFSTED-recognised after-school clubs that helped parents to balance work and family commitments, whilst providing pupils with study support, and offering them a broader range of experiences and interests.

Other schools were generally keen to receive innovative ideas for their after-school activities supported by CU and local partners. Some school leads were eager to participate because they wanted to establish after-school clubs and social action activities for the first time and participation in the project could be beneficial for involving parental support. The CU endorsement allowed schools to build a school profile for OFSTED inspections and parental engagement.

The implementation of social action activities was sometimes challenged by the geographical location of the schools. Schools in urban centres had various opportunities to engage with partnerships for social actions or approach various Learning Destinations with less cost in managing travelling. However, schools in rural areas needed more resources and motivation to create wider engagement opportunities for pupils.

The evaluation team visited various intervention schools to collect information on the CU activities. A general observation was that after-school clubs were popular and attended well by pupils. However, the social action activities themselves were not as frequent or fully integrated with after-school activities. The schools provided various opportunities for children to participate in sports, arts and crafts, singing and drama, cookery, sewing, board games and photography. The CU manager explained that such after-school activities where school staff has access and control are easier to conduct in a safe environment. However social action often requires preparatory work such as risk assessment, protocols for pupils' health and safety checks, and parental consent.

One school had gardening as an after-school club where pupils were helped to grow vegetables. The school arranged community days to sell the vegetables grown in the garden and raised money for donations to cancer research. A few schools organised community days to sell cupcakes and raised funds to support a children's hospital. One of the schools helped pupils in making and selling art and craft items and donations were made to the local home for elderly people. Several schools made packs for donations to food banks. Pupils were asked to collect items that are not used in their homes such as clothes, utensils and toys. The schools donated collected items to organisations such as Oxfam and Red Cross.

Pupils also participated in charity and fund-raising activities out of school, with help and support provided by parents, family and community members. These activities included charity events and collection services in a local church and participating in awareness walks.

The children enjoyed receiving a certificate of achievement in a formal graduation ceremony, with parental participation. The CU management ensured that the event was a special occasion for pupils. Pupils enjoyed wearing gowns and mortarboards and being photographed with their CU achievement certificates in hands. One pupil said:

> It is really so great. I felt so proud in wearing the graduation gown and scholar's hat. This has made me want to come to university for studies in the future.

Philosophy for Children results

The 'effect' sizes are presented here in terms of the post-intervention scores only, because as already noted the pre-intervention scores were obtained at slightly different ages for the two groups. The pre-intervention scores are not a fair comparison. They are included here for completeness, and as a caution showing the volatility of the small 'effect' sizes under different assumptions.

On the first headline indicator of impact – the self-reported response on communication with others – the P4C group is slightly ahead of the comparison group (Table 9.11). It is considerably further ahead when considering only the disadvantaged pupils known to be eligible for FSM (+0.33). This complements our earlier findings that, if P4C is deemed effective in raising attainment at Key Stage 2, this is especially true for FSM-eligible pupils.

However, it is important to note in Table 9.11 (and in some of those that follow) that the P4C group were already ahead of the comparison pupils at the outset. We cannot tell whether this pre-intervention difference is solely due to the six-month difference in age at that testing point (even though all indicators suggest a lowering of confidence in communication skills with age regardless of treatment group). This must reduce our trust in the scale of the post-intervention differences somewhat.

A similar picture appears for the second headline indicator of impact – the self-reported response on ability to work with others (Table 9.12). On post-test scores, the P4C group is ahead by a small amount, and this difference is considerably stronger for FSM-eligible pupils (+0.28). But again, the P4C group was ahead at the outset anyway and this weakens our trust in the scale of the post-intervention differences.

Table 9.13 shows the overall results in terms of 'effect' sizes for all 11 scaled attitude items. The P4C group are ahead in terms of three items – representing communication, teamwork, and social responsibility. They are behind in terms of one – happiness. And the differences are +/−0.05 or less on all other items. Considering only pupils known to be eligible for free school meals, the P4C group of disadvantaged pupils is ahead in terms of items representing communication, sociability, teamwork, self-confidence, social responsibility and empathy. They are slightly ahead in terms of self-reported resilience, not being afraid to try new things and feeling happy. There is almost no difference in terms of knowing where to get help, and the P4C group is behind in terms of wanting to be told what to do.

The outcomes on vignette results are presented in terms of differences in the odds ratios over time. Table 9.14 shows the changes in pupils responding with a

TABLE 9.11 Differences in social and communication skills, P4C, all pupils

I am good at explaining my ideas to other people	Pre-intervention mean	Standard deviation	Post-intervention mean	Standard deviation	'Effect' size
P4C	6.42	2.81	6.25	2.58	–
Comparison	6.03	2.64	6.00	2.29	–
Total	6.19	2.72	6.10	2.41	0.10

Note: P4C 968, comparison 1,469, total 2,437 cases

TABLE 9.12 Differences in co-operation, teamwork and resilience, P4C, all pupils

I can work with someone who has different opinions to me	Pre-intervention mean	Standard deviation	Post-intervention mean	Standard deviation	'Effect' size
P4C	7.26	3.03	7.16	2.77	–
Comparison	6.51	3.12	6.75	2.76	–
Total	6.81	3.11	6.91	2.77	0.15

TABLE 9.13 Overall post-test differences on all 11 items, P4C, all pupils and FSM-eligible pupils

	Post-intervention 'effect' size, all pupils	Post-intervention 'effect' size, FSM-eligible pupils
I am good at explaining my ideas to other people	+0.10	+0.23
I like meeting new people	+0.05	+0.06
I can work with someone who has different opinions to me	+0.15	+0.11
I can do most things if I try	+0.04	+0.10
Once I have started a task I like to finish it	−0.02	+0.10
I want to try and make my local area a better place	+0.08	+0.02
I like to be told exactly what to do	-0.04	-0.03
I am often afraid to try to new things	−0.02	-0.03
I feel happy most days	−0.09	-0.01
I try to understand other people's problems	+0.01	+0.08
I know where to go for help with a problem	−0.02	+0.08

TABLE 9.14 Vignette on empathy/generosity: percentage agreeing and pre- and post-intervention odds ratios, P4C, all pupils

	Pre-'empathy'	Pre-'not-empathy'	Pre-odds ratio	Post-'empathy'	Post-'Not-empathy'	Post-odds ratio
P4C	31%	69%	0.67	38%	62%	0.80
Comparison	40%	60%	–	41%	59%	–

sense of generosity/empathy for a struggling pupil (. . . it is fair that the teacher should spend more time helping Jacintha, even if the other pupils have to wait) as compared to the other two options (Jacintha should work harder and Jacintha should be taught in a separate class). The P4C group increased their odds noticeably whereas the comparison group did not.

The results for FSM-eligible pupils show an even greater increase in the selection of the 'empathy' option by P4C pupils. Although both groups increased this response slightly over time, in these tables the difference of six months between the groups at the pre-intervention survey cannot account for the difference.

The other vignette also shows an increase over time for P4C pupils compared to others, both when considering all pupils and for FSM-eligible pupils only. And again this cannot be explained in terms of the difference of six months at the outset. The finding confirms that from the scale items (above). However, the pilot study did not pick up how skewed the responses here would be, with well over 80% of pupils selecting only one of the three options. This makes the changes less convincing than with the first vignette.

In general the success of P4C sessions depends on the teacher's preparation of the session, enthusiasm to conduct the enquiry regularly, willingness to accept challenging arguments from pupils, and being aware of personal bias and readiness to accept justifications against personal beliefs and choices. Teachers and pupils perceived several benefits such as social and communication skills, respect for others and enjoyment.

P4C sessions were observed to be very different from ordinary primary classroom settings. They involve a different format of communication between teachers and pupils. Many of the pupils interviewed talked about how P4C gave them the opportunity to express themselves:

> I really enjoy P4C because I love to share my feelings in class because I feel my classmates and teacher will listen to me. I also enjoy looking at videos because we get to talk about things together.
>
> You can always express your feeling and you can never get judged or bullied for what you think.
>
> P4C is a great opportunity to share our feelings and share the things that are troubling us. I also enjoy talking about things happening around the world.

On the other hand, there were some pupils who were reticent about sharing their feelings publicly. Some said they were somewhat disturbed by the topics:

> I don't really like P4C that much because I don't really like talking so I get really bored when other people talk. But I like it when people talk about nice things.
>
> I don't like sharing my ideas in case people don't agree. In a way I do like P4C because I like listening to others points of review.
>
> I get to share my opinion with other p-eople and I like doing it with Miss *** and sometimes I get a little sad.

One of the biggest challenges to implementing the programme was finding regular gaps in school schedules to be devoted to P4C. Schools are given flexibility in how to incorporate P4C in their curriculum. Many integrated P4C in subjects like History, English and Personal, social and health education (PSHE). However, due to other curriculum activities and events such as OFSTED inspections, it was not always possible to maintain the regularity recommended by SAPERE (which is one lesson per week). A senior management team leader also reported that the national assessment system requires schools to achieve literacy and numeracy targets and unless those targets are directly addressed, curriculum time cannot be devoted to outside the curriculum. There was sometimes a tension between the school research lead and the other staff. Two of the 16 schools could not continue P4C on a full and regular basis because of changes in staff and school conversion into academies. In the schools where P4C was observed to be fully embedded, the senior leaders were found actively engaged with teachers and P4C trainers.

The process evaluation provided evidence that P4C sessions were focused on the development of a wide range of skills and concepts. One of the sessions was aimed at the creative thinking of pupils. The stimulus was to trigger imagination and allow pupils to think beyond the abilities of human senses. The teacher presented a stimulus in the form of a real object, a replica of the object, a picture of the object and an imaginary object. The pupils were then asked to say a few sentences individually about the forms of object presented and then asked to make questions in pairs. The top three voted questions were:

1. If we can't see many things does it mean that they don't exist?
2. Why are different things named the same?
3. Is it important to name things?

The follow-up discussion was based on the question that the pupils voted for. The teacher encouraged pupils to debate, using justification for their views. As pupils knew that there are often no right or wrong answers in a P4C session this seemed to encourage them to take part in the discussion. After the session ended the pupils resumed their chairs and places in the class. The teacher showed us her P4C planner and evaluation sheets. Detailed records were kept for each session, and individual pupil participation was closely monitored. The teacher reported that she found P4C a very valuable approach in the vocabulary development of pupils. She also reported that the benefits are much more profound for the disadvantaged pupils as they gained a lot of confidence and motivation through participating in the sessions.

Another P4C session was observed in which the teacher shared the stimulus of a picture-based story about a bird that could not fit into any other families of birds, due to its peculiar looks. The pupils shared their views very openly about what they thought a family meant to them. It seemed that the pupils were used to the rules of communication in P4C. No one talked over others and despite very contrasting opinions on the topic of discussion the pupils listened to each other openly and carefully. The teacher reported at the end of the session that it took a few sessions to embed the rules of communication. She said that P4C offered a great benefit for pupils in learning communication skills, and very swiftly it became a norm to listen and wait for a turn to speak. She said that P4C sessions are an opportunity for her to do things that otherwise get ignored, such as listening to individual pupil's point of view and sharing good practice in communication skills.

In a school where the class was made up of pupils from many different ethnic origins, the teacher used an Irish song about migrating to America in the hope of a better life as the stimulus. The following questions were proposed by pupils after discussion within groups of three to four:

1. Is the grass always green on the other side?
2. Does migration solve people's problems?
3. Why is hope so important?
4. If you are wealthy, will you always have a good life?

There were several debating points on the theme of migration and pupils shared their views openly. The teacher reported that she had conducted P4C quite regularly and it helped children to integrate with the school culture where there are pupils and teachers from different ethnic backgrounds and religions. She found that P4C gave pupils a voice of their own and confidence by encouraging them to justify their views.

Conclusions from the three wider outcomes trials

As with the previous two chapters, the headline results from all three trials are summarised in Table 9.15. Seen like this, and even linked to the prior studies, the evidence of benefits for non-cognitive outcomes is not strong. The most promising results are for P4C, especially for the most disadvantaged pupils and in terms of cost, but the groups were not randomised and these results are post-test only with no clear evidence of initial balance between the groups. Only the YU results have a positive NNTD after missing data, but the 'effect' sizes are still small for the cost involved.

In combination, the positive outcomes from all three trials suggest that this is an area of promise. If schools want to do these activities anyway, then any wider outcomes or even impact on attainment could be a bonus. For YU and CU at least, any benefits listed here will be a considerable underestimate because only a minority of the volunteers in treatment schools were able to take part.

The use of vignettes with less obvious socially desirable responses were successful, and perhaps show that what is needed now is research with better measures of social action outcomes than the self-reports adopted here and by the Cabinet Office. Such outcomes could be longer term life outcomes, such as employment, health, citizenship and general well being. These long-term measures would involve tracking individuals along their life course, and funders must be willing to bear the greater expense of a more realistic approach to assessing the wider outcomes of schooling.

TABLE 9.15 Summary of findings from the three trials

	Effect size	Effect size FSM-only	Quality of evidence	NNTD-attrition	Cost per pupil
Youth United – Self-confidence	0.10	0.09	4*	137	£500
Youth United – Teamwork	0.04	0.07	4*	39	£500
Children's University – Teamwork	0.03	0.02	4*	0	£300 (estimate)
Children's University – Social responsibility	0.07	0.39	4*	0	£300 (estimate)
P4C – Communication	0.10	0.33	2*	0	£16
P4C – Co-operation	0.15	0.28	2*	0	£16

PART IV
Conclusions

10

WHAT ARE THE LESSONS FOR THOSE CONCERNED WITH ROBUST EVALUATIONS?

There is an urgent need for decent research in education, and for its users and funders to demand a much higher quality of evaluation. The results of research can have a profound impact on children's future careers, earnings and happiness. Poor-quality studies are not just a waste of money. Many people, including teachers, parents and children invest a lot of their time participating in these studies. Policy-makers make decisions based on their misleading findings. And young people can be harmed by poor work. The quality of research matters to all involved, from commissioning studies to rolling out the results for struggling students. What can we learn from serious attempts to improve the quality of research and its reporting?

Substantive implications

What does not work?

There is now a considerable body of evidence that simply using commercial software or replacing teacher roles with IT/CAL is not effective. There are approaches that have been successful that do involve technology (and some are described elsewhere in this book) but it appears as though each approach works (or not) and may involve technology (or not). Simply having and using interactive boards, tablets, clickers and so on is not sufficient. Our review found 49 studies using IT/CAL that are not otherwise covered elsewhere (Gorard et al. 2016a). The better studies are clearly negative in that they show no benefit (or worse) for learning. There are indeed some studies suggesting that the use of technology instead of teachers is actually harmful.

Literacy programmes like READ180, Project CRISS and Writing Wings have not been shown to work. These have been evaluated more than once and none are convincingly found to be effective.

In addition, the following are probably not worth pursuing if the aim is *solely* to improve attainment – grade retention, setting and streaming, improving attitudes, aspirations or motivation alone, teacher's direct use of evidence, participation in arts, drama or music for improvement elsewhere, and behavioural interventions. If this is agreed, then these issues should not be promoted in literature, courses, resources or initial training for primary teachers. Given the number and range of possible interventions, unsuccessful ones should be avoided.

What is still unclear?

There has been considerable research on the value of teacher pedagogical and content knowledge. The aggregate result is mixed. It is not clear that intervening to make teachers themselves know more about their subject areas, or about theories on how to teach, makes much difference to pupil attainment. This may be because it is hard to alter teaching knowledge in a feasible way in an intervention. Several studies have attempted to enhance teachers' use of research evidence directly. This also does not seem to work, and suggests that evidence-informed teaching needs a conduit that translates the research into something more practical that teachers can use. It is probable that this must be more than access to information, like the Teaching and Learning Toolkit (although that may be considered more suitable for policy-makers and school leaders than class teachers). The current evidence on what works could be built into initial teacher preparation, texts, resources, and lesson plans – these are what need to be evidence-informed.

There are many approaches that offer some promise but either have not been robustly tested at an appropriate scale, or where they have been tested the aggregated results are mixed.

There is currently very little robust work on the impact of emphasising content (or Core) knowledge in teaching primary age children, and overall the current conclusion has to be that it is not known to be effective in terms of attainment in maths and literacy. Emphasising cultural, historical, geographical or other knowledge may have so far unknown intrinsic or long-term benefits however.

The evidence for enhanced immediate formative feedback in the classroom is still relatively, and somewhat surprisingly, weak. It is clearly an approach that 'good' teachers use but it is not so clear that the approach can be easily taught to others for them to use effectively such that it translates into better pupil attainment.

What appears to work?

In terms of the substantive results in this book we have found a range of specific interventions and protocols that have been used successfully with small groups or even individual pupils to help overcome problems in literacy (and to a lesser extent in maths). The evidence for teaching via phonics approaches is not quite as strong as some commentators envisage but the approach is successful – at least for struggling readers. Our trial of Fresh Start phonics adds significant support.

It appears that phonics works for young children who are not readers from an early age. This is not proposed as a whole class intervention, and the existing evidence base is largely about individual or small group teaching. The direct cost is minimal but the approach, as described, does mean having another trained staff member for each class.

The evidence for Switch-on Reading is slightly more secure. It has about the same impact as phonics interventions for the sub-set of pupils who are struggling to read. Again this is not a whole class treatment, but has the advantage over phonics in that the precise formal nature of the protocols for the seemingly related approaches of Reading Recovery and Switch-on Reading can be conducted in or out of class by trained teaching assistants (TAs). If deployed appropriately it is clear that TAs can contribute to class outcomes, and are cheaper than extra trained teachers. As discussed in relation to teachers' use of research evidence, it is this kind of evidence that is most easily digested and used when engineered into a simple observable protocol that appears to work, and which teachers and TAs can follow.

In fact, many of the successful interventions were largely conducted by teaching assistants (TAs). The future funding of TAs in England is unclear, and the evidence so far had been that just having TAs or using them as substitute teachers is rather costly and largely ineffective (Blatchford et al. 2012). Switch-on is an example of one way in which TAs might be deployed in schools to follow a set protocol and make a useful difference to the reading of pupils in transition from primary to secondary. Six other projects funded by the EEF involving TA-led literacy/numeracy interventions reported positive effects on children's learning, and were apparently particularly beneficial for disadvantaged children. These include the Nuffield Early Language Intervention with an effect size of +0.27 (Sibieta et al. 2016), REACH with an ES of +0.33 (Sibieta 2016), Catch Up® Numeracy with an effect of +0.21 (NFER 2014), and Catch Up® Literacy with an ES of +0.12 (Rutt 2015).

The evidence is just as secure for Accelerated Reader, which can be used as a whole class intervention or with individuals and small groups of struggling readers. Again the benefits are relatively small, but the overall evidence including that from the strongest evaluations is that it works, especially for the lowest attainers.

These different approaches to improving literacy may have a similar strength of 'effects' but in somewhat different tests of literacy. For example, a phonics approach will tend to improve word sounding more than fluency, decoding or spelling. There must be a larger number of specific interventions for literacy and other subject areas that could be deployed as evidence-informed, and could be implemented with the help of TAs (but which our reviews have not picked up or which have not been evaluated at scale). And given that the named approaches discussed here all have a similar impact, it is very possible that the precise protocol does not matter as much as might appear.

Indeed there are some indications from other evidence that within limits it is not the precise nature of the protocol that is being effective in any of these approaches. Rather, many coherent approaches to overcoming low attainment based on small group or individual attention or deployment of TAs could be equally effective. This is different to reducing class sizes. Altering class sizes within traditional limits, such as from 30 to 24, is not particularly helpful for raising attainment. The successful interventions of the kind being discussed here involve groups of only one to four pupils, while the same approaches used with whole classes, even small classes, may be only weakly effective or even ineffective. Similarly there is reasonably good evidence that within-class groupings for specific activities and events can be beneficial. The tiered approaches of Response to Intervention are an example, even though our evaluation of it led to insecure results. RTI or similar has been assessed in many subject areas across the primary age range. The effective elements appear to be the Tier 3 (individual or very small group) and Tier 2 (small group) work.

In summary, combining evaluations of specific interventions, more generic tiered teaching, and studies of grouping and individual attention there is a clear message that small is good – for at least some part of the teaching day. If the resources are available, then within-class tiers or groups given suitable tasks would form part of the work of the evidence-informed teacher. It is not our aim to suggest or promote specific commercially available products, and any examples given are only illustrations.

In contrast to an emphasis on subject knowledge and basic skills, it *is* possible to emphasise the reasoning skills of pupils. There is a considerable body of evidence now that such a focus has a small benefit for literacy and numeracy (as well as any possible intrinsic merits). There is also some promise from studies of the linked idea of teaching pupils strategies for meta-cognition (and self-regulation). Both approaches would involve a move away from content knowledge to some extent. Our review found 16 evaluations of which the majority, including all of the most robust studies, show at least small benefits for general attainment. This has to be seen by schools as a promising, cheap and currently evidence-informed way forward. Although several of these interventions involve a change to the layout and structure of classes, most of them are best undertaken in whole class groups with the teacher as facilitator ensuring that all pupils can contribute, while passing considerable control to the pupils themselves.

Of course, we can only provide summary evidence for approaches that have been evaluated and there may be many more that have not. But it is interesting to note a pattern that success in the interventions above comes from taking control away from teachers to some extent – either by giving more autonomy to children as in P4C or by adhering to a strict protocol as with Switch-on Reading. We are not advocating this – merely observing. If it is true that there are more and less successful teachers, then perhaps what our work so far shows is that trying to make the less successful ones behave like the more successful ones is not the way forward. Instead, improvement may be more likely either by passing more control to children as in circle-time philosophical discussions, or by passing control from teachers to an evidence-informed successfully trialled protocol such as in Fresh Start or similar. This is how evidence can most easily inform teaching – at least for primary pupils.

Further lessons for practitioners and teacher trainers

The purpose of educational research is largely to inform policy and practice. A high proportion of education research is either publicly funded or funded by charitable organisations, and therefore it follows that the outputs of such research should be made available to the people who want to consume (and help fund) the outcomes of the research. This not only saves time and money for schools and teachers, but also enhances the professional capacity of teachers for the benefit of learners. We argue that it is the ethical responsibility of academics to make their research output as comprehensible as possible to consumers of research. With the move towards open access in academic publishing, it is our hope that more of the academic papers that are relevant to classroom practice will become readily available for inspection by practitioners and the public. However, this also means that it is even more important for teachers to have access to training and development, in order to judge the quality of evidence and be equipped with the necessary research skills to test such evidence for themselves.

Our studies suggest that, although teachers can engage with research evidence, the process is complex and not necessarily successful in practice. This is partly because academic papers are not generally written for practical application and not meant for practitioners. Such papers do not usually give detailed descriptions of interventions and how they are to be implemented. This is especially true of meta-analyses and syntheses of evidence, which are compilations of many different studies using a variety of measures and involving a range of outcomes for participants of different ages. For practitioners to use such evidence therefore requires more than simply reading the papers. We argue that there needs to be a clear and unbiased conduit from primary evidence to proposed classroom practice (Nelson and O'Beirne 2014). Teachers need relevant resources and examples from the outset, as well as training to use the protocol and strategies associated with the intervention, as in P4C, Accelerated, Fresh Start and Switch-on.

These findings have implications for policy on teacher development. In their response to the Education Select Committee (House of Commons 2012), the UK government expressed the wish to encourage teachers to engage in and with research. There is, therefore, more to be done to support teachers as researchers and reflective practitioners. There was a suggestion in the government response to the House of Commons report on national curriculum reform (House of Commons 2009, paragraph 92) that resources, including a bank of pedagogical evidence, would be built to support and engage teachers in developing pedagogy in the classroom. However, it remains unclear as to what extent teachers have used or contributed to the resources or if the impact of these efforts has been independently and robustly evaluated.

While there is evidence that some teachers in the UK are already using research to inform their practice, what is less clear is whether teachers are able to interpret that research easily, and whether it is possible for teachers to contribute effectively to the knowledge base by undertaking research for themselves. Among the many recommendations in the UK's House of Commons report on national curriculum reform (2008-2009) was the call for the then Department of Children, Schools, and Families (now the Department for Education) to 'divert resources away from the production of guidance to the funding and dissemination of research findings to teachers in the spirit of informing local professional decision-making' (House of Commons 2009, p. 41).

How practitioners can run their own trials

Some commentators believe that teachers, as potential consumers of research, should be given the opportunity and the means not only to engage with the existing evidence, but also to conduct their own research to test the range of programmes they propose using in their classroom. A recent UK inquiry into the role of research in teacher education argued for teachers to be 'equipped to conduct their own research, individually and collectively, to investigate the impact of particular interventions or to explore the positive and negative effects of educational practice' (BERA-RSA 2014, p. 11). A review by the National Foundation for Educational Research (NFER) also argued for more evidence on the relative benefits of practitioner-led investigation.

This book has described interventions where teachers have tried to use research evidence directly to create an intervention. That approach was not successful, either in terms of the process or the impact. We have also described interventions where the evaluation was conducted by the schools and teachers themselves, with advice and guidance, and this was a much more promising approach. There are indications that it is possible for schools and teachers to undertake robustly-designed research that adds to the accumulation of knowledge about the effectiveness of particular approaches. However, in order to be able to carry out well-designed research, there is a need for teachers to be guided on important aspects of research craft, such as attention to bias and other threats to validity.

We were assigned as independent evaluators for the school-led trials. Our roles were to advise the school leads on the process of conducting research, randomisation and testing, and to aggregate the eventual results from all schools. Testing was done via an external company and we were provided with independent access to the results. Thus, one stage of the evaluation that schools never had complete control of was the testing.

Before our school-led trials started, we provided a workshop for each trial, attended by the school and cluster leads (Chapter 7). This step was seen as crucial by all parties. In any future RCTs by schools themselves such a meeting would be required. Schools need to understand that getting the highest quality result is more important than what that result is. Once this is understood, the 'craft' of an RCT becomes easier to explain. The workshop meeting also agreed on the timing of pre-tests, start of intervention, duration, frequency of intervention, ages of pupils and post-tests. Most important was agreement on a date for randomisation. Schools had to compromise from their original plans to some extent to allow greater co-ordination and so make aggregation of the individual school results feasible.

A second meeting was held before the post-testing phase. Here the evaluators learnt how to conduct the test and how to analyse and interpret the results. Again this meeting was useful to all parties, and cleared up a few misunderstandings. A few schools then felt able to calculate their own effect sizes, and as far as it is possible to tell, they did so correctly. Analysing trial results is not difficult.

In these trials the schools allowed the evaluators access to limited background data on each relevant pupil. If, in future, schools run their own trials it is possible to envisage a process whereby schools handle this step and no personal data on identifiable individuals is passed on.

Schools are reasonably good at implementing new packages, and all appeared to follow the programmes in both trials. However, it must be recalled that these schools were self-selected and chose these specific programmes. The situation might be worse if programmes were imposed on less willing schools. Schools were also generally good at monitoring attendance and progress. They produced little else in terms of a formal process evaluation (of the kind conducted by the evaluators). All appeared to believe strongly that the programmes were successful.

School leaders are able to take responsibility for the implementation of intervention in their schools and an evaluation at the same time. Their involvement, added to the fact that randomisation was at an individual level giving all schools a treatment group, meant that attrition was low in both trials. The experience of the evaluators is that the closer a trial is to the schools, with the fewest parties involved, and the lower the level of randomisation, the lower the attrition is. It is likely that randomisation at school level would fail, in a school-led trial, because the control schools would be more prone to dropping out.

In these school-led trials, permission to innovate was easier, no schools and few pupils dropped out after being deemed eligible, and there was no developer pushing the advantages of their product. In terms of managing the intervention school leaders were free to make decisions regarding venues for the intervention, purchasing materials, choice of equipment, timings and class adjustment without any developer's direct involvement.

In addition to the conduct of the trial, the process and training involved builds the capacity of practitioners in reading and critiquing research claims from other evaluations.

If conducting such research was seen as a part of schools' functions then the overall cost of research could go down. It may even be possible to create a range of nationwide ongoing trials with all willing schools contributing to an online database. The cost of robust evaluations could be reduced, making them more feasible across a range of situations. And, perhaps most promisingly, a series of large, ongoing, almost automatic trials could be conducted nationally, similar to those espoused by Goldacre (2012) for medical GP treatments.

On the other hand, it is not certain that schools can be trusted to conduct the randomisation themselves, perhaps because they allow practicalities and concern for some individuals to override the demands of the evaluation. This may be especially so when there is any conflict of interest, such as the involvement of the developer.

School leaders did not always appreciate the importance of some aspects of the evaluation. For example, when pressed they were happy to support the evaluators who were trying to locate and test missing pupils. But they did not do this on their own initiative, and had no real concept of the dangers from attrition (despite discussion of this in the training days).

It was observed that most staff involved became advocates for their programmes increasingly during the trial, and schools had already made arrangements to continue with and expand its use for future years. They did not always have the mental equipoise needed to conduct a fair test.

Lessons for researchers

Conducting reviews

The way in which the evidence from each trial is assessed in this book is not (yet) widely used. But this approach or something like it should be used. It is important to consider the quality of prior work much more carefully than at present in robust reviews of evidence. The approach described in Chapter 4 can fundamentally alter the conclusions drawn from an array of studies, and shows that many well-known reviews or syntheses of evidence have been misleading their readers by not considering issues of quality properly. The focus should be on the effect sizes coupled with issues such as design, scale, attrition, data quality and so on, as summarised in the sieve. It is crucial to consider the design of any study in relation to its research question, and a robust evaluation requires something as powerful as a randomised control trial (or regression discontinuity design). It is also crucial to consider the scale, the method of allocation to groups and its success, the level of missing data (which must be reported scrupulously), the measurement quality, and other threats such as teaching to the test. The NNTD is useful here in summarising several of these aspects along with the 'effect' size. There is certainly no role for significance testing or its hidden forms such as confidence intervals or multi-level modelling (Gorard 2016). Even if they worked as intended and their assumptions were met they address none of the issues above.

Conducting and reporting evaluations

Researchers, who really care about the welfare of the individuals they proclaim to help, should care more about achieving the safest result than in marketing the ideas behind the research like a commercial product. In other words, they should make the whole process of their research transparent in such a way that it can be replicated, and they should report all the results of their research, including the side effects, not just those that show positive effects. This aids reviewers and users of the research. It ought to be taken for granted, but sadly cannot be.

The biggest threat to the security of our trial findings was the high dropout, especially from control schools not providing test data. This is reasonably common, especially in large-scale randomised control trials. For example, in an evaluation of a literacy intervention called Quest, 45% of pupils in the treatment group and 15% in the control group did not take the post-test (Biggart 2015a). This arose due to miscommunication with schools. In addition, close to half of the original schools dropped out after allocation, due to issues with the programme. In another trial of an intervention called Tutoring with Alphie, there was even higher attrition – 70% from the treatment group and 73% from the control (Biggart 2015b). Again, this was partly due to teachers' dissatisfaction with the programme – which should be irrelevant to whether they provide the data necessary for the evaluation.

In our evaluation of the Word and World Reading programme (Gorard et al. 2015c), schools in both the control and treatment groups wrongly thought that since they did not intend to take up the programme after the trial, it was not necessary to post-test the pupils. Apparently, schools discussed this with the developer who agreed for them not to take the post-test. Some schools also routinely excluded pupils with special educational needs from tests. In the example of the Quest programme, schools thought that only pupils directly involved in Quest needed to take the post-test. In our evaluation of Youth United, some schools only tested pupils who opted to participate in the uniformed group even though the purpose of the trial was to compare the outcomes of those who were in the uniformed group with those who were not. And this was despite the schools receiving individually named tests for *all* eligible pupils.

Developers may be experts in their own interventions, but not necessarily experts in conducting evaluations. They also have a clear conflict of interest. Where evaluations have been conducted by developers themselves or commissioned by developers, important aspects of validity were not heeded, such as lack of randomisation of participants, and using volunteers for the programme instead (e.g. Brodsky 1994, Fagan and Iglesias 1999), having no comparison groups (e.g. Fiala and Sheridan 2003, Mobley 2012, McDonald and Fitzroy 2010, McDonald et al. 2006) or high or unreported attrition. The latter is very common. In some studies, how the participants were selected is not even reported. It cannot be assumed that programme developers understand how to conduct trials. Both the developers and those delivering the intervention need to be trained to understand the importance of complete and accurate data. Future evaluations could consider a pre-intervention workshop for schools about the process of evaluation, the importance of complete data, keeping attendance records (for assessing impact of dosage) and commitment to testing. The implications of failure to comply would need to be spelt out. It is, therefore, important for anyone conducting or involved in a trial to care more about the quality, validity and reliability of the findings than what the results are.

Having now completed a large number of evaluations with colleagues, we are in a position to make some informed recommendations to minimise the risk of spoiled trials. Direct communication between evaluators and schools (or other participants) was more efficient than having intermediaries. Information and instructions got passed quickly and acted upon promptly. Where the developer or another party lay between them this communication was more difficult. In the RTI trial with high dropout there were five parties involved: the EEF, the evaluators, the developers (CUREE), AFA3As and the schools. Future studies should have as few parties involved as possible as this additional layer of communication between the evaluators and the schools was not helpful. Our evaluations of the Fresh Start (Gorard et al. 2016c) and Accelerated Reader programmes (Siddiqui et al. 2015) demonstrated that when schools themselves conduct the trial and deliver the intervention, with no involvement of a third party (the programme developer), full and complete data were obtained with little or no attrition. This is also partly because schools received training prior to the trial on the craft of conducting a trial and the importance of data collection, and the implications of attrition were impressed upon them. Mostly, it was because the schools were all committed to the trial.

Such measures not only improve the security of findings, but also prevent unnecessary waste of funders' money and the time and effort put in by everyone concerned – pupils, teachers, staff, developers and evaluators. Any missing data or missing cases potentially bias the results and render the findings less secure. This means that the resources used will be wasted if we cannot draw any meaningful conclusions from the study.

Does theory matter?

Each of the interventions discussed in this book has a plausible theoretical explanation as to why it should work. The summer school, for example, provided additional direct tuition time from selected successful teachers, during the period over the summer when there is traditionally a learning 'loss'. Yet there is no solid evidence that this raised the attainment of the pupils who participated. The literacy software was admired by all those involved. Pupils liked it because they could work at their own pace. Teachers liked it because it freed them, and allowed them the flexibility to work on a one-to-one basis for an extended period with pupils who needed it. School leaders and parents liked it because the regular assessments provided evidence of progress. And yet, the pupils who did not use the software still made more progress. The advocates and observers were wrong.

As noted in the context of a much larger review of evidence, it seems as though having a plausible theoretical explanation does not matter that much when considering what works (Gorard et al. 2011). It may be reassuring, and it may help generate ideas for further research and development, but a theory (in the sense so often used by theorists) is not necessary for this kind of work (Gorard 2004b).

Does 'qualitative' evaluation work?

As explained earlier, all of our trials necessarily involved a process evaluation consisting of observations of the interventions in practice, and interviews with stakeholders, such as school leaders, staff, pupils, parents and developers. In-depth data is useful in understanding what goes on behind the scenes, what teachers and pupils actually do in the classroom, how they use the intervention, and the managerial and leadership support for the programme. All these provide clues as to why a programme may or may not be successful.

However, it is quite common for participants in trials to report that everything is going well even when the impact evaluation shows that the intervention has failed or is harmful (Khan and Gorard 2012). One important lesson from these studies is therefore not about impact itself, but about the conduct of such a trial.

It was remarkable not only that developers were always convinced that their intervention worked, but that generally all other parties were also. Put another way, there was no relationship between the eventual result of the impact evaluation and the views of stakeholders on whether the intervention worked or not. People involved just cannot tell whether something works, and therefore simply asking them is no kind of evaluation at all. Such 'qualitative' (as they are often termed by their advocates) evaluations of impact need to cease. Funders should stop supporting them and practitioners and policy-makers should stop heeding them.

Ethics committees

All of our studies described in this book were conducted in accordance with the British Educational Research Association's professional Code of Practice, and approved by Durham or Birmingham University's Ethics Committees. Schools agreed a memorandum of understanding that included the research, and schools sent opt-out consent letters to all parents. All participants in interviews and observations were informed that participation was voluntary and that they could withdraw consent at any stage. School visits were arranged with prior notice and with the co-operation of the school leads. Since, in many examples, the schools themselves conducted or initiated the research, the intervention was seen as something that the schools were doing anyway as part of normal school activity.

However, we observed again the tendency for ethics committees and regulations to focus on possible harm to participants in any research, and how they try to prevent this with bureaucratic processes of permissions and form-filling. They almost entirely ignore issues concerning the actual quality of any research, and what happens to the results. Much education research is either publicly (taxpayer) funded such as via EEF or IES, or charity funded such as via the Leverhulme or Nuffield Foundations. Where a piece of research turns out to have untrustworthy results (as that term is used throughout this book) that funding has been wasted. At best, this has opportunity costs because the funding could have been used more sensibly, whether on research or some other venture with a public benefit. But the situation is actually much worse than this. Much of the weak and untrustworthy research that is funded, conducted and published has unwarranted impacts in policy and practice. This means that public money is not just being wasted. It is being used to use to cause actual harm in the areas it is meant to improve.

Ethics committees need to be much more aware of, and active in, these issues. The participants in any study are a minority. Research damages or could damage a much larger number of people including those who fund it (all of us) and those subject to changes in education policy and practice (most of us). Conducting a trial in an education setting, such as trying to improve maths outcomes by improving teaching resources in a way that could have happened even if it was not being evaluated, raises few ethical issues for those participating. The complaint that some students will be denied the new approach is irrelevant, unless or until all innovation in schools is prohibited by ethics committees on the absurd ground that it is not being done in all schools at the same time. So, ethics committees need to worry less about regular education evaluations harming participants, and a lot more about the dangers of not doing them, and not doing them well. And about much of the rest of education research that is not contributing to anything, and is, frankly, a pointless waste of time and money.

Conclusion

There have been calls in recent years for evidence-informed policy and practice in the UK and in other developed countries. It is therefore pertinent and necessary that policy advisors and other consumers of research are able to evaluate and judge the quality of research that potentially informs policy and practice. It is hoped that the first part of this book, especially, will help in that regard.

The substantive results in the later part of this book can be added to a growing synthesis of evidence of what works, such as that represented by the Teaching and Learning Toolkit (EEF 2014). Our trials, including the first one ever completed for EEF, show that RCTs are feasible and useful in education. They have demonstrated that the EEF approach of filling in the existing gaps in later phases of the full research cycle (Chapter 2) is possible. The evaluations themselves were inexpensive, since the main cost was that of the intervention itself. The intervention was to happen anyway, as so many school interventions do every year. Therefore, the RCTs are simply 'piggy-backed' on the kind of activity that happens regularly in schools as part of normal routine. They generated no specific ethical or practical difficulties of the kind that those threatened researchers try to claim are intrinsic to rigorous evaluations. This work therefore forms part of the belated response to McIntyre and McIntyre (2000) and others as described in Chapter 2.

REFERENCES

Acharya, A. (2014) Forensic dental age estimation by measuring root dentin translucency area using a new digital technique. *Journal of Forensic Sciences*, 59, 3, 763–768.

Adams, M. and Bruck, M. (1993) Word recognition: The interface of educational policies and scientific research. *Reading and Writing: An Interdisciplinary Journal*, 5, 113–139.

Adeney K. and Carey S. (2011) How to teach the reluctant and terrified to love statistics: The importance of context in teaching quantitative methods in the social sciences. In Payne, G. and Williams, M. (Eds.) *Teaching quantitative methods: Getting the basics right.* London: SAGE, 85–98.

Ajegbo, K., Kiwan, D. and Sharma, S. (2007) *Curriculum review: Diversity and Citizenship.* London: DfES.

Al Otaiba, S., Connor, C., Folsom, J., Greulich, L., Meadows, J. and Li, Z. (2011) Assessment data informed guidance to individualize kindergarten reading instruction: Findings from a cluster randomized control field trial. *Elementary Schooling*, 111, 4, 535–560.

Anand, M. and Narasimha, Y. (2013) Removal of salt and pepper noise from highly corrupted images using mean deviation statistical parameter. *International Journal on Computer Science and Engineering*, 5, 2, 113–119.

Andrews, R., Dan, H., Freeman, A., McGuinn, N., Robinson, A. and Zhu, D. (2005) *The effectiveness of different ICTs in the teaching and learning of English (written composition) 5–16.* Research Evidence in Education Library, London: EPPI-Centre, Social Science Research Unit, Institute of Education, University of London, http://eppi.ioe.ac.uk/cms/Portals/0/PDF%20reviews%20and%20summaries/tda_ict_rv1.pdf?ver=2006-03-03-155323-573

Angrist J. and Lavy, V. (2002) New evidence on classroom computers and pupil learning. *The Economic Journal*, 112, 735–765.

Baenen, N., Bernhole, A. Dulaney, C. and Banks, K. (1997) Reading Recovery: Long-term progress after three cohorts. *Journal of Education for Students Placed at Risk*, 2, 2, 161.

Bai, Y., Mo, D., Zhang, L., Boswell, M., Rozelle, S. (2016) The impact of integrating ICT with teaching: Evidence from a randomized controlled trial in rural schools in China. *Computers and Education*, 96, 1–14.

Bakan, D. (1966) The test of significance in psychological research. *Psychological Bulletin*, 77, 423–437.

Bakker, M., van den Heuvel-Panhuizen, M. and Robitzsch, A. (2015) Effects of playing mathematics computer games on primary school students' multiplicative reasoning ability. *Contemporary Educational Psychology*, 40, 55–71.

Bebell, D. and Pedulla, J. (2015) Quantitative investigation into the impacts of 1:1 iPads on early learners' ELA and math achievement. *Journal of Information Technology Education-Innovations in Practice*, 14, 191–215.

Behaghel, L., Crepon, B., Gurgand, M. and Le Barbanchon, T. (2009) *Sample attrition bias in randomized surveys: A tale of two surveys.* IZA Discussion Paper 4162, http://ftp.iza.org/dp4162.pdf

BELL (2001) *BELL Accelerated Learning Summer Program 2001 evaluation report.* Dorchester, MA.

BELL (2002) *BELL Accelerated Learning Summer Program 2002 national evaluation report.* Dorchester, MA.

BELL (2003) *BELL Accelerated Learning Summer Program: 2003 program outcomes.* Dorchester, MA.

Bennett, R. (2015) *The effect of math in focus: The Singapore Approach on elementary students' mathematics achievement*, PhD Thesis. Union University US, ProQuest Information and Learning.

Benton, T. (2011) *Sticks and stones may break my bones but being left on my own is worse: An analysis of reported bullying at school within NFER attitude surveys.* Slough, UK: National Foundation for Educational Research.

BERA-RSA (2014) *The role of research in teacher education: Reviewing the evidence. Interim report of the BERA-RSA inquiry.* London: British Educational Research Association

Berger, J. and Sellke, T. (1987) Testing a point null hypothesis: The irreconcilability of p values and evidence (with comments). *Journal of the American Statistical Association*, 82, 1, 112–39.

Berk, R. and Freedman, D. (2001) *Statistical assumptions as empirical commitments.* www.stat.berkeley.edu/~census/berk2.pdf

Berkson, J. (1938) Some difficulties of interpretation encountered in the application of the chi-square test. *Journal of the American Statistical Association*, 33, 526–536.

Biggart, A. (2015a) *An evaluation of Quest, a whole-group literacy intervention.* London: Education Endowment Foundation.

Biggart, A. (2015b) *An evaluation of Tutoring with Alphie, a computer literacy-tutoring programme.* London: Education Endowment Foundation.

Birdwell, J, Birnie, R. and Meham, R. (2012) The state of the service nation: Youth social action in the UK. London: DEMOS

Birdwell, J., Scott, R. and Reynolds, R. (2015) *The double benefit of youth social action could help to tackle some of our most social problems: Service Nation 2010.* London: DEMOS

Black, P. (2000) Research and the development of educational assessment. *Oxford Review of Education*, 26, 3/4, 407–419.

Black, P. and Wiliam, D. (1998) *Inside the black box: Raising standards through classroom assessment.* London: GL Assessment.

Blatchford, P., Webster, R. and Russell, A. (2012) *Challenging the role and deployment of teaching assistants in mainstream schools.* Report to the Esmee Fairbairn Foundation.

Blok, H., Oostdam, R., Otter, M., and Overmaat, M. (2002) Computer-assisted instruction in support of beginning reading instruction: A review. *Review of Educational Research*, 72, 1, 101–130.

Boeck, T., Makadia. N., Johnson, C., Cadogan, N., Salim, Hogar, Cushing, J. (2009) *The impact of volunteering on social capital and community cohesion.* Leicester: Youth Action Network.

Booth, C., Shrimpton, H., Candy, D., Di Antonio, E., Hale, C. and Leckey, C. (2015) *National Citizen Service 2014 Evaluation.* Ipsos/MORI, www.ipsos-mori.com/Assets/Docs/Publications/sri-ncs-2014-evaluation.pdf

Boring, E. (1919) Mathematical vs. scientific importance. *Psychological Bulletin*, 16, 335–338.

Borman, G. and Dowling, N. (2006) Longitudinal achievement effects of multiyear summer school: Evidence from the Teach Baltimore randomized field trial. *Educational Evaluation and Policy Analysis*, 28, 1, 25–48.

Borman, G., Benson, J. and Overman, L. (2009) A randomised field trial of the Fast ForWord Language computer-based training program. *Educational Evaluation and Policy Analysis*, 31, 82–106.

Botting, N. and Conti-Ramsden, G. (2000) Social and behavioural difficulties in children with language impairment child language. *Teaching and Therapy*, 16, 105–120.

Bottino, R., Ott, M. and Benigno, V. (2009) Digital mind games: Experience-based reflections on design and interface features supporting the development of reasoning skills. Proceedings of the 3rd European Conference on Games Based Learning, 53–61.

Bradbury, S. and Kay, T. (2005) *Evaluation of the pupil centred stages of phase one of the Step into Sport project.* Loughborough: Institute of Youth Sport.

Braster, S. and Dronkers, J. (2013) *The positive effects of ethnic diversity in class on the educational performance of pupils in a multiethnic European metropole.* London: Centre for Research and Analysis of Migration.

Brighouse, H. (2008) Education for a flourishing life. *Yearbook of the National Society for the Study of Education*, 107, 1, 58–71.

Broadfoot, B. (1985) The impact of educational research. *Research Intelligence*, May 1985, 10–11.

Brodsky, S. (1994) *An urban family math collaborative* (CASE-09094) New York: City University of New York.

Brooks, G. (2003) *Sound Sense: The phonics element of the National Literacy Strategy. A report to the Department for Education and Skills.* DfES website, 20/8/03, www.standards.dfes.gov.uk/pdf/literacy/gbrooks_phonics.pdf

Brooks, G. (2007) *What works for pupils with literacy difficulties? The effectiveness of intervention schemes*, London: DCSF Publications

Brooks, G., Harman, J. and Harman, M. (2003) *Catching up at Key Stage 3: An evaluation of the Ruth Miskin [RML2] pilot project 2002/2003.* A report to the Department for Education and Skills. Sheffield: University of Sheffield.

Brooks, G., Miles, J., Torgerson, C. and Torgerson, D. (2006) Is an intervention using computer software effective in literacy learning? A randomised controlled trial. *Educational Studies*, 32, 2, 133–143.

Brummelman, E., Thomaes, S., Orobio de Castro, B., Overbeek, G. and Bushman, B. (2014) 'That's not just beautiful – that's incredibly beautiful!': The adverse impact of inflated praise on children with low self-esteem. *Psychological Science*, DOI: 10.1177/09567976135114251.

Brunello, G., and Schlotter, M. (2011) Non-cognitive skills and personality traits: Labour market relevance and their development in education and training systems. IZA Discussion paper, http://ftp.iza.org/dp5743.pdf

Brunton-Smith, I., Carpenter, J, Kenward, M. and Tarling, R. (2014) Multiple imputation for handling missing data in social research. *Social Research Update*, 65, Autumn 2014.

Bullock, J. (2005) *Effects of the Accelerated Reader on reading performance of third, fourth, and fifth-grade students in one western Oregon elementary school.* University of Oregon; 0171 Advisor: Gerald Tindal. DAI, 66 (07A), 56–2529.

Caggiano, J. (2007) *Addressing the learning needs of struggling adolescent readers: The impact of a reading intervention program on students in a middle school setting.* Unpublished EdD dissertation. The College of William and Mary (Virginia).

Camilli, G. (1996) Standard errors in educational assessment: a policy analysis perspective, *Education Policy Analysis Archives*, 4, 4.

Campbell, J. (2002) *An evaluation of a pilot intervention involving teaching philosophy to upper primary children in two primary schools, using the Philosophy for Children methodology.* PhD thesis: University of Dundee.

Cantrell, S., Almasi, J., Carter, J., Rintamaa, M. and Madden, A. (2010) The impact of a strategy-based intervention on the comprehension and strategy use of struggling adolescent readers. *Journal of Educational Psychology*, 102, 2, 257–280.

Carneiro, P., Crawford, C. and Goodman, A. (2007) *The impact of early cognitive and non-cognitive skills on later outcomes*, London: Centre for Economics of Education.

Carr, D. (2015) The paradox of gratitude. *British Journal of Educational Studies*, 63, 4, 429–446 10.1080/00071005.2015.1011077.

Carvalho, C., Santos, J., Conboy, J. and Martins, D. (2014) Teachers' feedback: Exploring differences in students' perception. *Procedia - Social and Behavioral Sciences*, 159, 169–173.

Carver, R. (1978) The case against statistical significance testing, *Harvard Educational Review*, 48, 378–399.

Chamberlain, J., Hillier, J. and Signoretta, P. (2015) Counting better? An examination of the impact of quantitative method teaching on statistical anxiety and confidence, *Active Learning in Higher Education*, 16, 1, 51–66.

Chambers, B., Slavin, R., Madden, N., Abrami, P., Karanzalis, M. and Gifford, R. (2011) Small-group computer-assisted tutoring to improve reading outcomes for struggling first and second graders. *Elementary School Journal*, 111, 4, 625–640.

Chanfreau, J., Lloyd, C., Byron, C., Roberts, C., Craig, R., De Feo, D. and McManus, S. (2008) *Predicting wellbeing.* NatCen Social Research, prepared for the UK Department of Health, www.natcen.ac.uk/media/205352/predictors-of-wellbeing.pdf

Chanfreau, J., Tanner. E., Callanan, M., Laing, K., Skipp, A. and Todd, L. (2016) *Out of school activities during primary school and KS2 attainment.* Centre for Longitudinal Studies Working Paper 2016/1, www.nuffieldfoundation.org/sites/default/files/files/CLS%20WP%202016%20(1)%20-%20Out%20of%20school%20activities%20during%20primary%20school%20and%20KS2%20attainment.pdf

Chaplin, D. and Capizzano, J. (2006) *Impacts of a summer learning program: A random assignment study of Building Education Leaders for Life (BELL)*, Washington, DC: The Urban Institute, www.urban.org/UploadedPDF/411350_bell_impacts.pdf

Chatfield, C. (1991) Avoiding statistical pitfalls, Statistical Science, 6, 240–268.

Cheung, A. and Slavin, R. (2012) Effective Reading Programs for Spanish-Dominant English Language Learners (ELLs) in the Elementary Grades: A Synthesis of Research. *Review of Educational Research*, 82(4): 351–395.

Cheung, A. and Slavin, R. (2015) *How methodological features affect effect sizes in Education.* Baltimore, MD: Johns Hopkins University, Center for Research and Reform in Education

Chowdry, H., Crawford, C., Dearden, L., Joyce, R., Sibieta, L., Sylva, K. and Washbrook, E. (2010) Poorer children's educational attainment: How important are attitudes and behaviour? Joseph Rowntree Foundation, www.jrf.org.uk/sites/default/files/jrf/migrated/files/poorer-children-education-full.pdf

Christodoulou, D. (2014) *Seven myths about education.* London: Routledge.

Clark, C. (2013) *Accelerated Reader and young people's reading. Findings from the National Literacy Trust's 2012 annual literacy survey on reading enjoyment, reading behaviour outside class and reading attitudes*. London: National Literacy Trust, www.literacytrust.org.uk/assets/0001/9353/AR_and_young_people_s_reading.pdf

Clark, M., Gleeson, P., Tuttle, C., and Silverberg, M. (2015) Do charter schools improve student attainment? *Educational Evaluation and Policy Analysis*, 37, 4, 419–436.

Clay, M. (1991) *Becoming literate: The construction of inner control*. Auckland: Heinemann.

Clegg, J., Hollis, C. and Rutter, M. (1999) A survey of the nature and extent of bully / victim problems in junior / middle and secondary schools. *Educational Research*, 35, 3–25.

Coe, M., Hanita, M., Nishioka, V., Smiley, R. (2011) *An investigation of the impact of the 6+1 Trait Writing Model on grade 5 student writing achievement: Final report*. Washington DC: National Center for Education Evaluation and Regional Assistance, Institute of Education Sciences, US Department of Education.

Coe, R., Aloisi, C., Higgins, S. and Major, L.E. (2014) *What makes great teaching? Review of the underpinning research*. London: Sutton Trust.

Cohen, J. (1994) The earth is round (p<.05). *American Psychologist*, 49, 12, 997–1003.

Coles, J. (2012) *An evaluation of the teaching assistant led Switch-on literacy intervention*. Unpublished MA thesis, University of London Institute of Education.

Collado, D., Lomos, C. and Nicaise, I. (2014) The effects of classroom socioeconomic composition in student's civic knowledge in Chile. *School Effectiveness and School Improvement*, 26, 3, 415–440.

Colom, R., Moriyón, F., Magro, C. and Morilla, E. (2014) The long-term impact of Philosophy for Children: A longitudinal study (Preliminary Results). *Analytic Teaching and Philosophical Praxis*, 35, 1.

Connolly, P. (2013) *Analysis of randomised contolled trials*. EEF Evaluators Conference, https://www.google.co.uk/url?sa=t&rct=j&q=&esrc=s&source=web&cd=1&cad=rja&uact=8&ved=0ahUKEwjHidTEiMLSAhVrAsAKHSv3B6EQFggkMAA&url=https%3A%2F%2Fv1.educationendowmentfoundation.org.uk%2Fuploads%2Fpdf%2FSession_4_-_analysis_and_reporting.pptx&usg=AFQjCNFxznudstJ7QwZcxKN1FJ034QPqqA&sig2=sgTmPBvnGE06z2F7Alq2WA&bvm=bv.148747831,d.ZGg

Cooper, H., Charlton, K., Valentine, J. and Muhlenbruck, L. (2000) Making the most of summer school: a meta-analytic and narrative review. *Monographs of the Society for Research into Child Development*, 65, 1.

Co-operative StreetGames Young Volunteers (2014) *The Cooperative StreetGames Young Volunteer Programe. Evaluation report for year six: 2012–2013*. London: Street Games.

Core Knowledge (2014) *E.D. Hirsch and cultural literacy*, www.coreknowledge.org.uk/culturalliteracyck.php

Core Knowledge Foundation (2000) In Oklahoma City, a rigorous scientific study shows the positive equity effects of Core Knowledge, www.coreknowledge.org/our-schools/results-research/research-studies/

Coughlan, S. (2013) Gove sets out 'core knowledge' curriculum plans. *BBC News*, 6 February 2013, www.bbc.co.uk/news/education-21346812

Cox D. (1958) *Planning of experiments*. New York: Wiley.

Cox, M., Abbott, C., Webb, M., Blakeley, B., Beauchamp, T. and Rhodes, V. (2003) *ICT and pedagogy: A review of the research literature*, ICT in Schools Research and Evaluation Series 18. Coventry/London: Becta/DfES, https://kclpure.kcl.ac.uk/portal/en/publications/ict-and-pedagogy--a-review-of-the-research-literature--a-report-to-the-dfes-isbn-1844781356(18f80036-ce8c-470e-9573-acc63c4f8979)/export.html

Creemers, B. (1994) *The effective classroom*. London: Cassell.

Cuddeback, G.. Wilson, E., Orme, J. and Combs-Orme, T. (2004) Detecting and statistically correcting sample selection bias. *Journal of Social Service Research*, 30, 3, 19–30.

Cummings, G. (2014) The new statistics: why and how, *Psychological Science*, 25, 1, 7-29.

Cunningham, M., Kerr, K., McEune, R., Smith, P. and Harris, S. (2004) *Laptops for Teachers: An evaluation of the first year of the initiative.* ICT in Schools Research and Evaluation Series 19. Coventry/London: Becta/DfES, www.becta.org.uk/page_documents/research/lft_evaluation.pdf

Daniel, L. (1998) Statistical significance testing: A historical overview of misuse and misinterpretation with implications for the editorial policies of educational journals. *Research in the Schools,* 5, 2, 23–32.

Darling-Hammond, L. (2015) Can value added add value to teacher evaluation? Educational Researcher, 44, 2, 132–137.

Dartnow, A., Borman, G. and Springfield, S. (2000) School reform through a highly specified curriculum: Implementation and effects of the Core Knowledge Sequence. *The Elementary School Journal,* 101, 2, 167–192.

De Corte, E., Verschaffel, L. and Van De Ven, A. (2001) Improving text comprehension strategies in upper primary school children: A design experiment. *British Journal of Educational Psychology,* 71, 4, 531–559.

Decristan, J., Klieme, E., Kunter, M., Hochweber, J., Buttner, G., Fauth, B., Hondrich, A., Rieser, S., Hertel, S. and Hardy, I. (2015) Embedded formative assessment and classroom process quality: How do they interact in promoting science understanding? *American Educational Research Journal,* 52, 6, 1133–1159.

Dee, T. (2014) Social identity and achievement gaps: Evidence from an affirmation intervention. *Journal of Research on Educational Effectiveness,* 8, 2, 149–168.

Deming, W. (1975) On probability as a basis for action. *American Statistician,* 29, 146–152.

DEMOS (2015) *61% of ethnic minority kids in England – and 90% in London – begin Year 1 in schools where ethnic minorities are the majority of the student body,* www.demos.co.uk/press-release/61-of-ethnic-minority-kids-in-england-and-90-in-london-begin-year-1-in-schools-where-ethnic-minorities-are-the-majority-of-the-student-body/

Department for Education (DfE) (2012a) £10 million literacy catch-up programme for disadvantaged pupils. DfE: National Statistics, www.gov.uk/government/news/10-million-literacy-catch-up-programme-for-disadvantaged-pupils

Department for Education (DfE) (2012b) A profile of pupil exclusions in England. Research Report DFE-RR190. London: DfE

Department for Education (DfE) (2013) *Statistical first release: National Curriculum Assessments at Key Stage 2 in England, 2013* (revised). DfE: National Statistics, www.gov.uk/government/uploads/system/uploads/attachment_data/file/ 264987/SFR51_2013_KS2_Text.pdf

Department for Education (DfE) (2015) *Children looked after in England including adoption: 2014 to 2015.* London: DfE, www.gov.uk/government/statistics/children-looked-after-in-england-including-adoption-2014-to-2015

Department for Education (DfE) (2016) *Behaviour and discipline in schools: Advice for headteachers and school staff.* London: DfE.

Department for Education and Employment (DfEE) (2000) *Research into teacher effectiveness: A model of teacher effectiveness.* Research Report 216 by Hay McBer. London: DfEE

Department of Health (2012) *Preventing suicide in England: A cross-government outcomes strategy to save lives,* www.gov.uk/government/uploads/system/uploads/attachment_data/file/430720/Preventing-Suicide-.pdf

Doherr, E. (2000) *The demonstration of cognitive abilities central to cognitive behavioural therapy in young people: Examining the influence of age and teaching method on degree of ability.* PhD thesis: University of East Anglia.

Dolton, P., Lindeboom, M. and Van den Berg, G. (2000) *Survey attrition: A taxonomy and the search for valid instruments to correct for biases,* http://www.fcsm.gov/99papers/berlin.html

Dong, N. and Lipsey, M. (2011) *Biases in estimating treatment effects due to attrition in randomised controlled trials*. SREE Conference, http://eric.ed.gov/?id=ED517992

Duckworth, A. and Scott Yeager, D. (2015) Measurement matters: Assessing personal qualities other than cognitive ability of educational purposes. *Educational Researcher*, 44, 4, 237–251.

Duke of Edinburgh (2010) *The impact of the Duke of Edinburgh's award on young people*. Windsor: Duke of Edinburgh.

Duke, J. (2011) *The Accelerated Reader Program in conjunction with best-practice reading instruction: The effects on elementary-school reading scores*. PhD thesis, Capella University, USA.

Dumville, J., Torgerson, D. and Hewitt, C. (2006) Reporting attrition in randomised controlled trials. *BMJ* 332, 7547, 969–971.

Dyfed County Council (1994) *Improving reading standards in primary schools project*. Dyfed County Council, Wales.

Dynarski, M., Agodini, R., Heaviside, S., Novak, T., Carey, N., Campuzano, L., et al. (2007) *Effectiveness of reading and mathematics software products: Findings from the first pupil cohort* (Publication 2007–4005). Washington, DC: U.S. Department of Education, Institute of Education Sciences, available from http://ies.ed.gov/ncee/pdf/20074005.pdf

Dziura, J., Post, L., Zhao, Q, Fu, Z. and Peduzzi, P. (2013) Strategies for dealing with missing data in clinical trials: From design to analysis. *Yale Journal of Biology and Medicine*, 86, 3, 343–358.

Education Endowment Foundation (2014) *Classification of the security of findings from EEF evaluations*, https://v1.educationendowmentfoundation.org.uk/uploads/pdf/Classifying_the_security_of_EEF_findings_FINAL.pdf

Education Endowment Foundation (2015) *Education Endowment Foundation pupil premium toolkit*, http://educationendowmentfoundation.org.uk/uploads/pdf/Feedback_Toolkit_references.pdf

Egger, M., Schneider, M., Davey Smith, G. (1998) Meta-analysis: Spurious precision?, *BMJ*, 316, 140–144.

Ehri, L., Nunes, S., Stahl, S. and Willows, D. (2001) Systematic phonics instruction helps students learn to read: Evidence from the National Reading Panel's meta-analysis, *Review of Educational Research*, 71, 3, 393–447.

Elamir, E. (2015) New formulae and uses of the mean deviation. *International Journal of Business and Statistical Analysis*, 2, 1, 1–9.

Facemire, N. (2000) *The effect of the accelerated reader on the reading comprehension of third graders*. MA dissertation, Salem-Teikyo University.

Fagan, J. and Iglesias, A. (1999) Father involvement program effects on fathers, father figures, and their head start children: A quasi-experimental study. *Early Childhood Research Quarterly*, 14, 2, 243–269.

Faggella-Luby, M. and Wardwell, M. (2011) RTI in a middle school: Findings and practical implications of a Tier 2 reading comprehension study. *Learning Disability Quarterly*, 34, 1, 35–49.

Fair, F., Haas, L., Gardosik, C., Johnson, D., Price, D. and Leipnik, O. (2015) Socrates in the schools from Scotland to Texas: Replicating a study on the effects of a Philosophy for Children program. *Journal of Philosophy in Schools*, 2, 1, 5–16.

Falie, D. and David, L. (2010) New algorithms of the absolute deviation covariance and correlation, *IEEEXplore*, http://ieeexplore.ieee.org/xpl/tocresult.jsp?reload=true&isnumber=7499908&sortType%3Dasc_p_Sequence%26filter%3DAND(p_Publication_Number%3A97)%26pageNumber%3D43%26rowsPerPage%3D75&pageNumber=43

Falk, R. and Greenbaum, C. (1995) Significance tests die hard: The amazing persistence of a probabilistic misconception. *Theory and Psychology*, 5, 75–98.

Family, Kids and Youth (2015) *Youth social action journey fund evaluation: Report of research results.* London: Youth United.

Farmer, E. and Lutman, E. (2009) Case management and outcomes for neglected children returned to their parents: A five year follow-up study. Report to the Department for Children, Schools and Families. University of Bristol.

Fiala, C. and Sheridan, S. (2003) Parent involvement and reading: Using curriculum-based measurement to assess the effects of paired reading. *Psychology in the Schools*, 40, 6, 613– 626. DOI: 10.1002/pits.10128.

Fidler, F., Thomson, N., Cumming, G., Finch, S. and Leeman, J. (2004) Editors can lead researchers to confidence intervals, but can't make them think: Statistical reform lessons from medicine. *Psychological Science*, 15, 2, 119–126.

Field, A. (2013) *Discovering statistics using IBM SPSS statistics.* 4th Ed. London: Sage.

Filho, D., Paranhos, R., da Rocha, E., Batista, M., da Silva, J., Santos, M. and Marino, J. (2013) *When is statistical significance not significant?*, www.scielo.br/pdf/bpsr/v7n1/02.pdf

Fleming, J., Mitchell, W. and McNally, M. (2014) Can markets make citizens? *Journal of School Choice*, 8, 2, 213–236.

Fogelman, K. (1995) Why is citizenship so important? *Citizenship*, 4, 19–23.

Fountas, I., and Pinnell, G. (2006) Teaching for comprehending and fluency: Thinking, talking and writing about reading, K-8. Portsmouth, NH: Heinenmann.

Freedman, D. (2004) Sampling. In M. Lewis-Beck, A. Bryman and T. Liao (Eds.), *Sage encyclopaedia of social science research methods.* Thousand Oaks, CA: Sage, 987–991.

Fuchs, L. and Fuchs, D. (1986) Effects of Systematic Formative Evaluation: A Meta-Analysis, *Exceptional Children*, 53, 199-208.

Galton M., Gray J. and Ruddock J. (1999) *The impact of school transitions and transfers on pupil progress and attainment.* DfEE Research Report 131. Norwich: HM's Stationery Office.

Galuschka, K., Ise, E., Krick, K. and Schulte-Körne, G. (2014) Effectiveness of treatment approaches for children and adolescents with reading disabilities: A meta-analysis of randomized controlled trials. *PLoS One*, 26, 9. DOI: 10.1371/journal.pone.0089900

Gibbs, B., Shafer, K. and Miles, A. (2015) Inferential statistics and the use of administrative data in US educational research. *International Journal of Research and Method in Education.* DOI: 10.1080/1743727X.2015.1113249

Ginsburg, A. and Smith, M. (2016) *Do randomized controlled trials meet the 'gold standard'?* American Enterprise Institute, www.aei.org/publication/do-randomized-controlled-trials-meet-the-gold-standard/

Girlguiding (2012–2013) *Girlguiding impact report 2012–2013.* London: Youth United.

Glass, G. (2014) Random selection, random assignment and Sir Ronald Fisher. *Psychology of Education Review*, 38, 1, 12–13.

Glass, G. (2016) One hundred years of research: Prudent aspirations. *Educational Researcher*, 45, 2, 69–72.

Glover, A. and Sparks, J. (2009) *The impact of Combined Cadet Force contingents in state secondary schools in Wales.* Newport: University of Wales.

Goldacre, B. (2012) *Bad Pharma.* London: HarperCollins.

Goldacre, B. (2013) *Building evidence into education.* London: Department for Education, www.gov.uk/government/uploads/system/uploads/attachment_data/file/193913/Building_evidence_into_education.pdf

Good, R., Simmons, D., and Smith, S. (1998) Effective academic interventions in the United States: Evaluating and enhancing the acquisition of early reading skills. *School Psychology Review*, 27, 45–56.

Goodman, A. and Gregg, P. (2010) *Poorer children's educational attainment: How important are attitudes and behaviour?* York: Joseph Rowntree Foundation.

Goodman, A., Joshi, H., Nasim, B. and Tyler, C. (2015) Social and emotional skills in childhood and their long-term effects on adult life. *Early Intervention Foundation*, www.eif.org.uk/wp-content/uploads/2015/03/EIF-Strand-1-Report-FINAL1.pdf

Goodman, G. (1999) *The Reading Renaissance/Accelerated Reader Program.* Pinal County school-to-work evaluation report, Tucson, AZ: Creative Research, Inc. (ERIC Document Reproduction Service ED427299).

Goolsbee, A. and Guryan, J. (2005) The impact of internet subsidies for public schools. *Review of Economics and Statistics*, 88, 2, 336–347.

Gorard, S. (2002a) Ethics and equity: Pursuing the perspective of non-participants. *Social Research Update*, 39, 1–4.

Gorard, S. (2003a) Understanding probabilities and re-considering traditional research methods training. *Sociological Research Online*, 8, 1, 12 pages.

Gorard, S. (2003b) *Quantitative methods in social science: The role of numbers made easy.* London: Continuum.

Gorard, S. (2004a) The British Educational Research Association and the future of educational research. *Educational Studies*, 30, 1, 65–76.

Gorard, S. (2004b) Scepticism or clericalism? Theory as a barrier to combining methods. *Journal of Educational Enquiry*, 5, 1, 1–21.

Gorard, S. (2005) Revisiting a 90-year-old debate: The advantages of the mean deviation. *The British Journal of Educational Studies*, 53, 4, 417–430.

Gorard, S. (2006) Towards a judgement-based statistical analysis. *British Journal of Sociology of Education*, 27, 1, 67–80.

Gorard, S. (2009) Misunderstanding and misrepresentation: a reply to Schagen and Hutchison, *International Journal of Research and Method in Education*, 32, 1, 3-12.

Gorard, S. (2010a) Serious doubts about school effectiveness. *British Educational Research Journal*, 36, 5, 735–766.

Gorard, S. (2010b) Measuring is more than assigning numbers. In Walford, G., Tucker, E. and Viswanathan, M. (Eds.), *Sage handbook of measurement.* Los Angeles: Sage, 389–408.

Gorard, S. (2013a) *Research design: Robust approaches for the social sciences.* London: Sage.

Gorard, S. (2013b) The propagation of errors in experimental data analysis: A comparison of pre- and post-test designs. *International Journal of Research and Method in Education*, 36, 4, 372–385.

Gorard, S. (2014) A proposal for judging the trustworthiness of research findings. *Radical Statistics*, 110, 47–60.

Gorard, S. (2015a) Rethinking "quantitative" methods and the development of new researchers. *Review of Education*, 3, 1, 72–96. DOI: 10.1002/rev3.3041

Gorard, S. (2015b) An absolute deviation approach to assessing correlation. *British Journal of Education, Society and Behavioural Sciences*, 5, 1, 73–81.

Gorard, S. (2015c) *Introducing the mean absolute deviation 'effect' size. International Journal Research and Methods in Education*, 38, 2, 105–114.

Gorard, S. (2015d) *A proposal for judging the trustworthiness of research findings.* ResearchED, January 2015, www.workingoutwhatworks.com/en-GB/Magazine/2015/1/Trustworthiness_of_research

Gorard, S. (2016) Damaging real lives through obstinacy: Re-emphasising why significance testing is wrong. *Sociological Research On-line*, 21, 1, www.socresonline.org.uk/21/1/2.html

Gorard, S. and Gorard, J. (2016) What to do instead of significance testing? Calculating the 'number of counterfactual cases needed to disturb a finding'. *International Journal of Social Research Methodology*, http://tandfonline.com/doi/full/10.1080/13645579.2015.1091235

Gorard, S., and See, B. H. (2011) How can we enhance enjoyment of secondary school? The student view. *British Educational Research Journal, 37*, 4, 671–690.

Gorard, S. and Smith, E. (2010) *Equity in Education: an international comparison of pupil perspectives*, London: Palgrave

Gorard, S., See, B. H. and Davies, P. (2011) *Do attitudes and aspirations matter in education? A review of the research evidence.* Saarbrucken: Lambert Academic Publishing.

Gorard, S., Siddiqui, N. and See, B. H. (2015a) An evaluation of the 'Switch-on reading' literacy catch-up programme. *British Educational Research Journal*, 41, 4, 596–612.

Gorard, S., Siddiqui, N. and See, B. H. (2015b) How effective is a summer school for catch-up attainment in English and maths? *International Journal of Educational Research*, 73, 1–11, www.sciencedirect.com/science/article/pii/S0883035515301932

Gorard, S., See, B. H. and Morris, R. (2016a) *Review of effective teaching approaches in primary schools:* Main report of findings. London; DfE.

Gorard, S., Siddiqui, N. and See, B. H. (2016b) An evaluation of Fresh Start as a catch-up intervention: And whether teachers can conduct trials. *Educational Studies*, 42, 1, 98–113.

Gorard, S., See, B. H. and Siddiqui, N. (2016c) *Youth United: Youth social action trial.* Evaluation Report and Executive Summary, EEF.

Gorard, S., Siddiqui, N. and See, B. H. (2016d) Can 'Philosophy for Children' improve primary school attainment. *Journal of Philosophy of Education* (forthcoming).

Gorard, S., Siddiqui, N. and See, B. H. (2017) Can 'Philosophy for Children' improve primary school attainment. *Journal of Philosophy of Education*, http://onlinelibrary.wiley.com/doi/10.1111/1467-9752.12227/abstract.

Gorard, S., with Adnett, N., May, H., Slack, K., Smith, E. and Thomas, L. (2007) *Overcoming barriers to HE.* Stoke-on-Trent: Trentham Books.

Gorard, S., with Taylor, C. (2004) *Combining methods in educational and social research.* London: Open University Press.

Gottfried, M. (2014) Does classmate ability influence students' social skills? *School Effectiveness and School Improvement.* DOI: 10.1080/09243453.2014.988731

Gov.UK (2012) *£10 million to boost literacy*, www.gov.uk/government/news/10-million-to-boost-literacy-for-year-sevens

Graves, A. W., Brandon, R., Duesbery, L. McIntosh, A. and Pyle, N. B. (2011) The effects of tier 2 literacy instruction in sixth grade: Toward the development of a Response-to-Intervention Model in middle school. *Learning Disability Quarterly*, 34, 1, 73–86 (full paper not available, analysis based on abstracts).

Green, C., Taylor, C. and Hean, S. (2016) Beyond synthesis: Augmenting systematic review procedures with practical principles to optimise impact and uptake in educational policy and practice *International Journal of Research and Method in Education*, 39, 3, 329–344.

Greenland, S., Senn, S., Rothman, K., Carlin, J., Poole, C., Goodman, S. and Altman, D. (2016) Statistical tests, p-values, confidence intervals, and power: A guide to misinterpretations. *European Journal of Epidemiology*, 31, 4, 337–350.

Greenwald, A. (1975) Consequences of prejudice against the null hypothesis. *Psychological Bulletin*, 82, 1–20.

Gupta, N. D., and Simonsen, M. (2010) Non-cognitive child outcomes and universal high quality child care. *Journal of Public Economics*, 94, 1, 30–43.

Gutman, L., and Schoon, I. (2013) The impact of non-cognitive skills on outcomes for young people. Education Endowment Foundation, http://educationendowmentfoundation.org.uk/uploads/pdf/Non-cognitive_skills_literature_review.pdf

Gutman, L. and Vorhaus, J. (2012) *The impact of pupil behaviour and wellbeing on educational outcomes.* London: DfE.

Gutman, L. (1985) The illogic of statistical inference for cumulative science. *Applied Stochastic Models and Data Analysis*, 1, 3–10.

Hanley, P., Slavin, R. and Elliott, L. (2015) *Thinking, doing and talking science. Evaluation report and summary*. London: Education Endowment Foundation.

Hansen, M. and Hurwitz, W. (1946) The problem of non-response in sample surveys. *Journal of the American Statistical Association*, 41, 517–529.

Hao, Y., Flowers, H., Monti, M. and Qualters, J. (2012) U.S. census unit population exposures to ambient air pollutants. *International Journal of Health Geographics* 2012, 11, 3. doi:10.1186/1476–072X-11–3

Harris, R, and Ratcliffe, M. (2005) Socio-scientific issues and the quality of exploratory talk – what can be learned from schools involved in a 'collapsed day' project? *The Curriculum Journal*, 16, 4, 439–453.

Hartshorne, M. (2007) *The cost to the nation of children's poor communication: Scotland edition*. London: I CAN.

Harvard Family Research Project (2006) *Evaluation of the BELL (Building Educated Leaders for Life) Accelerated Learning Summer Program*, www.hfrp.org/out-of-school-time/ost-database-bibliography/database/bell-accelerated-learning-summer-program/evaluation-1–2002-national-evaluation-report

Haste, H. (1996) *Understanding voluntary organisations*. London: Penguin.

Hattie, J. (1992) What works in Special Education. Presentation to the Special Education Conference, May 1992, www.education.auckland.ac.nz/webdav/site/education/shared/hattie/docs/special-education.pdf

Hattie, J. and Timperley, H. (2007) The power of feedback. *Review of Educational Research*, 77, 1, 81–112.

Heckman, J., and Rubinstein, Y. (2001) The importance of non-cognitive skills: Lessons from the GED testing program. *American Economic Review*, 91, 2, 145–149.

Hedayati, M. and Ghaedi, Y. (2009) Effects of the Philosophy for Children Program through the Community of Inquiry method on the improvement of interpersonal relationship skills in primary school students. *Childhood & Philosophy*, 5, 9, 199–217.

Higgins, S. (2015) A recent history of teaching thinking, in Wegerif, R., Li, L. and Kaufman, J. C. (Eds.) *The Routledge international handbook of research on teaching thinking*. New York: Routledge, 19–28.

Hill, M., Stafford, A., Seaman, P., Ross, N. and Daniel, B. (2007) *Parenting and resilience*. York: Joseph Rowntree Foundation.

Hillage, J., Pearson, R., Anderson, A. and Tamkin, P. (1998) *Excellence on research in schools*. Sudbury: DfEE.

Hirsch, D. (2007) *Chicken and egg: child poverty and educational inequalities*. London: Campaign to End Child Poverty, www.endchildpoverty.org.uk/index.html

Hirsch, E. (1987) *Cultural literacy: What every American needs to know*. Boston: Houghton Mifflin.

Hižak J. and Logožar R. (2011) A derivation of the mean absolute distance in one-dimensional random walk. *Technical Journal*, 5, 1, 10–16.

Ho, LS, and Ip, P. (2016) What accounts for the decline of happiness of children as they grow into their teens: A Hong Kong case study. *Pacific Economic Review*. doi: 10.1111/1468–0106.12145

Hoenig, J. and Heisey, D. (2001) The abuse of power. *The American Statistician*, 55, 1, 19–24.

Holliman, A. J. and Hurry, J. (2013) The effects of Reading Recovery on children's literacy progress and special educational needs status: a three-year follow-up study. *Educational Psychology* 33, 6, 719-733.

Hopfenbeck, T. and Stobart, G. (2015) Large scale implementation of assessment for learning. *Assessment in Education*, 22, 1, 1–2.

Horsfall, S. and Santa, C. (1994) *Project CRISS: Validation report for the program effectiveness panel.* Unpublished manuscript. In WWC (2010) *Project CRISS® (CReating Independence through Student-owned Strategies)* What Works Clearinghouse Intervention Report. Washington, DC: US Department of Education, Institute of Education Sciences

Hoskins, B., Janmaat, J., Han, C. and Muijs, D. (2014) Inequalities in the education system and the reproduction of socioeconomic disparities in voting in England, Denmark and Germany. *Compare*, 44, 5, 801–825. doi: 10.1080/03057925.2014.912796

House of Commons (2009) *National Curriculum: Fourth report of session 2008–2009*, London: The Stationery Office Limited.

House of Commons (2012) *Great teachers: Attracting, training and retaining the best. Government response to the committee's ninth report of session 2010–2012. First special report of session 2012–2013.* London: The Stationery Office Limited.

House of Commons Education and Skills Committee (2005) *Teaching children to read: Eighth report of session 2004–05*, www.publications.parliament.uk/pa/cm200405/cmselect/cmeduski/121/121.pdf

Hubbard, R. and Meyer, C. (2013) The rise of statistical significance testing in public administration research and why this is a mistake. *Journal of Business and Behavioral Sciences*, 25, 1.

Humphrey, N., Lendrum, A. and Wigelsworth, M. (2010) Social and emotional aspects of learning (SEAL) programme in secondary schools: National evaluation. London: DfE.

Hunter, J. (1997) Needed: A ban on the significance test. *Psychological Science*, 8, 1, 3–7.

Hyland, T. (2015) The limits of mindfulness. *British Journal of Educational Studies, early view.* doi:10.1080/00071005.2015–1051946

Institute of Education Sciences (IES) (2008) *What Works Clearing House Intervention Report: Accelerated Reader.* Washington, DC: US Department of Education.

Institute for the Advancement of Philosophy for Children (IAPC) (2002) IAPC research: experimentation and qualitative information, in Trickey, S. and Topping, K. J. (2004) *Philosophy for children: a systematic review, Research Papers in Education*, 19, 3, 365-380.

Interactive Inc. (2002) *An efficacy study of READ 180, a print and electronic adaptive intervention program: Grades 4 and above.* New York, NY: Scholastic Inc. Evaluated in WWC (2009) *READ 180.* What Works Clearinghouse Intervention Report. Washington, DC: US Department of Education, Institute of Education Sciences.

Ioannidis, J. (2005) Why most published research findings are false. *PLoS Med*, 2, 8, e124, www.ncbi.nlm.nih.gov/pmc/articles/PMC1182327/

Iverson, S. and Tunmer, W. (1993) Phonological processing skills and the Reading Recovery program. *Journal of Educational Psychology*, 85, 1, 112–126.

James-Burdumy, S., Mansfield, W., Deke, J., Carey, N., Lugo-Gil, J., Hershey, A., Douglas, A., Gersten, R., Newman-Gouchar, R., Dimino, J. and Faddis, B. (2009) *Effectiveness of selected supplemental reading comprehension interventions: impacts on a first cohort of fifth-grade students* (NCEE 2009–4032). Washington, DC: National Center for Educational Evaluation and Regional Assistance, Institute of Education Sciences, U.S. Department of Education.

Jeffreys, H. (1937) *Theory of probability.* Oxford: Oxford University Press.

Jimenez, J. E., Rodriguez, C., Crespo, P., Gonzalez, D., Artiles, C. and Alfonso, M. (2010) Implementation of Response to Intervention (RtI) Model in Spain: An example of a collaboration between Canarian universities and the department of education of the Canary Islands. *Psicothema*, 22, 4, 935–942.

Johnson, M., Lipscomb, S. and Gill, B. (2014) Sensitivity of teacher value-added estimates to student and peer control variables. *Journal of Research on Educational Effectiveness*, 8, 1, 60–83. doi: 10.1080/19345747.2014.967898

Johnson, R. and Howard, C. (2003) The effects of the Accelerated Reader program on the reading comprehension of pupils in grades 3, 4, and 5. *The Reading Matrix*, 3, 3, 87–96.

Johnston, R. and Watson, J. (2004) Accelerating the development of reading, spelling and phonemic awareness skills in initial readers. *Reading and Writing: An Interdisciplinary Journal*, 17, 4, 327–357.

Johnston, R., McGeown, S., and Watson, J. (2012) Long-term effects of synthetic versus analytic phonics teaching on the reading and spelling ability of 10-year-old boys and girls, *Reading and Writing*, 25, 6, 1365–1384.

Jonsson, A., Lundahl, C., and Holmgren, A. (2015) Evaluating a large-scale implementation of Assessment for Learning in Sweden. *Assessment in Education*, 22, 1, 104–121.

Kelly, P., Gomez-Bellenge, F-X and Chen, J. (2008) Learner outcomes for English language learner low readers in an early intervention. *Tesol Quarterly*, 42, 2, 235–260.

Kerins, M., Trotter, D. and Schoenbrodt, L. (2010) Effects of a Tier 2 intervention on literacy measures: Lessons learned. *Child Language Teaching and Therapy*, 26, 3, 287–302.

Kern, H. Stuart, A., Hill, J. and Green, D. (2016) Assessing methods for generalizing experimental impact estimates to target populations *Journal of Research on Educational Effectiveness*, 9, 1, 103–127.

Khan, M. and Gorard, S. (2012) A randomised controlled trial of the use of a piece of commercial software for the acquisition of reading skills. *Educational Review*, 64, 1, 21–36.

Kim, J. (2006) Effects of a voluntary summer reading intervention on reading achievement: Results from a randomized field trial, *Educational Evaluation and Policy Analysis*, 28, 4, 335–355.

Kim, J., Samson, J. Fitzgerald, R. and Hartry, A. (2010) A randomized experiment of a mixed-methods literacy intervention for struggling readers in grades 4–6: Effects on word reading efficiency, reading comprehension and vocabulary, and oral reading fluency. *Reading and Writing: An Interdisciplinary Journal*, 23, 9, 1109–1129.

King, B., and Kasim, A. (2015) *Evaluation of Rapid Phonics*. London: Education Endowment Foundation, https://educationendowmentfoundation.org.uk/our-work/projects/rapid-phonics/

Kirkman, E., Sanders, M. and Emanuel, N. (2015) Evaluating Youth Social Action: An interim report. London: Behavioural Insights Team.

Kirkman, E., Sanders, M., Emanuel, N. and Larkin, C. (2016) Does participating in social action boost the skills young people need to succeed in adult life? Evaluating Youth Social Action: Final report. London: Behavioural Insights Team.

Kline, R. (2004) *Beyond significance testing: Reforming data analysis methods in behavioral research*. Washington, DC: American Psychological Association.

Kluger, A. and DeNisi, A. (1996) The effects of feedback interventions on performance: A historical review, a meta-analysis, and a preliminary feedback intervention theory. *Psychological Bulletin*, 119, 2, 254–284.

Knox, E. and Conti-Ramsden, G. (2003) Bullying risks of 11-year-old children with Specific Language Impairment (SLI): Does school placement matter? *International Journal of Language and Communication Disorders* Vol. 38.

Krashen, S. (2007) Accelerated Reader: Once again, evidence still lacking. *Knowledge Quest* 36, 1, September/October.,

Kuhberger, A., Fritz, A. and Schemdl, T. (2014) Publication bias in psychology. *PLOSone*. doi: 10.137/journal.pome.0105825

Lanes, D., Perkins, D., Whatmuff, T., Tarokh, H. and Vincent, R. (2005) *A survey of Leicester City Schools using the RML1 and RML2 literacy programme*. Leicester: Leicester City LEA (mimeograph).

Lang, L., Schoen, R., LaVenia, M., Oberlin, M. (2014) Mathematics Formative Assessment System—Common Core State Standards: A randomized field trial in kindergarten and first grade. Society for Research on Educational Effectiveness. SREE Spring Conference, 6–8 March 2014, Washington DC, http://files.eric.ed.gov/fulltext/ED562773.pdf

Larrain, A., Howe, C., and Cerda, J. (2014) Argumentation in whole-class teaching and science learning. *Psykhe: Revista de la Escuela de Psicología*, 23, 2, 1–15.

Le Fanu J. (1999) *The rise and fall of modern medicine*, New York: Little, Brown.

Lecoutre, B. and Poitevineau, J. (2011) *The significance test controversy and the Bayesian alternative*, www.encyclopediaofmath.org/index.php/The_significance_test_controversy_and_the_bayesian_alternative

Lei, J., and Zhao, Y. (2005) Technology uses and pupil achievement: A longitudinal study. *Computers and Education*, 49, 284–296.

Leroux, A., Vaughn, S., Roberts, G., and Fletcher, J. (2011) Findings from a three-year treatment within a response to intervention framework for students in grades 6 with reading difficulties. Paper presented at the Society for Research on Educational Effectiveness Conference, www.eric.ed.gov/PDFS/ED518866.pdf

Lester, L. and Cross, D. (2015) The relationship between school climate and mental and emotional wellbeing over the transition from primary to secondary school. *Psychology of Well-being*, 51, 1, 9–20.

Li, Q. and Ma, X. (2010) A meta-analysis of the effects of computer technology on school students' mathematics learning. *Educational Psychology Review*, 22, 215–243.

Li, Y. and Arce, G. (2004) A maximum likelihood approach to least absolute deviation regression. *EURASIP Journal on Applied Signal Processing*, 12, 1762–1769.

Lindner, J., Murphy, T. and Briers, G. (2001) Handling non-response in social science research. *Journal of Agricultural Education*, 42, 3, 43–53.

Lipko-Speed, A., Dunlosky, J. and Rawson, K. (2014) Does testing with feedback help grade-school children learn key concepts in science?, *Journal of Applied Research in Memory and Cognition*, 3, 3, 171–176.

Lipsey, M., Puzio, K., Yun, C., Hebert, M., Steinka-Fry, K., Cole, M., Roberts, M., Anthony, K. and Busick, M. (2012) *Translating the statistical representation of the effects of education interventions into more readily interpretable forms*. Washington DC: Institute of Education Sciences.

Loftus, G. (1991) On the tyranny of hypothesis testing in the social sciences. *Contemporary Psychology*, 36, 102–105.

Lysakowski, R., and Walberg, H. (1982) Instructional effects of cues, participation, and corrective feedback: A quantitative synthesis. *American Educational Research Journal*, 19, 559–578.

MacBeath, J. (2012) *Evaluation of the Children University: First report*. Cambridge: University of Cambridge.

MacBeath, J. and Waterhouse, J. (2008) *Evaluation of the Children University: First report*. Cambridge: University of Cambridge.

Malmberg, L. and Flouri, E. (2011) The comparison and interdependence of maternal and paternal influences on young children's behavior and resilience. *Journal of Clinical Child and Adolescent Psychology*, 40, 3, 434–444.

Manning, N. and Edwards, K. (2014) Does civic participation for young people increase political participation? A systematic review. *Educational Review*, 66, 1, 22–45.

Marks, G. (2015a) Are school-SES effects statistical artefacts? *Oxford Review of Education*, 41, 1, 122–144. doi: 10.1080/03054985.2015.1006613

Marks, G. (2015b) The size, stability and consistency of school effects. *School Dffectiveness and School Improvement*, 26, 3, 397–414.

Marting, K., Sharp, C. and Mehta, P. (2013) *The impact of the summer schools programme on pupils.* Report to National Foundation for Educational Research, https://educationendowmentfoundation.org.uk/uploads/pdf/EEF_Evaluation_Report_-_Summer_Active_Reading_Programme_-_October_2014.pdf

Mathis, D. (1996) *The effect of the Accelerated Reader Program on reading comprehension.* US Department of Education, http://files.eric.ed.gov/fulltext/ED398555.pdf

Matsudaira, J. (2008) Mandatory summer school and student achievement. *Journal of Econometrics*, 142, 2, 829–850.

Matthews, R. (2001) Methods for assessing the credibility of clinical trial outcomes. *Drug Information Journal*, 35, 1469–1478.

Maxwell, B., Connolly, P., Demack, S., O'Hare, L., Stevens, A., and Clague, L. (2014) *Summer active reading programme: Evaluation report and executive.* London: Educational Endowment Foundation.

May, H., Gray, A., Gillespie, J., Sirinides, P., Sam, C., Goldsworthy, H., Armijo, M. and Tognatta, N. (2013) *Evaluation of the i3 scale-up of Reading Recovery.* University of Delaware.

May, H., Gray, A., Sirinides, P., Goldsworthy, H., Armijo, M., Sam, C. Gillespie, J. and Tognatta, N. (2015) Year one results from the multisite randomized evaluation of the i3 scale-up of Reading Recovery. *American Educational Research Journal*, 52, 3, 547–581.

McArthur, G., Eve, P., Jones, K., Banales, E., Kohnen, S., Anandakumar, T., Larsen, L., Marinus, E., Wang, H. C. and Castles, A. (2012) Phonics training for English-speaking poor readers. *Cochrane Database of Systematic Reviews*, 12. doi: 10.1002/14651858.CD009115.pub2

McDonald L. and Fitzroy, S. (2010) *Families and Schools Together (FAST): Aggregate FASTUK evaluation report of 15 schools in 15 local education authorities (LEAs) across the UK.* London: Middlesex University.

McDonald, L., Moberg, D.P., Brown, R., Rodriguez-Espiricueta I., Flores, N.I., Burke, M.P. and Coover, G. (2006) After-School Multi-Family groups: A randomised controlled trial involving low-income, urban, Latino children. *Children and Schools*, 28, 1, 25–34.

McIntyre, D. and McIntyre, A. (2000) *Capacity for research into teaching and learning.* Swindon: Report to the ESRC Teaching and Learning Research Programme.

Meehl, P. (1967) Theory - testing in psychology and physics: A methodological paradox. *Philosophy of Science*, 34, 103–115.

Meir, S. and McCann, J. (2016) An evaluation of P4C, in Anderson, B. (ed) *Philosophy for Children: Theories and praxis in teacher education.* Oxon: Routledge.

Mercer, N., Wegerif, R. and Dawes, L. (1999) Children's talk and the development of reasoning in the classroom. *British Educational Research Journal*, 25, 1, 95–111.

Merrell, C., and Kasim, A. (2015) *Evaluation of Butterfly Phonics.* London: Education Endowment Foundation, www.realaction.org.uk/wp-content/uploads/2014/07/Butterfly_Phonics_Final-EEF-report.pdf

Meyer, B., Wijekumar, K., Middlemiss, W., Higley, K., Lei, P.W., Meier, C. and Spielvogel, J. (2010) Web-based tutoring of the structure strategy with or without elaborated feedback or choice for fifth- and seventh-grade readers. *Reading Research Quarterly*, 45, 1, 62–92.

Mitra, S. (2012) *Beyond the hole in the wall.* London: TED Books.

Mobley, J. (2012) The impact of home-school collaboration on student achievement in K-5 reading and math. EdD thesis, Walden University.

Moon, G., Twigg, L. and Horwood, J. (2010) The societal impact of cadet forces. A report prepared for the Council for Reserved Forces' and Cadets' Associations. London: The Council of RFCA.

Morgan, R. (2008) *Children on bullying: A report by the Children's Rights Director of England.* London: OFSTED.

Moriyón, F. and Tudela, E. (2004) What we know about research in philosophy with children, https://philoenfant.org/2015/10/30/resume-de-103-recherches-en-philosophie-pour-les-enfants/ June 25 2016

Morrison, D. and Henkel, R. (1969) Significance tests reconsidered. *American Sociologist,* 4, 131–140.

Moss, G. (2013) Research, policy and knowledge flows in education: What counts in knowledge mobilization? *Contemporary Social Science,* 8, 3, 237–248. doi: 10.1080.21582041. 2013.767466

Murtonen, M. and Lehtinen, E. (2003) Difficulties experienced by education and sociology students in quantitative methods courses. *Studies in Higher Education,* 28, 2, 171–185

Nash, R. (2004) Science as a theoretical practice: A response to Gorard from a sceptical cleric. *Journal of Educational Enquiry,* 5, 2, 1–18.

National Educational Research Policy and Priorities Board (2000) *Second policy statement with recommendations on research in education.* Washington DC: NERPP.

National Foundation for Educational Research (NFER) (2014) *Catch Up Numeracy. Evaluation report and executive summary.* London: EEF.

National Research Council (1999) *Improving student learning: A strategic plan for educational research and its utilization.* Washington DC: National Academy Press.

National Science Foundation (2002) *Scientific research in education.* Washington DC: National Academy Press.

Nelson, J. and O'Beirne, C. (2014) *Using evidence in the classroom: What works and why?* Upton Park, Slough: National Foundation for Educational Research.

Nester, M. (1996) An applied statistician's creed. *Applied Statistics,* 45, 4, 401–410.

Nichols, J. (2013) *Accelerated Reader and its effect on fifth-grade students' reading comprehension.* Doctoral dissertation, Liberty University.

Nickerson, R. (2000) Null hypothesis significance testing: A review of an old and continuing controversy. *Psychological Methods,* 5, 2, 241–301.

Nix, T. and Barnette, J. (1998) The data analysis dilemma: Ban or abandon. A Review of null hypothesis significance testing. *Research in the Schools,* 5, 2, 3–14.

NYC Core Knowledge Early Literacy Pilot (2012) K-Grade 2 Results, www.coreknowledge. org/mimik/mimik_uploads/documents/712/CK%20Early%20Literacy%20Pilot%20 3%2012%2012.pdf

Oakes, M. (1986) *Statistical inference: A commentary for the social and behavioural sciences.* Chichester: Wiley

O'Brien, S. (2014) 'Graceful failure': The privatization of resilience. *International Studies in Sociology of Education,* 24, 3, 260–273.

Ockenden, N. and Stuart, J. (2014) Review of evidence on the outcomes of youth volunteering, social action and leadership. Institute of Volunteering Research. London: NCVO.

OFSTED (2004) *ICT in schools: The impact of government initiatives.* School Portraits Eggbuckland Community College. London: Ofsted, http://217.35.77.12/archive/england/papers/education/pdfs/3652.pdf

OFSTED (2015) School inspection handbook Handbook for inspecting schools in England under section 5 of the Education Act 2005, www.gov.uk/government/publications/school-inspection-handbook-from-september-2015

Olsson, C., McGee, R., Nada-Raja, S. and Williams, S. (2013) A 32-year longitudinal study of child and adolescent pathways to well-being in adulthood. *Journal of Happiness Studies*, 14, 3, 1069–1083.

Pampaka, M., Hutcheson, G. and Williams, J. (2016) Handling missing data. *International Journal of Research and Method in Education*, 39, 1, 19–37.

Parr, A. and Bonitz, V. (2015) Role of family background, student behaviors, and school-_ related beliefs in predicting high school dropout. *The Journal of Educational Research*, 108, 6, 504–514.

Patalay, P., Fink, E., Fonagy, P. and Deighton, J. (2016) Unpacking the associations between heterogeneous externalising symptom development and academic attainment in middle childhood. *European Child and Adolescent Psychiatry*, 25, 5, 493–500.

Paufler, N. and Amrein-Beardsley, A. (2014) The random assignment of students into elementary classrooms. *American Educational Research Journal*, 51, 2, 328–362.

Paul, T., VanderZee, D., Rue, T. and Swanson, S. (1996) Impact of the Accelerated Reader technology-based literacy program on overall academic achievement and school attendance. Paper presented at the National Reading Research Centre Conference on Literacy and Technology for the 21st Century, Atlanta, GA, October 4, 1996.

Pavonetti, L., Brimmer, K. and Cipielewski, J. (2000) Accelerated Reader [R]: What are the lasting effects on the reading habits of middle school students exposed to Accelerated Reader [R] in elementary grades? Paper presented at the Annual Meeting of the National Reading Conference, Scottsdale, AZ, November 29–December 2, 2000.

Peak, J. and Dewalt, M. (1994) Reading achievement: Effects of computerized reading management and enrichment. *ERS Spectrum*, 12(1), 31–34.

Pearl, J. (2014) Causes of effects and effects of causes. *Sociological Methods and Research*, 44, 1, 149–164.

Pelgrum, W. (2001) Obstacles to the integration of ICT in education: Results from a worldwide educational assessment, *Computers and Education*, 37, 163–178.

Peress, M. (2010) Correcting for survey nonresponse using variable response propensity. *Journal of the American Statistical Association*, www.rochester.edu/College/faculty/mperess/Nonresponse.pdf

Phelan, J., Choi, K., Vendlinkski, T., Baker, E. and Herman, J. (2011) Differential improvement in student understanding of mathematical principles following formative assessment intervention. *Journal of Educational Research*, 104, 5, 330–339.

Pigott, T., Valentince, J., Polanin, J., Williams, R. and Canada, D. (2013) Outcome-reporting bias in education research. *Educational Researcher*, 42, 8, 424–432.

Pikulski, J. and Chard, D. (2005) Fluency: Bridge between decoding and comprehension, *The Reading Teacher*, 58, 6, 510–519.

Pinnell, G., DeFord, D. and Lyons, C. (1988) *Reading Recovery: Early intervention for at-risk first graders*. Educational Research Service Monograph. Arlington, VA: Educational Research Service.

Pinnell, G., Lyons, C., DeFord, D., Bryk, A. and Seltzer, M. (1994) Comparing instructional models for the literacy education of high risk first graders. *Reading Research Quarterly*, 29, 1, 8–39.

Piper, B. and Korda, M. (2011) Early Grade Reading Assessment (EGRA) Plus: Liberia. Program Evaluation Report, RTI International.

Pittard, V, Bannister, P and Dunn, J (2003) *The big pICTure: The impact of ICT on attainment, motivation and learning*. London: DfES, http://webarchive.nationalarchives.gov.uk/20130401151715/http://www.education.gov.uk/publications/eOrderingDownload/DfES%200796%20200MIG2507.pdf

Platt, J. (2012) Making them count: How effective has official encouragement of quantitative methods been in British sociology? *Current Sociology*, 60, 5, 690–704.

Powney, M., Williamson, P., Kirkham, J. and Kolamunnage-Dona, R. (2014) A review of the handling of missing longitudinal outcome data in clinical trials. *Trials*, 15, 237. doi: 10.1186/1745–6215-15–237.

Puma, M., Tarkow, A. and Puma, A. (2007) *The challenge of improving children's writingability: A randomised evaluation of Writing Wings.* Washington DC: Institute of Education Sciences, US Department of Education.

Quintelier, E. and Hooghe, M. (2013) The relationship between political participation intentions of adolescents and a participatory democratic climate at school in 25 countries. *Oxford Review of Education.* doi: 10.1080/03054985.2013.830097.

Rahilly, T. and Hendry, E. (2014) *Promoting the wellbeing of children in care.* London: NSPCC.

Raudenbush, S. (2015) Value-added: A case study of the mismatch between education research and policy. *Educational Researcher*, 44, 2, 138–141.

Rees, G., Pople, L. and Goswami, H. (2011) Understanding children's well-being. Links between family economic factors and children's subjective well-being: Initial findings from Wave 2 and Wave 3 quarterly surveys. London: The Children's Society.

Reznitskaya, A., Glina, M., Carolan, B., Michaud, O., Rogers, J. and Sequeria, L. (2012) Examining transfer effects from dialogic discussions to new tasks and contexts. *Contemporary Educational Psychology*, 37, 4, 288–306.

Roksa, J., Trolian, T., Pascarella, E., Kilgo, C., Blaich, C. and Wise, K. (2017) Racial inequality in critical thinking skills: The role of academic and diversity experiences. *Research in Higher Education*, 58, 2, 117–140.

Rosas, R., Nussbaum, M., Cumsille, P., Marianov, V., Correa, M., Flores, P., Grau, V., Lagos, F., Lopez, X., Lopez, V., Rodriguez, P. and Salinas, M. (2003) Beyond Nintendo: Design and assessment of educational video games for first and second grade students. *Computers and Education*, 40, 1, 71–94.

Rose J. (2006) *Independent review of the Teaching of Early Reading.* London: DFES, http://www .literacytrust.org.uk/assets/0000/1175/Rose_Review.pdf

Rose, D. and Dalton, B. (2002) Using technology to individualize reading instruction. In C. Block, L. Gambrell and M. Pressley (Eds.), *Improving comprehension instruction: Rethinking research, theory, and classroom practice.* San Francisco: Jossey Bass Publishers, 257–274.

Rosenberg, M. (1965) *Society and the adolescent self-image.* Princeton, NJ: Princeton.

Rosenthal, R. (1979) The 'file drawer problem' and tolerance for null results. *Psychological Bulletin*, 86, 638–641.

Ross, S., Nunnery, J. and Goldfeder, E. (2004) A randomized experiment on the effects of Accelerated Reader/Reading Renaissance in an urban school district: Preliminary evaluation report. Memphis, TN: The University of Memphis, Centre for Research in Educational Policy.

Rouse, C., and Krueger, A. (2004) Putting computerized instruction to the test: A randomised evaluation of a 'scientifically-based' reading program. *Economics of Education Review*, 23, 323–338.

Rozeboom, W. (1960) The fallacy of the null hypothesis significance test. *Psychological Bulletin*, 57, 416–428.

Rudd, P. and Wade, P. (2006) *Evaluation of renaissance learning mathematics and reading programs in UK specialist and feeder schools* (Final Report). Slough, UK: National Foundation for Educational Research, www.nfer.ac.uk/publications/SRY01/SRY01_home.cfm

Rutt, S. (2015) *Catch Up® Literacy. Evaluation report and executive summary.* London: EEF.

Sainsbury, M., Whetton, C., Keith, M. and Schagen, I. (1998) Fallback in attainment on transfer at age 11: evidence from the Summer Literacy Schools evaluation. *Educational Research*, 40, 1, 73–81.

Sari, S., Roslan, H. and Shimamura, T. (2012) Noise estimation by utilizing mean deviation of smooth region in noisy image. Fourth International Conference on Computational Intelligence, Modelling and Simulation, http://eprints.uthm.edu.my/3265/1/487 1a232.pdf.

Sasseville, M. (1994) Self-esteem, logical skills and philosophy for children. *Thinking*, 4, 2, 30–32.

Schacter, J. and Jo, B. (2005) Learning when school is not in session: A reading summer day-camp intervention to improve the achievement of exiting first-grade students who are economically disadvantaged. *Journal of Research in Reading*, 28, 2, 158–169.

Scheerens, J. (1992) *Effective schooling: Research, theory and practice*. London: Cassell.

Scheerens, J. (1999) School effectiveness in developed and developing countries: A review of the research evidence. web.worldbank.org/archive/website00237/WEB/DOC/JAAP699.DOC

Schmidt, F. (1996) Statistical significance testing and cumulative knowledge in psychology: Implications for training of researchers. *Psychological Methods*, 1, 115–129.

Schmidt, F. and Hunter, J. (1997) Eight common but false objections to the discontinuation of significance testing in the analysis of research data. In L. A. Harlow, S. A. Mulaik, and J. H. Steiger (Eds.), *What if there were no significance tests?* Mahwah, NJ: Lawrence Erlbaum Associates, 37–64.

Schmidt, W., Burroughs, N., Zoido, P. and Houang, R. (2015) The role of schooling in perpetuating educational inequality: An international perspective. *Educational Researcher*, 44, 7, 371–386.

Scholastic Research (2008) *Desert Sands unified school district, CA*. New York, NY: Scholastic Inc.

Schoon, I. (2006) *Risk and resilience: Adaptations in changing times*. Cambridge: Cambridge University Press.

Schuepbach, M. (2014) Effects of extracurricular activities and their qualities on primary school-age students' achievements in mathematics in Switzerland. *School Effectiveness and School Improvement*, 26, 2, 279–295.

Schuller, T. (2007) *Capacity building in educational research: Sketching an international picture*, www.scotedreview.org.uk/media/scottish-educational-review/articles/198.pdf

Schwartz, R. (2005) Literacy learning of at-risk first-grade students in the Reading Recovery early intervention. *Journal of Educational Psychology*, 97, N2, 257–267.

Scott, L. (1999) *The Accelerated Reader program, reading achievement, and attitudes of students with learning disabilities*. Unpublished doctoral dissertation, Georgia State University, Atlanta (ERIC Document Reproduction Service ED 434431).

Sebba, J., Berridge, D., Luke, N., Fletcher, J., Bell, K., Strand, S., and O'Higgins, A. (2015). The educational progress of looked after children in England: linking care and educational data. Nuffield Foundation, www.nuffieldfoundation.org/sites/default/files/files/EducationalProgressLookedAfterChildrenOverviewReportNov2015.pdf

See, B. H. and Gorard, S. (2014) Improving literacy in the transition period: A review of the existing evidence on what works. *British Journal of Education, Society and Behavioural Science*, 4, 6, 739–754.

See, B. H., Gorard, S. and Siddiqui, N. (2015a) Best practice in conducting RCTs: Lessons learnt from an independent evaluation of the Response-to-Intervention programme. *Studies in Educational Evaluation*, 47, 83–92.

See, B. H., Gorard, S. and Siddiqui, N. (2015b) Can teachers use research evidence in practice? A pilot study of the use of feedback to enhance learning. *Educational Research*. www.tandfonline.com/doi/full/10.1080/00131881.2015.1117798

See, B. H., Gorard, S. and Siddiqui, N. (2016) Can teachers use research evidence in practice?: A pilot study of the use of feedback to enhance learning, *Educational Research*, 58, 1, 56-72.

See, B. H., Gorard, S. and Siddiqui, N. (2017) Can explicit teaching of knowledge improve reading attainment?: An evaluation of the core knowledge curriculum, *British Educational Research Journal*, forthcoming.

Senn, S. (2002) Power is indeed irrelevant in interpreting completed studies. *BMJ*, 325, 1304.

Shadish, W., Cook, T. and Campbell, D. (2002) *Experimental and quasi-experimental designs for generalized causal inference*. Belmont: Wadsworth.

Shannon, L., Styers, M., and Siceloff, E. (2010) *A final report for the evaluation of Renaissance Learning's Accelerated Reader Program*. Charlottesville, VA: Magnolia Consulting.

Shannon, L., Styers, M., Wilkerson, S. and Peery, E. (2014) *Computer-assisted learning in elementary reading: A randomized control trial*, Charlottesville, VA: Magnolia Consulting.

Shannon, L., Styers, M., Wilkerson, S., and Peery, E. (2015) Computer-assisted learning in elementary reading: A randomized control trial. *Computers in the Schools*, 32, 1, 20–34.

Shapiro, L. and Solity, J. (2008) Delivering phonological and phonics training within whole-class teaching. *British Journal of Educational Psychology*, 78, 4, 597–620.

Shayer, M. and Adhami, M. (2010) Realizing the cognitive potential of children 5–7 with a mathematics focus: Post-test and long-term effects of a 2-year intervention. *British Journal of Educational Psychology* 80, 3, 363–379.

Sheikh, K. and Mattingly, S. (1981) Investigating nonresponse bias in mail surveys. *Journal of Epidemiology and Community Health*, 35, 293–296.

Sibieta, L. (2016) *REACH Evaluation report and executive summary*. London: EEF, https://educationendowmentfoundation.org.uk/public/files/Support/Campaigns/Evaluation_Reports/EEF_Project_Report_REACH

Sibieta, L., Kotecha, M and Skipp, A. (2016) *Nuffield Early Language Intervention. Evauation report and executive summary*. London: EEF.

Siddiqui, N., Gorard, S. and See, B. H. (2014) Is a summer school programme a promising intervention in preparation for transition from primary to secondary school? *International Education Studies*, 7, 7, 125–135.

Siddiqui, N., Gorard, S. and See, B. H. (2015) Accelerated Reader as a literacy catch-up intervention during the primary to secondary school transition phase. *Educational Review*, 68, 2, 139–154.

Siddiqui, N., Gorard, S. and See, B. H. (2016a) Children's University: *Youth Social Action Trial*. Evaluation Report and Executive Summary, EEF.

Siddiqui, N., Gorard, S. and See, B. H. (2016b) *The wider outcomes of P4C*. Report to the Nuffield Foundation.

Silverstein, G., Frechtling, J. and Miyoaka, A. (2000) *Evaluation of the use of technology in Illinois public schools: Final report* (prepared for Research Division, Illinois State Board of Education). Rockville, MD: Westat.

Simmons, J., Nelson, L. and Simonsohn, U. (2011) False-positive psychology: Undisclosed flexibility in data collection and analysis allows presenting anything as significant. *Psychological Science*, 11, 1359–66. doi: 10.1177/0956797611417632

Siraj-Blatchford, I. and Taggart, B. (2014) *Exploring effective pedagogy in primary schools: Evidence from research*. London: Pearson.

Sivin-Kachala, J., and Bialo, E. (2000) *2000 research report on the effectiveness of technology in schools* (7th ed.). Washington DC: Software and Information Industry.

Skiba, R., Casey, A., and Center, B. (1985–1986) Nonaversive procedures in the treatment of classroom behavior problems. *Journal of Special Education*, 19, 459–481.

Slavin, R. and Smith, D. (2009) The relationship between sample sizes and effect sizes in systematic reviews in education. *Educational Evaluation and Policy Analysis*, 31, 4, 500–506.

Slavin, R., Lake, C., Chambers, B., Cheung, A. and Davis, S. (2009) Effective reading programmes for the elementary grades: A best evidence synthesis, *Review of Educational Research*, 79, 4, 1391–1466.

Slavin, R., Lake, C., Davis, S. and Madden, N. (2011) Effective programs for struggling readers: A best evidence synthesis, *Educational Research Review*, 6 (1): 1–26.

Smith, A. and Bates, M. (1992) Confidence limit analyses should replace power calculations in the interpretation of epidemiologic studies. *Epidemiology*, 3, 5, 449–452.

Smith, E. and Gorard, S. (2005) 'They don't give us our marks': The role of formative feedback in student progress. *Assessment in Education*, 12, 1, 21–38.

Social and Character Development Research Consortium (2010) *Efficacy of schoolwide programs to promote social and character development and reduce problem behavior in elementary school children* (NCER 2011–2001). Washington, DC: National Center for Education Research, Institute of Education Sciences, U.S. Department of Education.

Sprague, K., Hamilton, J., Coffey, D., Loadman, W., Lomax, R., Moore, R., Faddis, B. and Beam, M. (2010) Using randomized clinical trials to determine the impact of reading intervention on struggling adolescent readers: Reports of research from five nationally funded striving readers grants. Papers presented at the Society for Research on Educational Effectiveness Conference (no details about place and date of conference), www.sree.org/conferences/2010/program/abstracts/208.pdf

Spybrook, J., Shi, R. and Kelcey, B. (2016) Progress in the last decade: An examination of the precision of cluster randomized trials funded by the US Institute of Education Sciences. *International Journal of Research and Method in Education*, 39, 3, 255–267.

Stang, A., Poole, C. and Kuss, O. (2010) The ongoing tyranny of statistical significance testing in biomedical research. *European Journal of Epidemiology*, 25, 4, 225–230.

Starbuck, W. (2016) 60th anniversary essay: How journals could improve research practices in social science. *Administrative Science Quarterly*, 61, 2, 165–183.

Statham, J. and Chase, E. (2010) *Childhood wellbeing: A brief overview.* Loughborough: Childhood Wellbeing Research Centre.

Straw, S. and Macleod, S. (2015) Evaluation of STEMNET's operations and impact. 2011– 2015 Summary Report. Slough: NFER.

Stringfield, S., Dartnow, A., Borman, G. and Rachuba, L. (2000) *National evaluation of Core Knowledge Sequence implementation final report. Report 49.* Baltimore: CRESPA, John Hopkins University.

Sturgis, P., Brunton-Smith, I., Kuha, J. and Jackson, J. (2014) Ethnic diversity, segregation and the social cohesion of neighbourhoods in London. *Ethnic and Racial Studies*, 37, 8, 1286–1309.

Swain, J., Cara, O. and Litster, J. (2013) Doing philosophy in schools: An evaluation report prepared by the Institute of Education, University of London, philosophy-foundation .org/asset/download/416

Tanner, E., Brown, A., Day, N., Kotecha, M., Low, N., Morrell, G., Turczuk, O., Brown, V., Collingwood, A., Chowdry, H., Greaves, E., Harrison, C., Johnson, G. and Purdon, S. (2011) *Evaluation of Every Child: A Reader.* London: NatCen.

Taylor, C. (2002) The RCBN consultation exercise: Stakeholder report. Occasional Paper 50, Cardiff University School of Social Sciences.

Televantou, I., Marsh, H., Kyriakides, L., Nagengast, B., Fletcher, J. and Malmberg, L. (2015) Phantom effects in school composition research. *School Effectiveness and School Improvement*, 26, 1, 75–101.

Terzian, M. and Moore, K. (2009) *What works for summer learning programs for low-income children and youth?* Washington: Child Trends, www.researchgate.net/publication/242573051_ WHAT_WORKS_FOR_SUMMER_LEARNING_PROGRAMS_FOR_LOW-INCOME_CHILDREN_AND_YOUTH_Preliminary_Lessons_from_Experimental_Evaluations_of_Social_Interventions_1

The Good Childhood (2015) *The subjective well-being of children in the UK*. London: The Children's Society.

The Guardian (2012, October 15) US idea of 'cultural literacy' and key facts child should know arrives in UK. www.theguardian.com/education/2012/oct/15/hirsch-core-knowledge-curriculum-review

Thompson, B. (2004) The "significance" crisis in psychology and education. *The Journal of Socio-Economics*, 33, 607–613.

Tok, S. and Mazı, A. (2015) The effect of Stories for Thinking on reading and listening comprehension: A case study in Turkey, *Research in Education*, 93, 1, 1–18.

Tomlinson, M., Walker, R. and Williams, G. (2008) *The relationship between poverty and childhood well-Being in Great Britain*. Barnet Papers in Social Research. Oxford: Department of Social Policy and Social Work.

Tooley, J. with Darby, D. (1998) *Educational research: a critique*. London: OFSTED.

Topping, K. (2014) *What kids are reading: The book reading habits of students in British Schools 2014: An Independent Study*. United Kingdom: Renaissance Learning Inc.

Topping, K. and Trickey, S. (2007) Collaborative philosophical inquiry for schoolchildren: Cognitive gains at 2-year follow-up. *British Journal of Educational Psychology*, 77, 4, 787–796.

Torgerson, C. (2003) *Systematic reviews*. London: Continuum

Torgerson C. and Zhu D. (2003) *A systematic review and meta-analysis of the effectiveness of ICT on literacy learning in English, 5–16*. Research Evidence in Education Library. London: EPPI-Centre, Social Science Research Unit, Institute of Education, University of London.

Torgerson, C., Brooks, G. and Hall, J. (2006) *A systematic review of the research literature on the use of phonics in the teaching of reading and spelling*. London: DfES, Research Report 711, https://czone.eastsussex.gov.uk/sites/gtp/library/core/english/Documents/pho-nics/A%20Systematic%20Review%20of%20the%20Research%20Literature%20on%20the%20Use%20of%20Phonics%20in%20the%20Teaching%20of%20Reading%20and%20Spelling.pdf

Torgerson, C., Torgerson, D., Jefferson, L., Buckley, H., Ainsworth, H., Heaps, C. and Mitchell, N. (2014) *Discover summer school: Evaluation report and executive summary*. London: Educational Endowment Foundation, 2–25, https://educationendowmentfoundation.org.uk/uploads/pdf/EEF_Evaluation_Report_-_Discover_Summer_School_-_May_2014.pdf

Torgerson, D., Torgerson, C., Ainsworth, H., Buckley, H., Heaps, C., Hewitt, C. and Mitchell, N. (2014b) Improving writing quality. Evaluation report and executive summary. London: Education Endowment Foundation.

Trickey, S. and Topping, K. (2004) Philosophy for children: A systematic review. *Research Papers in Education*, 19, 3, 365–380.

Trickey, S. and Topping, K. (2006) Collaborative philosophical enquiry for school children socio-emotional effects at 11 to 12 years. *School Psychology International*, 27, 5, 599–614.

Truckenmiller, A., Eckert, T., Codding, R. and Petscher, Y. (2014) Evaluating the impact of feedback on elementary aged students' fluency growth in written expression: A randomized controlled trial. *Journal of School Psychology*, 52, 6, 531–548.

Tryon, W. (1998) The inscrutable null hypothesis. *American Psychologist*, 53, 796.

Tseng, C-M. (2014) *The effects of the science writing heuristic (SWH) approach versus traditional instruction on yearly critical thinking gain scores in grade 5–8 classrooms.* PhD thesis, University of Iowa, USA.

Tu, Y.K., Gunnell, D. and Gilthorpe, M. (2008) Simpson's Paradox, Lord's Paradox, and Suppression Effects are the same phenomenon – the reversal paradox. *Emerging Themes in Epidemiology* 2008, 5, 2. doi:10.1186/1742–7622-5–2.

Vadasy, P. and Sanders, E. (2011) Efficacy of supplemental phonics-based instruction for low-skilled first graders: How language minority status and pretest characteristics moderate treatment response. *Scientific Studies of Reading*, 15, 6, 471–497.

Vadasy, P., Nelson, J. and Sanders, E. (2013) Longer term effects of a Tier 2 kindergarten vocabulary intervention for English learners. *Remedial and Special Education*, 34, 2, 91–101.

Vaughn, S. and Fletcher, J. (2012) Response to intervention with secondary school students with reading difficulties. *Journal of Learning Disabilities*, 4, 3, 244–256.

Vollands, S., Topping, K. and Evans, R. (1996) *Experimental evaluation of computer assisted self-assessment of reading comprehension: Effects on reading achievement and attitude.* ERIC Document, ED 408 567.

Vollands, S., Topping, K. and Evans, R. (1999) Computerized self-assessment of reading comprehension with the Accelerated Reader: Action research. *Reading and Writing Quarterly*, 15, 3, 197–211.

Volunteer Now (2014) *Evaluation of the impact of volunteering in the uniformed organisations in N Ireland.* Belfast: Volunteer Now.

Walford, G. (2002) Editorial. *British Journal of Educational Studies*, 50, 4, 415–418.

Walster, G. and Cleary T. (1970) A proposal for a new editorial policy in the social sciences. *The American Statistician*, 241, 16–19.

Wandt, E., Adams, G.W., Collett, D. M., Michael, W. B., Ryans, D. G., and Shay, C. B. (1965) *An evaluation of educational research published in journals.* Report of the Committee on Evaluation of Research, American Educational Research Association, unpublished report.

Ward, F., Thurston, M and Alford, S. (2009) *RESPECT: A personal development programme for young people at risk of social exclusion. Final report.* Chester: University of Chester.

Watts, D. (1991) Why is introductory statistics difficult to learn? *The American Statistician*, 45, 4, 290–291.

Waxman, H., Lin, M., and Michko, G. (2003) *A meta-analysis of the effectiveness of teaching and learning with technology on pupil outcomes.* North Central Regional Educational Laboratory, http://treeves.coe.uga.edu/edit6900/metaanalysisNCREL.pdf

IES (2008) *Accelerated Reader. WWC intervention report.* IES, http://ies.ed.gov/ncee/wwc/interventionreport.aspx?sid=12

What Works Clearinghouse (2010) *Sound partners.* US Department of Education: Institute of Education Sciences, https://ies.ed.gov/ncee/wwc/EvidenceSnapshot/475

What Works Clearinghouse (2013) *Reading Recovery*, http://ies.ed.gov/ncee/wwc/interventionreport.aspx?sid=420

Wheldall, K. (2000) Does Rainbow Repeated Reading add value to an intensive literacy intervention programme for low-progress readers? An experimental evaluation. *Educational Review*, 52, 1, 29–36.

White, P. (2009) *Developing research questions: a guide for social scientists.* London: Palgrave.

White, B. and Frederiksen, J. (1998) Inquiry, modelling and meta-cognition: Making science accessible to all students. *Cognition and Instruction*, 16, 1, 3–118.

White, R., Williams, I. and Haslem, M. (2005) *Performance of District 23 students participating in Scholastic READ 180.* Washington, DC: Policy Studies Associates. Evaluated in WWC (2009) *READ 180.* What Works Clearinghouse Intervention Report. Washington: US Department of Education, Institute of Education Sciences.

Whitehurst-Hall, J. (1999) *The impact of the Core Knowledge Curriculum on the achievement of seventh and eighth grade students.* PhD thesis, University of Georgia, USA.

Williams, M., Sloan, L., Cheung, S., Sutton, C., Stevens, S. and Runham, L. (2016) Can't count or won't count? Embedding quantitative methods in substantive sociology curricula: A quasi-experiment. *Sociology*, 50, 3, 435–452.

Williams, S. (1993) *Evaluating the effects of philosophical enquiry in a secondary school.* The Village Community School Philosophy for Children Project.

Williams, S. and Wegerif, R. (2004) *Radical encouragement: Creating cultures for learning.* Birmingham: Imaginative Minds.

Winsper, C., Lereya, T., Zanarini, M. and Wolke, D. (2012) Involvement in bullying and suicide-related behavior at 11 years: A prospective birth cohort study. *Journal of the American Academy of Child and Adolescent Psychiatry*, 51, 3, 271–282.

WISERD (2013) Confidence intervals and tests about one mean, http://wiserd.ac.uk/files/2613/7881/9558/QRDI-W1-ConfidenceIntervalsOneSampleTTests.pdf

Wolf, M. and Katzir-Cohen, T. (2001) Reading fluency and its intervention. *Scientific Studies of Reading*, 5, 3, 211–239.

Wood, M., Barter, C. and Berridge, D. (2011) *Standing on my own two feet: Disadvantaged teenagers, intimate partner violence and coercive control.* London: NSPCC, www.nspcc.org.uk/globalassets/documents/research-reports/standing-own-two-feet-report.pdf

Woods, D.E. (2007) *An investigation of the effects of a middle school reading intervention on school dropout rates.* Unpublished doctoral dissertation. Virginia Polytechnic Institute and State University (Blacksburg).

Worth, J., Sizmur, J., Ager, R. and Styles, B. (2015) *Improving numeracy and literacy. Evaluation report and summary.* London: Education Endowment Foundation.

Wrigley, J. (1976) Pitfalls in educational research. *Research Intelligence*, Autumn 1976, 2, 2, 2–4.

WWC (2009) *READ 180. What Works Clearinghouse Intervention Report.* Washington, DC: US Department of Education, Institute of Education Sciences.

WWC (2010) *Project CRISS® (CReating Independence through Student-owned Strategies) What Works Clearinghouse Intervention Report.* Washington, DC: US Department of Education, Institute of Education Sciences.

Wyse, D. and Goswami, U. (2008) Synthetic phonics and the teaching of reading. *British Educational Research Journal*, 34. 6, 691–710.

Xiao, Z., Kasim, A. and Higgins, S. (2016) Same difference? Understanding variation in the estimation of effect sizes from trial data. *International Journal of Educational Research*, 77, www.sciencedirect.com/science/article/pii/S0883035515304808

Yates, F. (1964) Sir Ronald Fisher and the design of experiments, *Biometrics* 20, 307–321.

Young, T. (2012) Free schools: The research lab of state education, *The Guardian*, 3 October 2012, www.theguardian.com/teacher-network/2012/oct/03/free-schools-research-development-education

INDEX

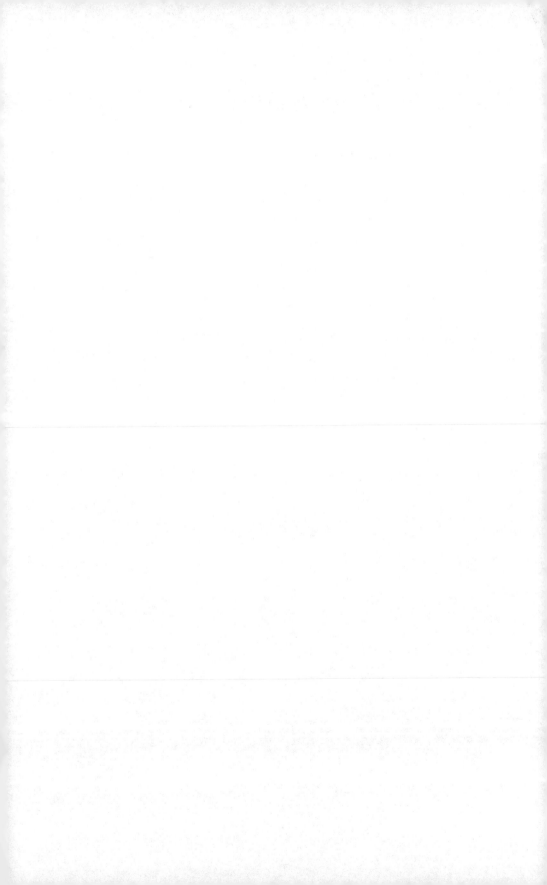